# THE PLUNDER OF ART

H. BHISHAM PAL

ABHINAV PUBLICATIONS

abhinav publications

*First Published in India 1992*





Publishers
Abhinav Publications
E-37, Hauz Khas,
New Delhi-110016

ISBN 81-7017-285-3

Lasertypeset by
Shagun Composers
92-B, Krishna Nagar, Street No. 4
Safdarjung Enclave
New Delhi-110029

Printer
Mehta Offset Works
Mehta House
16-A Narina II
New Delhi - 110 028

# CONTENTS

# INTRODUCTION

A nation's ancient treasures and monuments are the soul of its history and culture. They are part of a nation's pedigree and mute chroniclers of change and refinement as society moves through a process of challenge and response into its current character and mores.

India has a rich past. Temples and other edifices are standing monuments which prove beyond doubt the existence of a rich culture and lively society. These places contribute much to enrich the culture of the soil, for it was here that devastation as well as construction moved almost side by side. History was written and rewritten, made and remade. Hordes of invaders kept the people and their Hindu rulers engaged in battlefields, yet their faith in their religion was never lost. Invasion, no doubt, moulded the people's way of life but it helped them rely on their religion in a more vigorous form for solace and contentment. Hindu temples were pulled down by the invaders but they were rebuilt sooner than they were destroyed. The idols from these temples were taken to safer places by the people so that they could continue to pursue their religious faith. Despite the passing of many centuries, these temples have remained intact to tell us the story of the past.

These invasions left deep marks in the minds of the people which is visible even today. During this momentous period of history, various cultures fused. They enriched various forms of Indian architecture—Mughal, Jain and Rajput. The architecture became more graceful, engravings enchanting and paintings beautiful.

Religion has always been a great source of inspiration in India. Buddhism, Jainism, Shaivism and Vaishnavism have all left behind important buildings which indicate the sway these religions had over the minds of the people and their rulers. They are works of beauty and have about them an aura of religious fervour which inspired not only those who provided the necessary funds but also the craftsmen who built them. The charm of these great buildings is eternal.

Temple architecture has its origin in the small shrines erected to give a fillip to the religious feelings of the people. These small stone structures later took the form of big shrines, where people began to congregate. Early temples consisted of a single cell having a portico attached to them. The 4th and the 5th centuries ushered in a golden era in the architectural history of India.

In the 5th century, the masons began to experiment with new designs in temple buildings. Superstructures of stones were erected on the ceilings, which looked like pyramids with either straight or curvilinear sides. According to Rawson, 'one characteristic and constant feature of the Indian temple, from the earliest times was an ornate frame on the exterior of the cell door bearing sculptured figures of the purifying river goddesses Ganga and Yamuna at the base of Jambs, an ornate lintel usually with the figure of the Goddess of good fortune in the centre and a series of small panels of amorous couples ranged up to the Jambs.' From about A.D. 600, it became conventional to employ a great deal of figure sculpture chiefly in panels of narrative, or iconic relief, ceiling, ornament, friezes of flying celestials and vegetation and water deities on the brackets of the column capitals.

The impact of Hindu, Buddhist and Mughal architecture is clearly visible in the temples and other monuments of India. The temples were built not only to meet the religious needs of the people but also to satisfy the spiritual urge of the rulers. Defaced and mutilated figures in these shrines tell us of pathetic tales of barbarity of the iconoclast invaders.

The religious fervour among Hindus, Jains and Buddhists never waned despite harassment during the Muslim suzerainty over India. The British did not interfere as far as religion was concerned. In spite of all the difficulties and humiliations meted out at the hands of invaders and bigots, the religious feeling continued with vigour and enthusiasm. Iconoclasm could not shake the faith and will of the worshippers. New shrines are still being constructed. Men come and go but religion and its monuments remain.

The temples at Khajuraho, Konarak, Ramgarh and Ranakpur are notable for their erotic sculptures. One really wonders, why these temples have sculptures displaying varied postures of sexual union? It is not unusual to find a western beholder standing aghast at the sight of such erotic sculptures which have no place in the Christian Church. A foreigner suddenly finds himself confronted with the sacred principles of SUCHITA on the one hand and frank sexual representations on the other. The explanation is found in Hindu mythology. The creation of universe is based upon the consummation of the male and female. An open representation of this sexual union is not a symbol of degeneration of licentiousness but it signifies the philosophy of creation. The coital scenes in Jain temples are meant to lead one towards alienation from society, i.e., Vairagya, and not to indulge in sensual life.

Whatever may be the origin of erotic sculptures it is certain that these marvels in stone were products of sublime inspiration. There can be no two opinions that philosophy and religion were the base of these exquisite pieces of sculpture. It would be unjust to consider them as patterns of sex behaviour, representing the moral and social degradation of the age. These monuments were dedicated to the discovery of truth and beauty. In fact, the coital scenes were to serve as a 'catharsis' to the worshippers.

Temples depicting erotic scenes have specially attracted the interest of affluent foreigners who want to decorate their mansions and art galleries with art objects. The antique smugglers have been plundering the rich heritage of their country for the sake of huge sums of money. From Khajuraho alone over 100 erotic sculptures valued at several million dollars were stolen and smuggled abroad to decorate the drawing rooms of rapacious antique hunters. These included the figures carved in buff-colour sandstone portrayed as 'Apsaras' in playful moods, nymphs standing in erotic poses, couples in loving embrace and female figures arranged in intricate formations. There is no doubt that the aesthetic excellence of Indian art from the prehistoric times has had a world-wide appeal both for the public and for the art collectors.

The Buddhist stupa at Sanchi, the temples of Khajuraho, Konarak, Rajasthan, Himachal Pradesh and Tamil Nadu and the various forts in the country have attracted world-wide tourist interest. However, the arrangements made for their preservation and protection are woefully inadequate.

Throughout Indian history, creativity in art and architecture has been sustained by State patronage. Buddhist art developed with the support of Emperor Ashoka; Hindu art reached its apex during the golden age of the Gupta Empire; new experiments in Rajput art owed their inspiration to Rajput rulers and the emergence of Moghul art had the patronage of the Moghul emperors. Thus, art repositories have almost invariably been owned by patrons of art; and there have been very few art collectors other than the government, the former princely states and a few wealthy landlords. In fact, art galleries, museums and archives required large and economically unproductive investments. Only the affluent princes and big landlords had the resources for the upkeep of these art galleries.

The complex social changes that took place in India in the wake of independence progressively affected these erstwhile patrons of art. The Indian Constitution is committed to the evolution of a socialistic pattern of society, placing a major emphasis on the reduction of inequalities among citizens, which has had a bearing on the level of resources available for important private art acquisitions and patronage. Concurrently, the significance of the fabulous prices offered for antiques in foreign markets was not lost upon major art collectors in India—the more so as their changed status often entailed the loss of personal pride in their art collections. This, together with actual or expected tax problems—especially with regard to estate taxation (death duties)—, produced a role reversion from art buying to art selling, presumably often for (undeclared) foreign currency (UNSDRI No. 13).

The experts have pondered over the reasons for antique thefts and their smuggling to foreign countries. They believe, it is not exactly one of simple theft by petty people out to earn a quick buck. It is basically a phenomenon that can be explained by psychologists. They term it as 'acquisition of culture' by people who lack it. India, Italy and old Russia are among the few nations with a long glorious past where the arts had been a passion of their rulers. As in India, the Romans and the people of Caucasia enshrined their gods in stone and metal for worship as much as for their aesthetic appeal. Then came a decline and the past was being forgotten, but it was not so everywhere. Britain, France and Spain rose to power in the medieval darkness. They conquered countries of far and near and traded with them and soon the history of the victim country became the grandeur of the ruler's homes. The process was repeated four hundred years later—that is in the 20th century—when the United States of America and a few European nations amassed so much wealth that they could buy or steal the culture which they lacked. In the thirties, the national museums and State governments of the USA went on a treasure hunt. They bought copiously valuable treasures in India from unscrupulous traders and the money-hungry princes. Unfortunately, no permission was needed under the law of the land. To cite an example, some years ago, Jose Casteneda, a Mexican lawyer-turned-antique collector visited an art gallery in Paris. He could not resist himself from stealing a rare manuscript of 17th century Azeto Codex. Back home, when he was arrested in Cancun with the priceless manuscript, he explained to the law enforcing agency that he was simply enriching his country's heritage. Under Mexico's patrimony law, the manuscript had become government property. France requested for its return and also Casteneda's extradition. The Government of Mexico did not yield to France's request. Instead, the Mexican media hailed the smuggler as a national hero.

Today, antique-collection has become one of the most absorbing pastimes the world over. It is also probably one of man's oldest pastimes going far back into history, beginning with the despoiling of India's temple treasures. Antiques wisely acquired have often earned handsome, if not spectacular, profits for their collectors. Apart from the profit motive most antique collectors have found that the years they have spent searching for various objects of interest have widened their horizons of knowledge. Businessmen saw antique collection as a prospective gold mine and today, antiques are globally recognised as safe investments. As a result of these factors, priceless objects have sometimes mysteriously disappeared and an entire new generation of antique collectors has emerged. Yet, just a couple of generations ago, people collected priceless objects merely for their aesthetic value and for decorating their homes. What are antiques and what is so special about them?

To an ardent collector, an antique must be at least 100 years old, invariably bearing high aesthetic and historic value. Items of all past eras and their decorative arts fall into this category. Traditional objects that have,attracted collectors, include porcelain, silver, chinaware, tapestries, jewellery, sculpture, bronzes, paintings, miniatures and furniture pieces. Many a time nostalgia, sentiment, a desire for continuity with the past, or a simple reminder of a bygone era might strike a delicate chord. And that is it—an antique collector is born.

People in India have always been firm believers in things of enduring value. With her highly developed ancient civilisation and culture, India has witnessed several foreign invasions through the centuries. These have left indelible marks upon our rich heritage. Today, imposing temples, mosques, churches, forts and palaces bear witness to the intricate sculpture that was once executed on a massive scale. These were made to last for posterity at a time when the world lacked literacy and printing techniques. Industrial arts including inlay work and carvings were practised by groups of craftsmen who passed on their skills through generations.

If we look at the principal public and private art collections, art galleries and museums of the western countries, we find that Indian art, in comparison to that of Egypt, China, Greece and Europe, was least represented and appreciated prior to the independence of

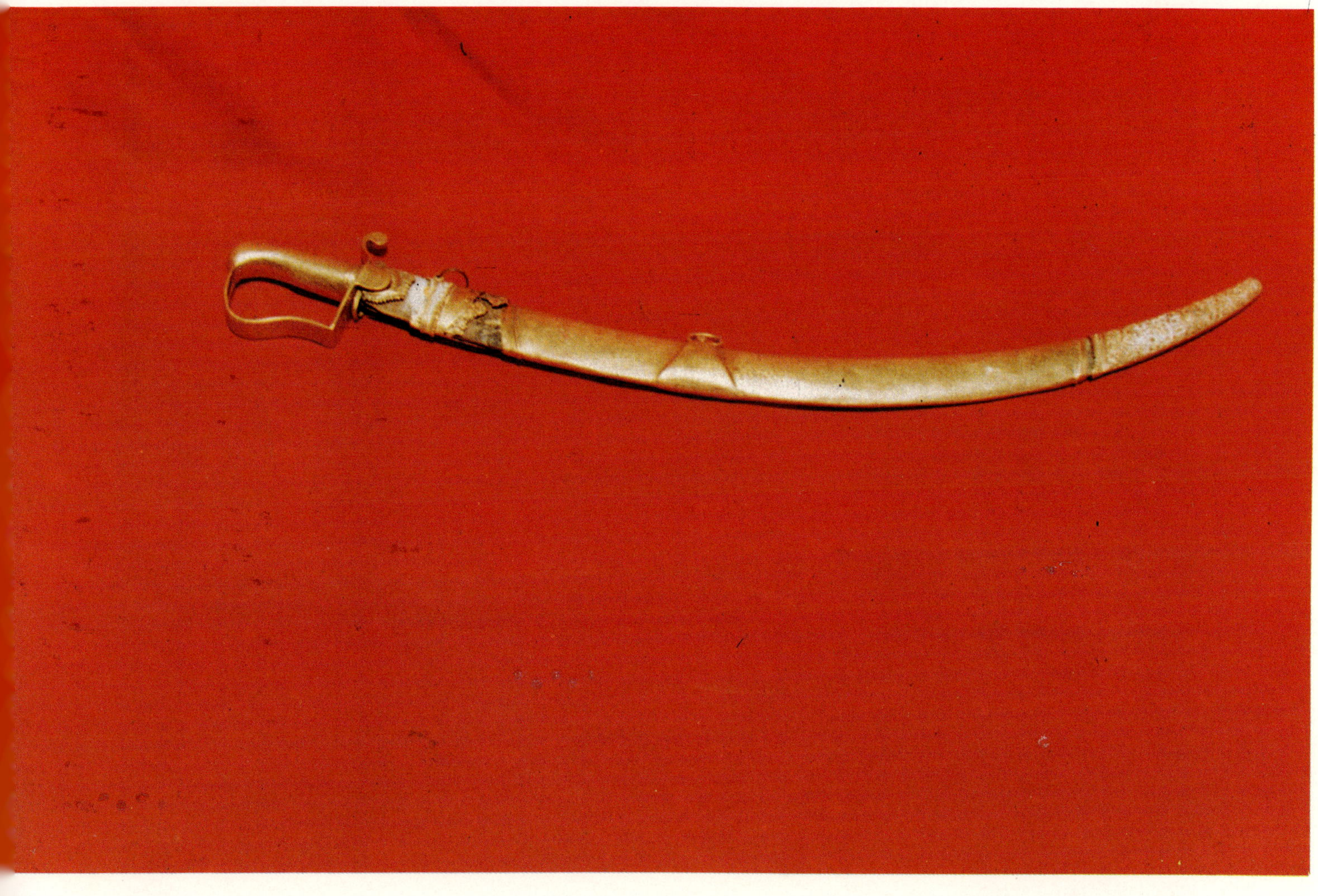

Tipu's Sword.

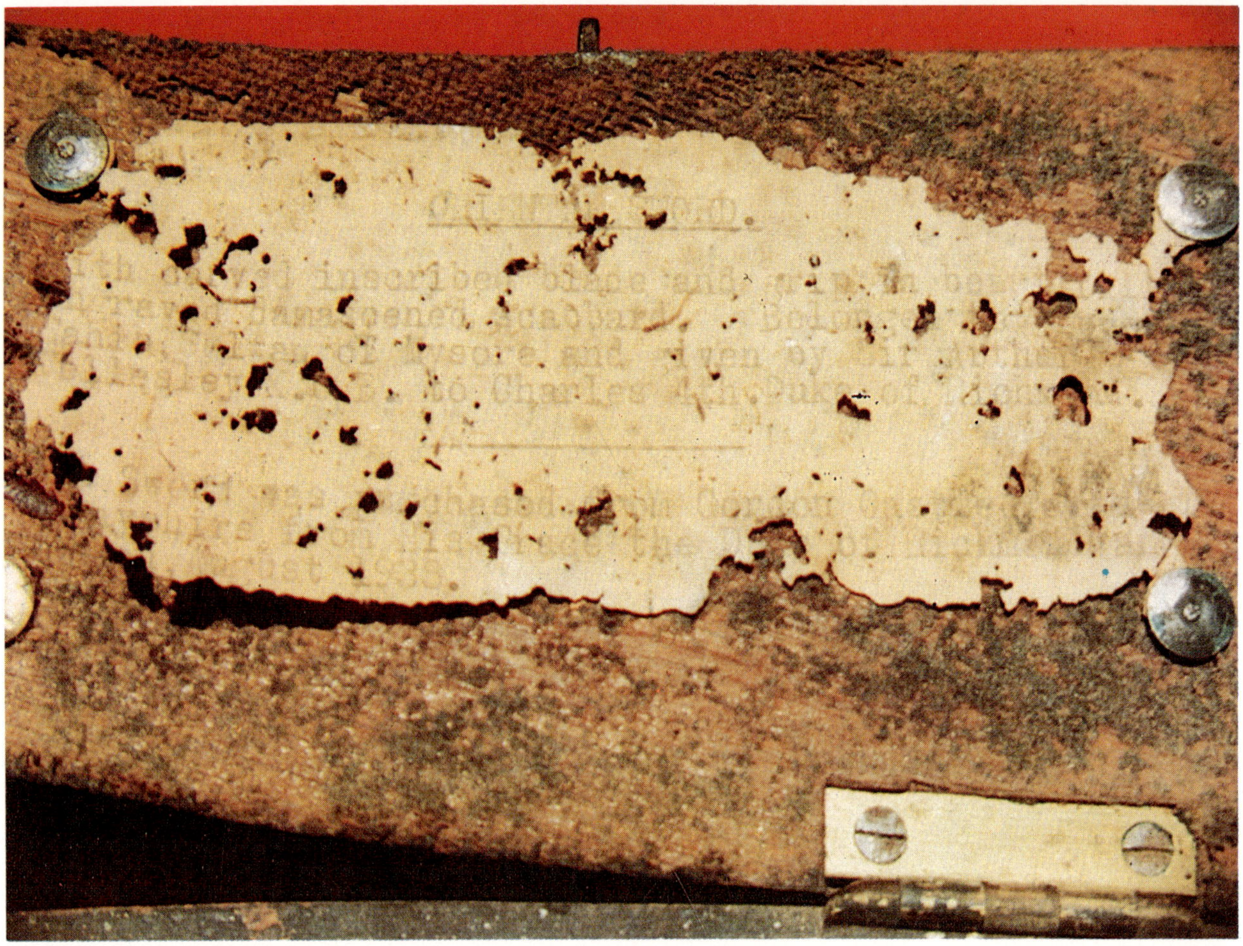

Cover of the Cupboard of the Sword.

Writings on the cover.

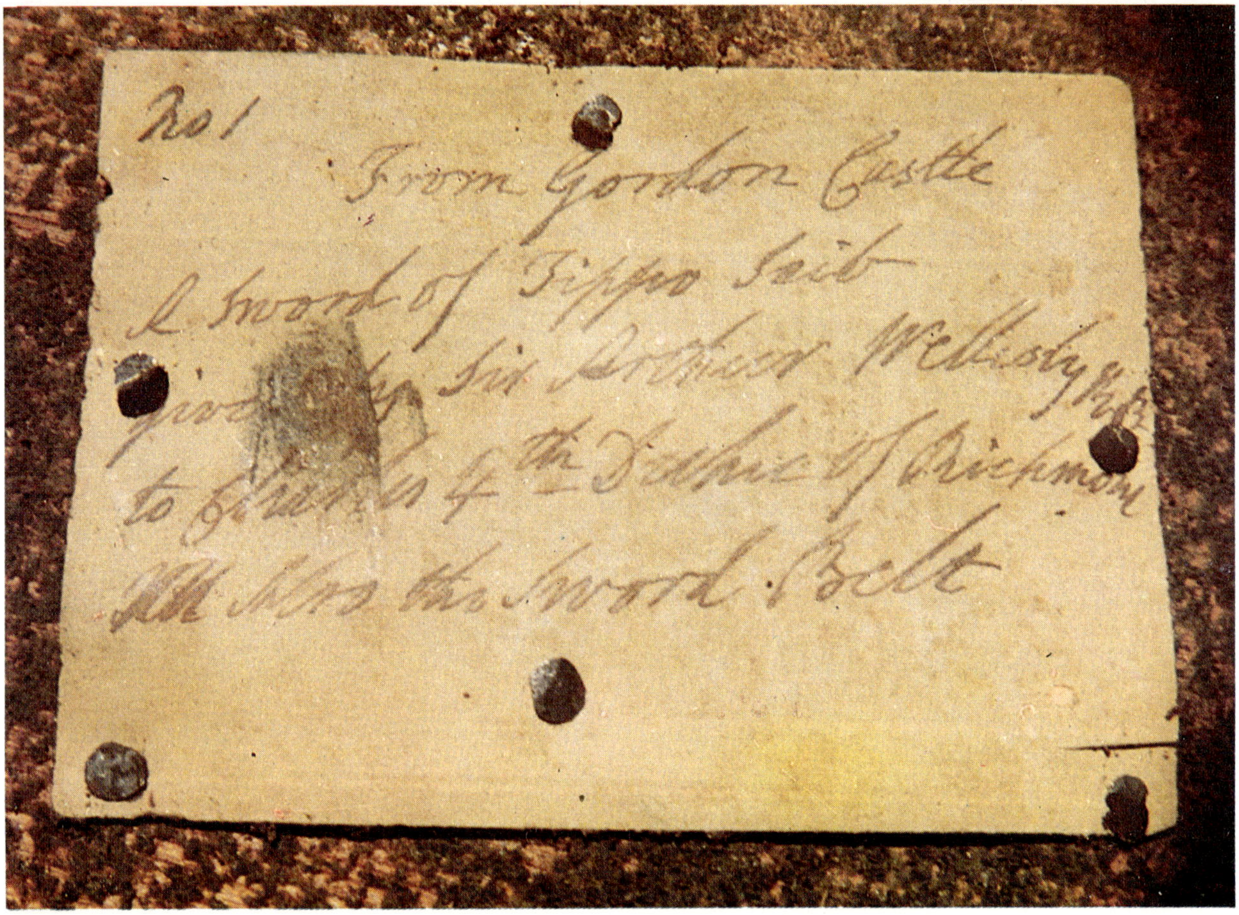

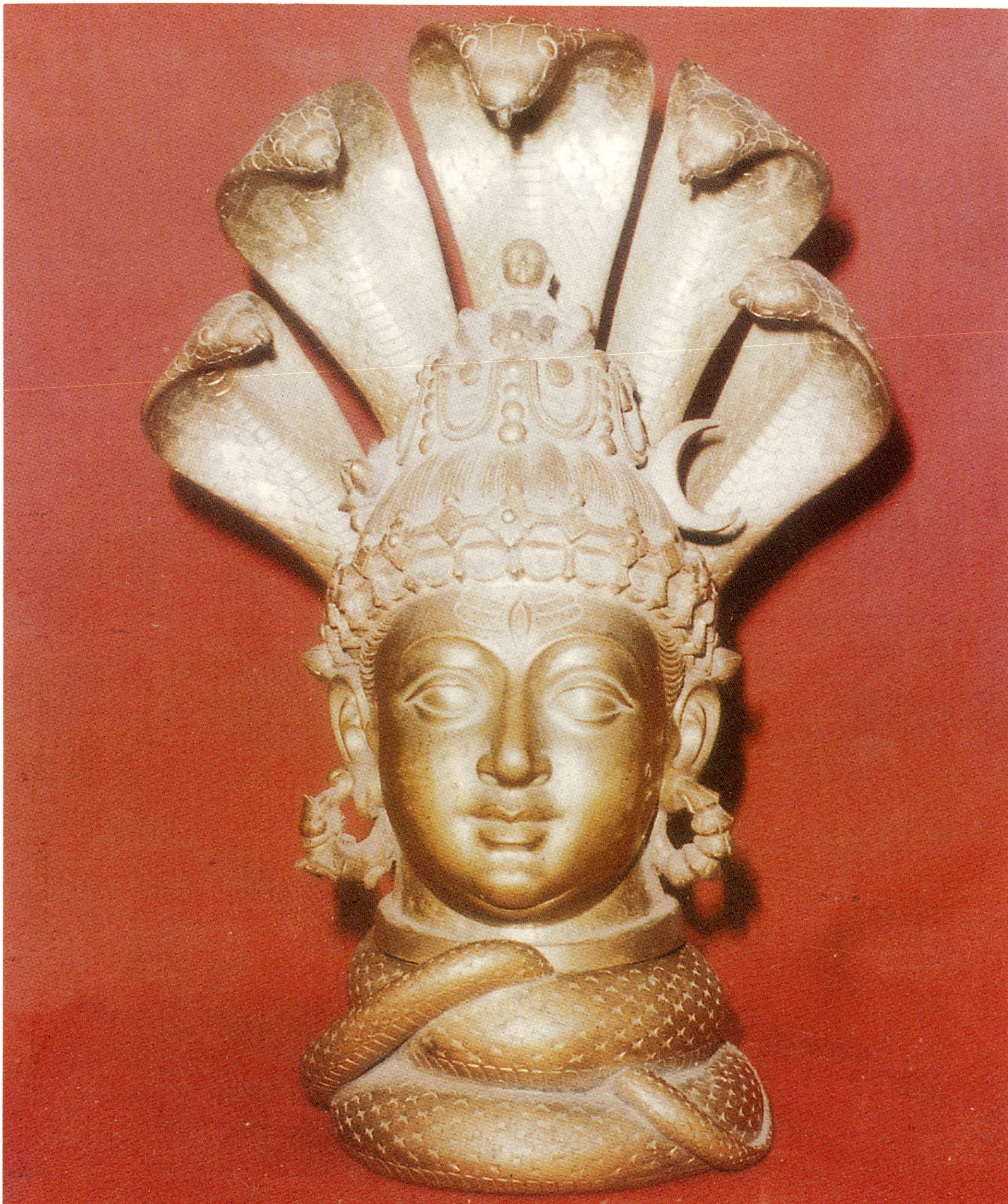

Lord Chander Mouli Iswara—300 years old Pancha Loha Idol.

A painting depicting the rituals of Goddess Chamundeswari.

A Walking Stick.

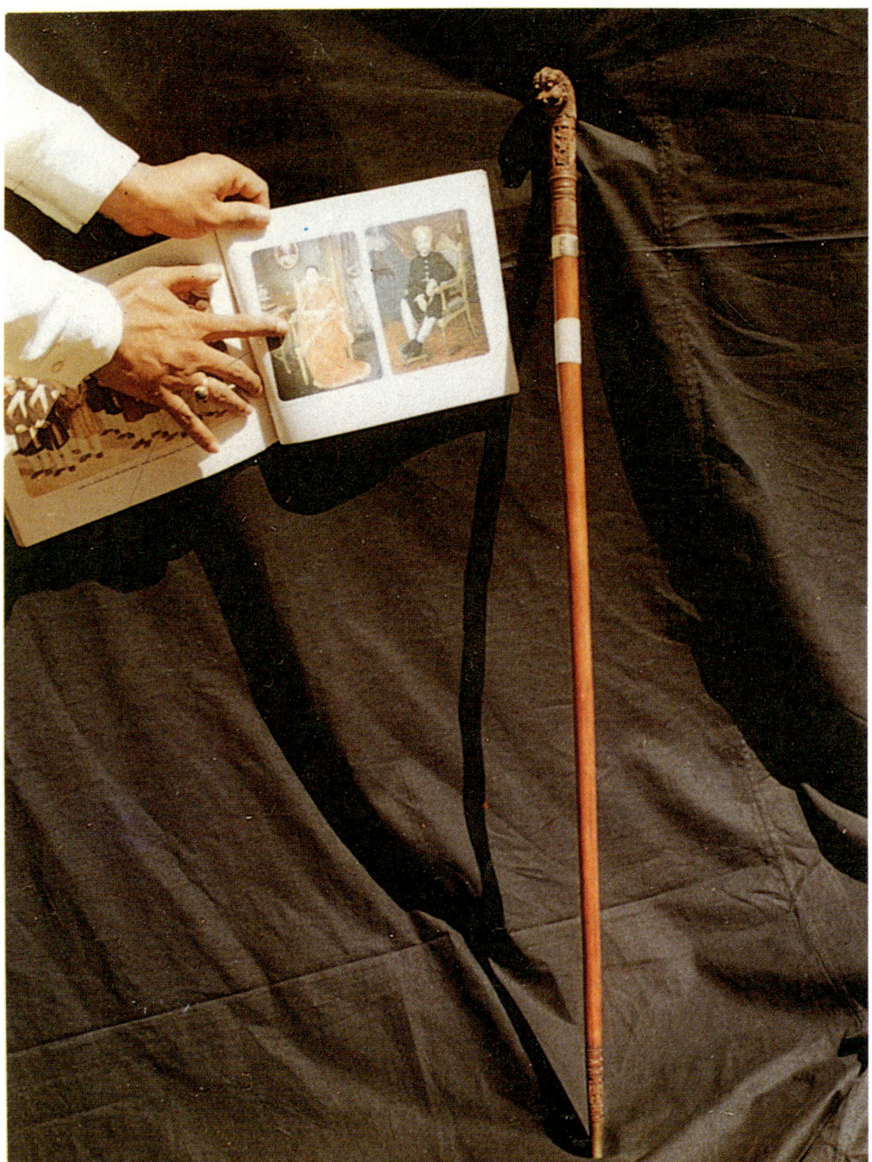

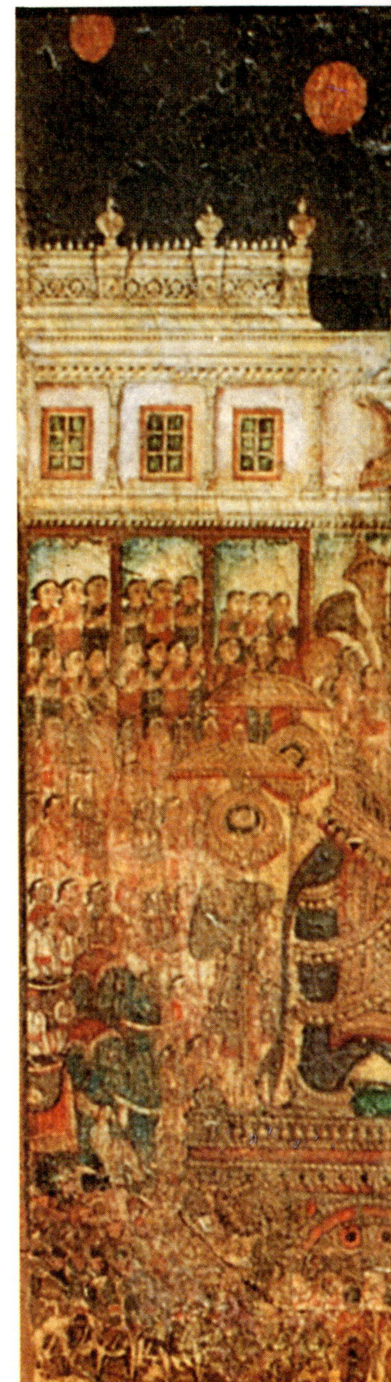

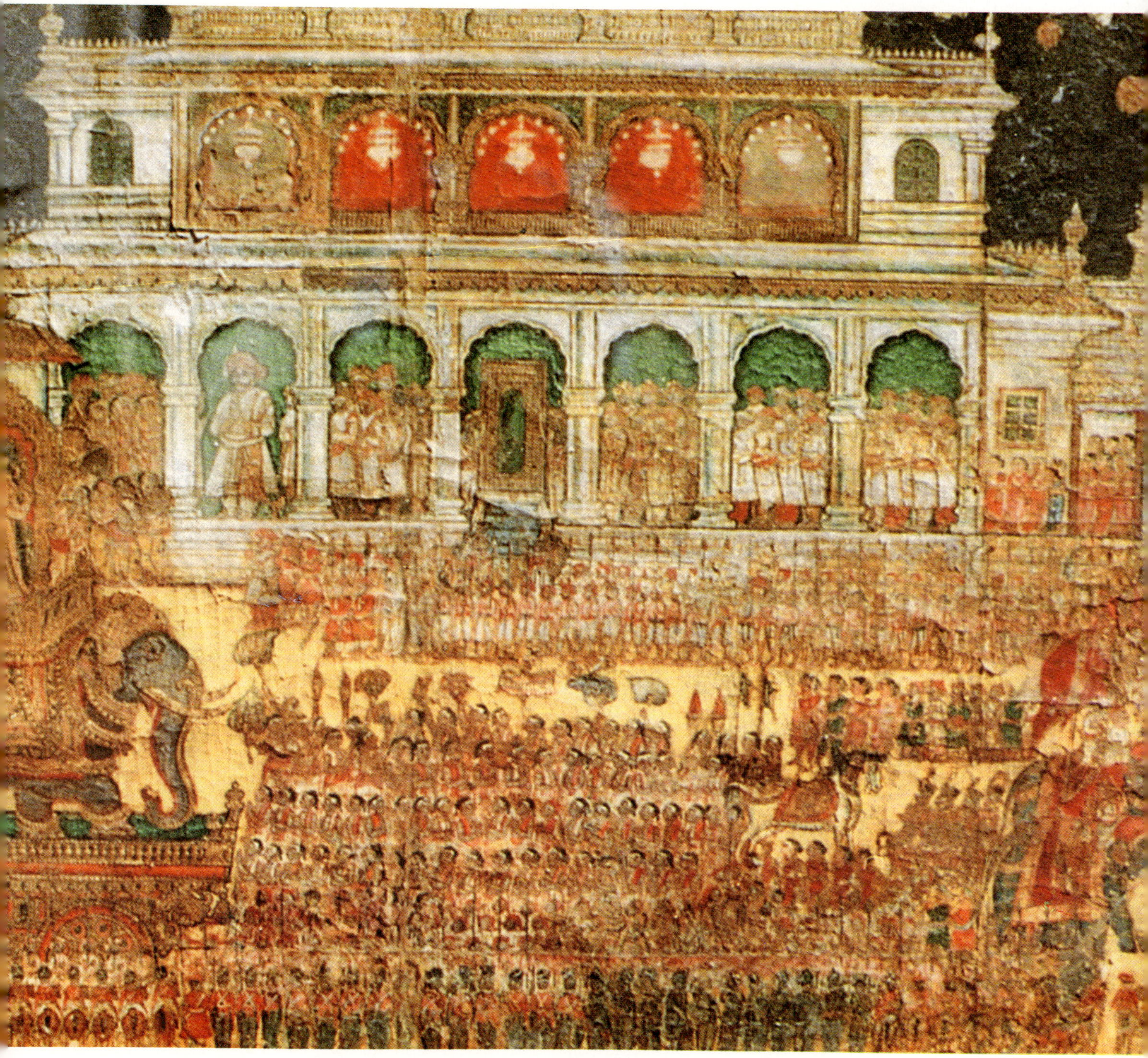

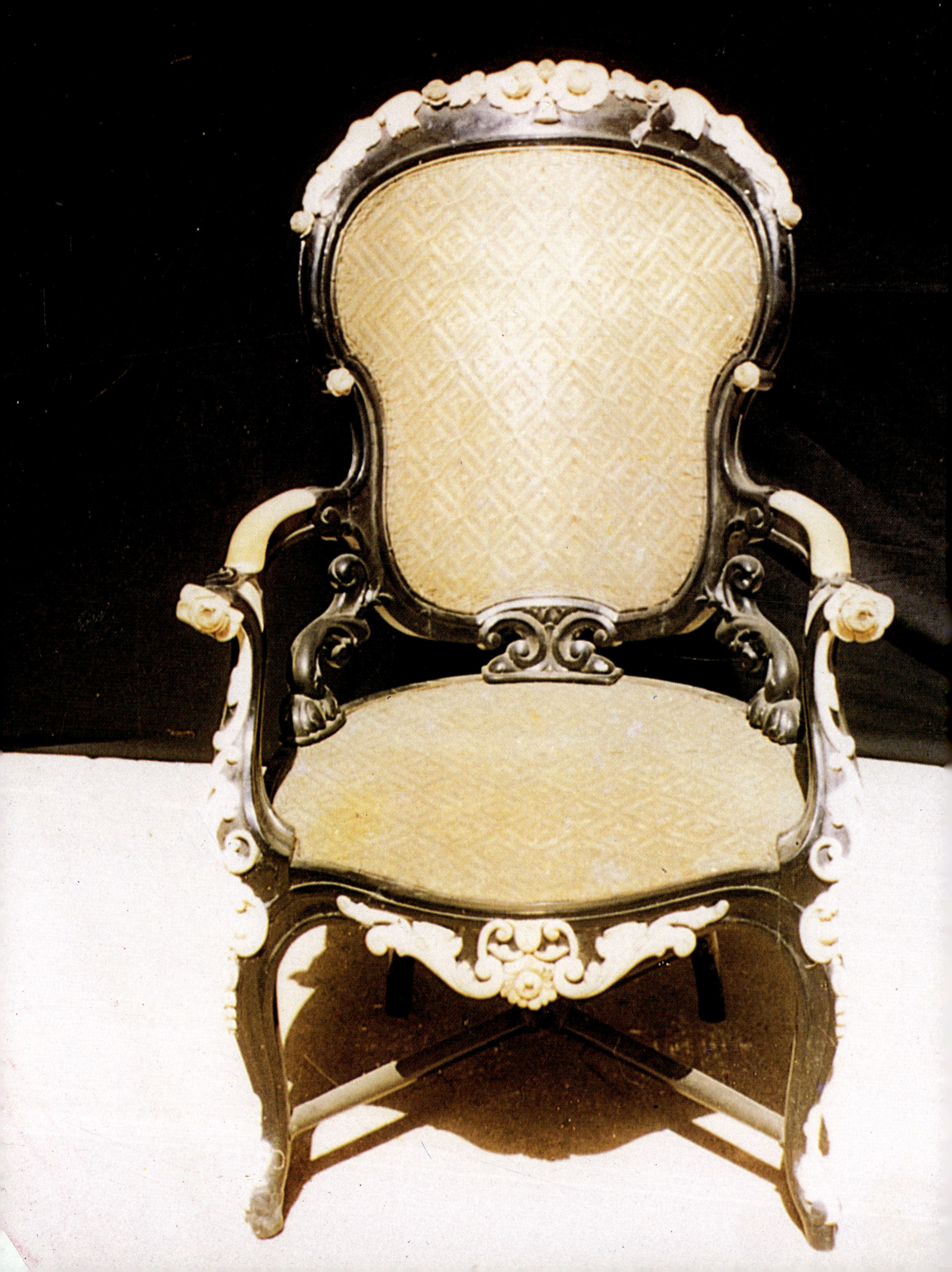

A rosewood chair inlaid with Ivory Carving.

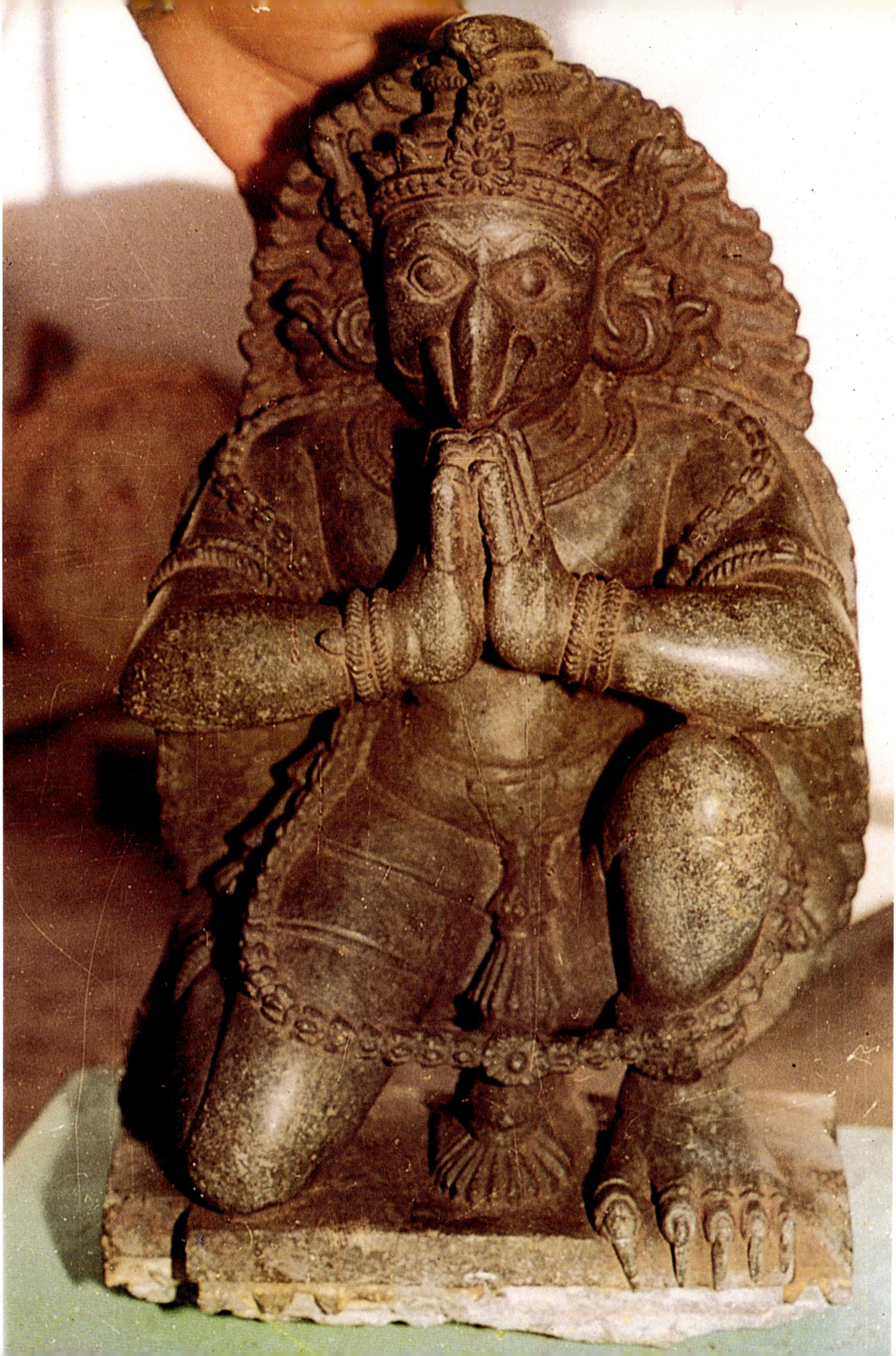

Lord Garuda with folded hands stolen from Puri Temple.

Antiques relating to 2nd to 13th Century recovered from Delhi.

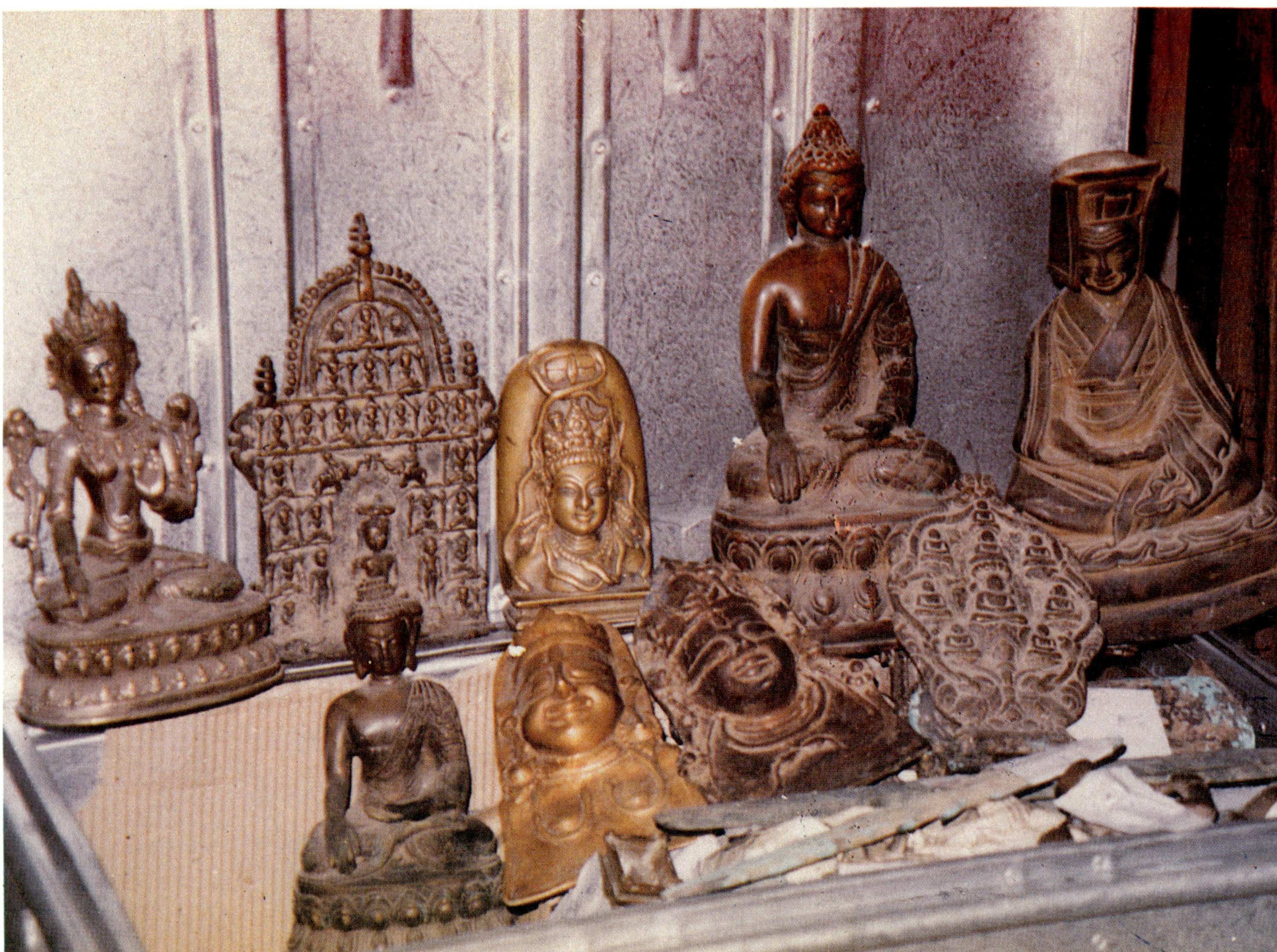

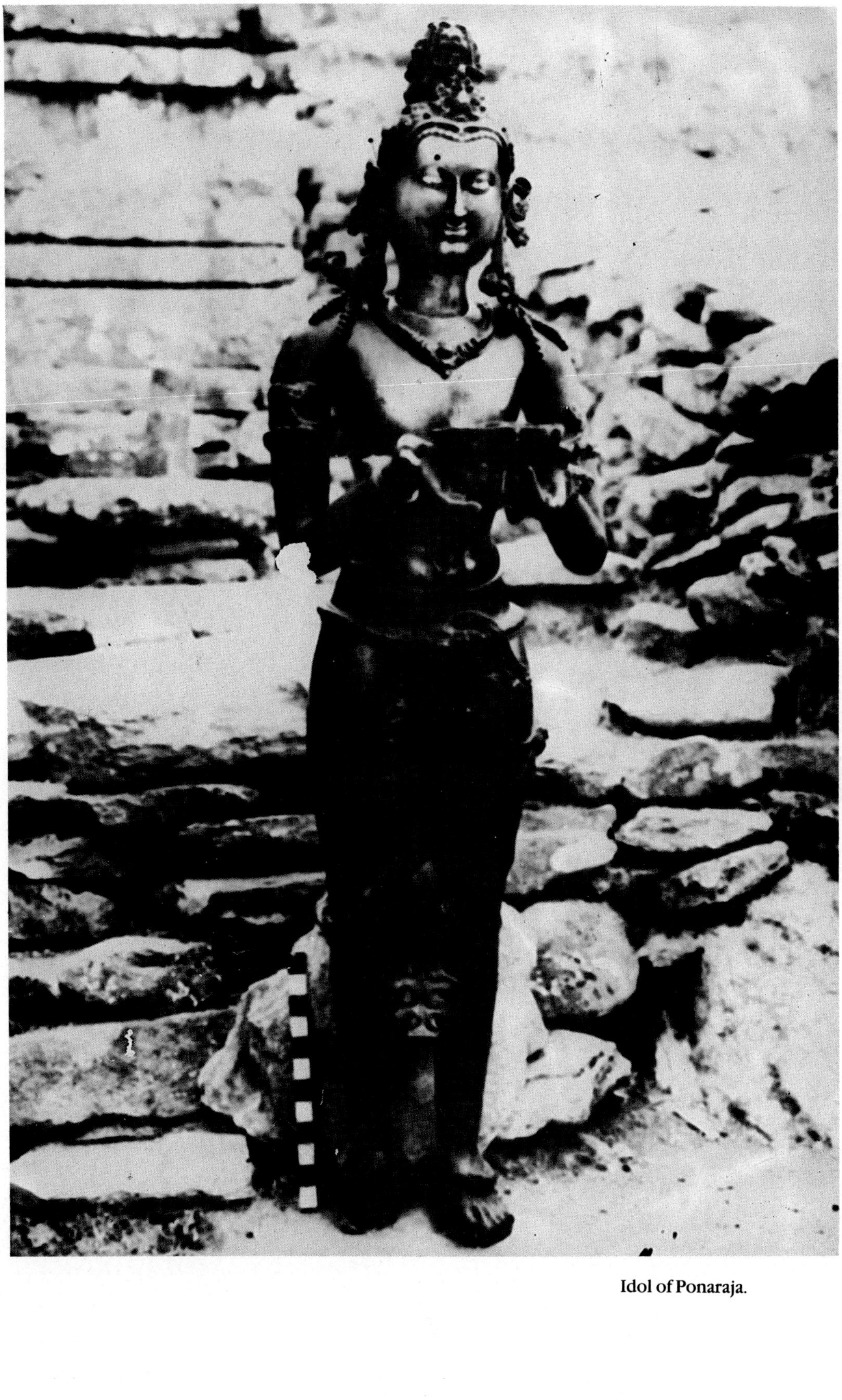

Idol of Ponaraja.

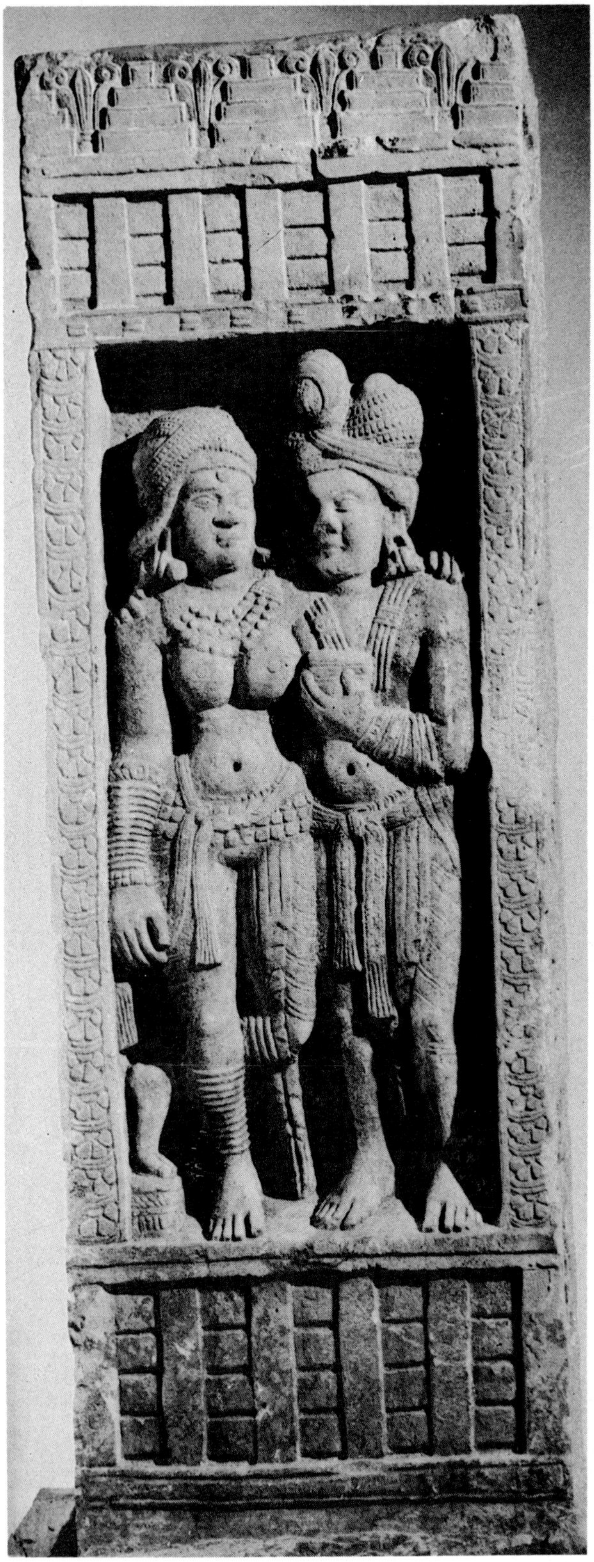

A panel of Yaksha and Yakshini.

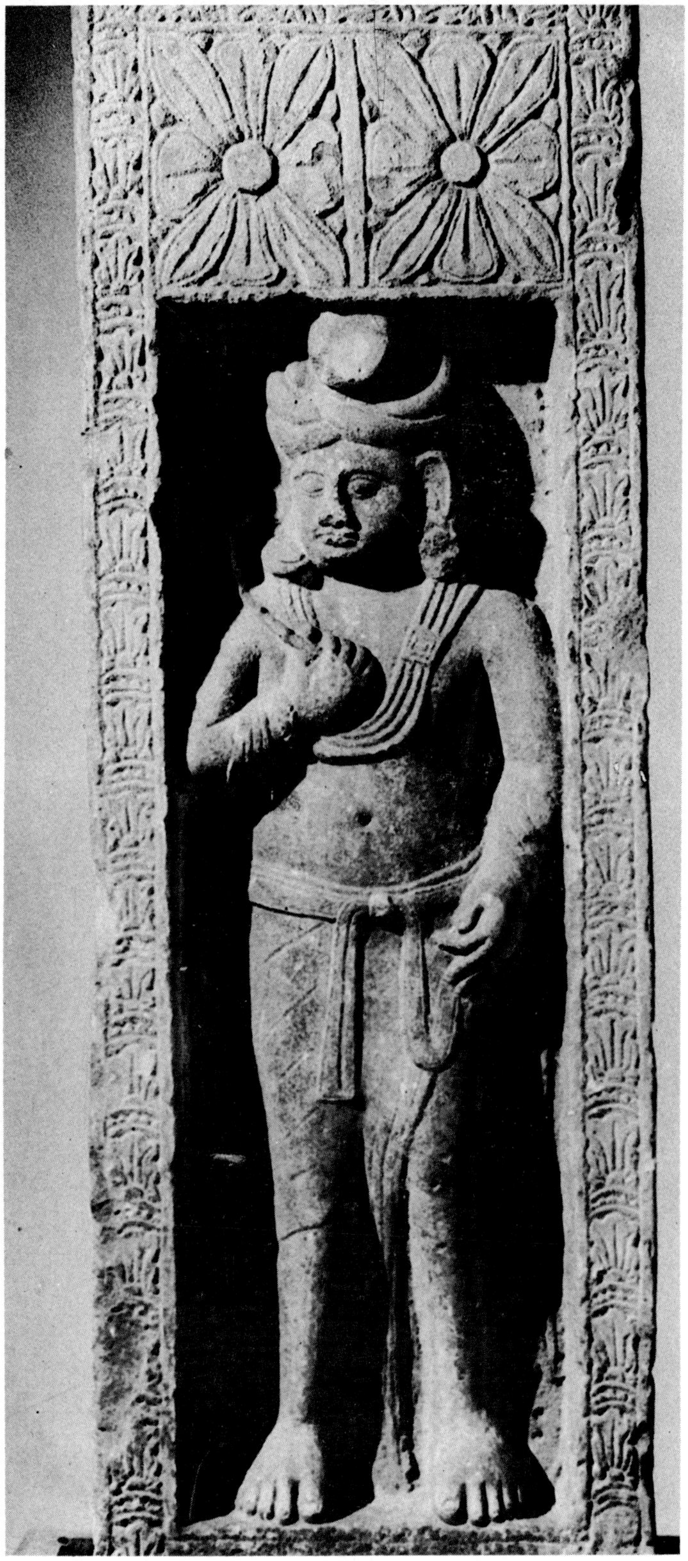

A Stolen Panel.

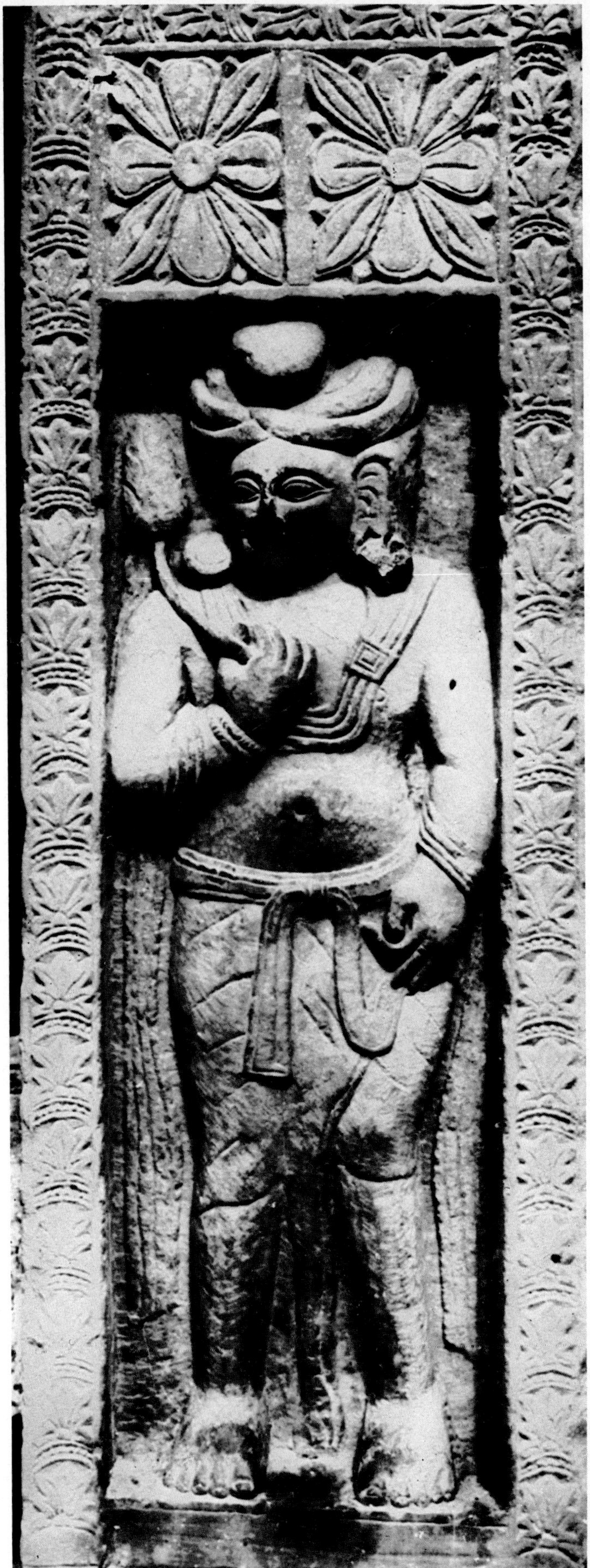

Yaksha in standing posture.

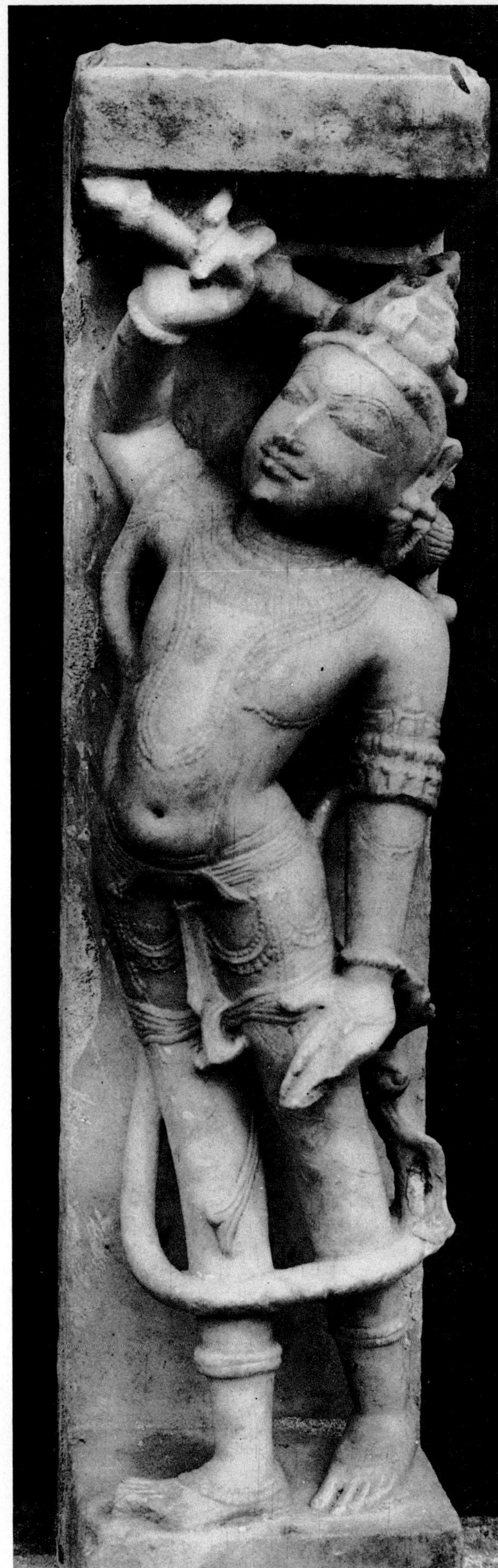

An idol of 'Chanwardhari' made of white marble belonging to 11th-12th century A.D. seized by CBI from village Mukundpura of Rajasthan.

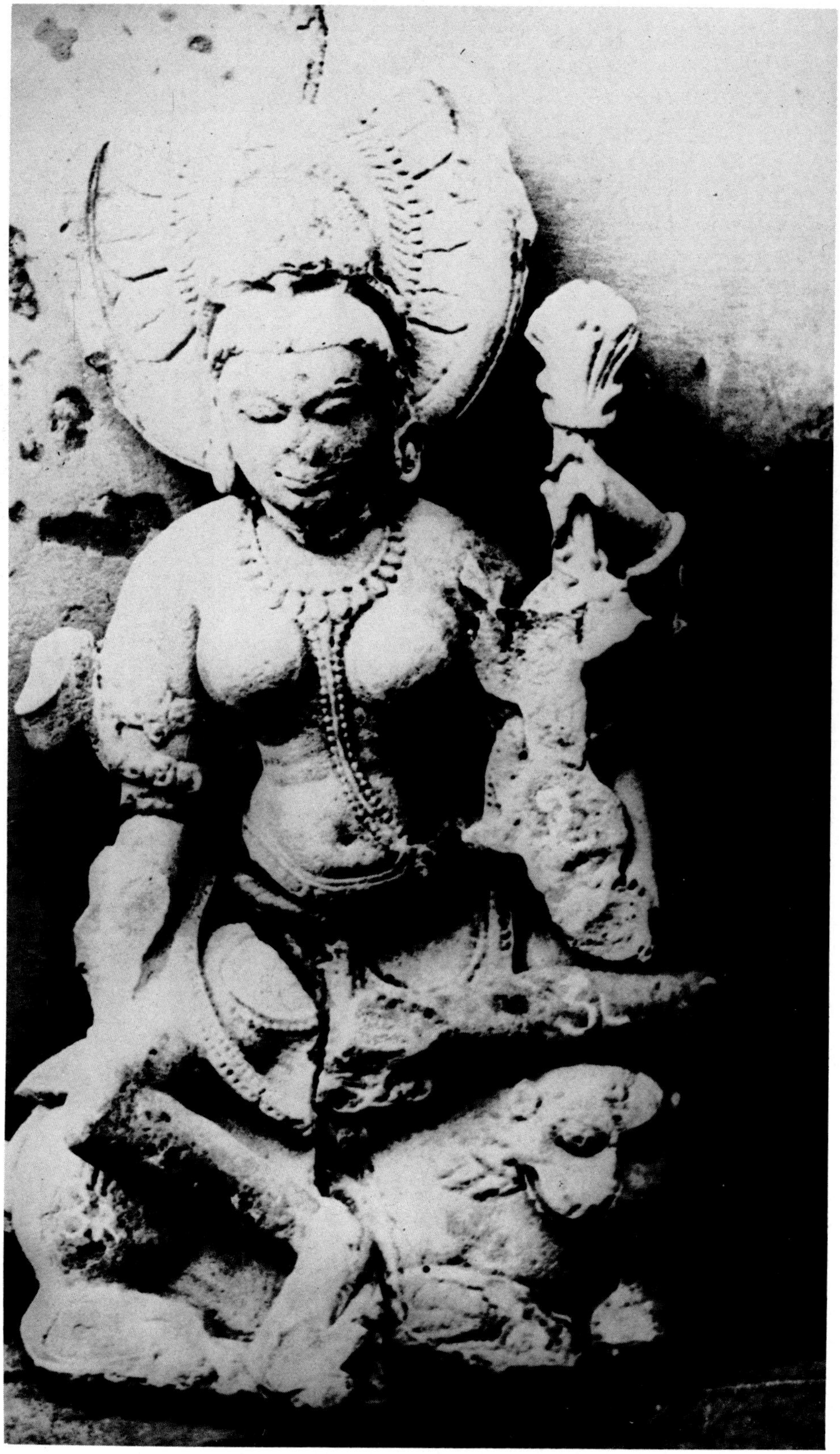

Tripura Sundari—Durga.

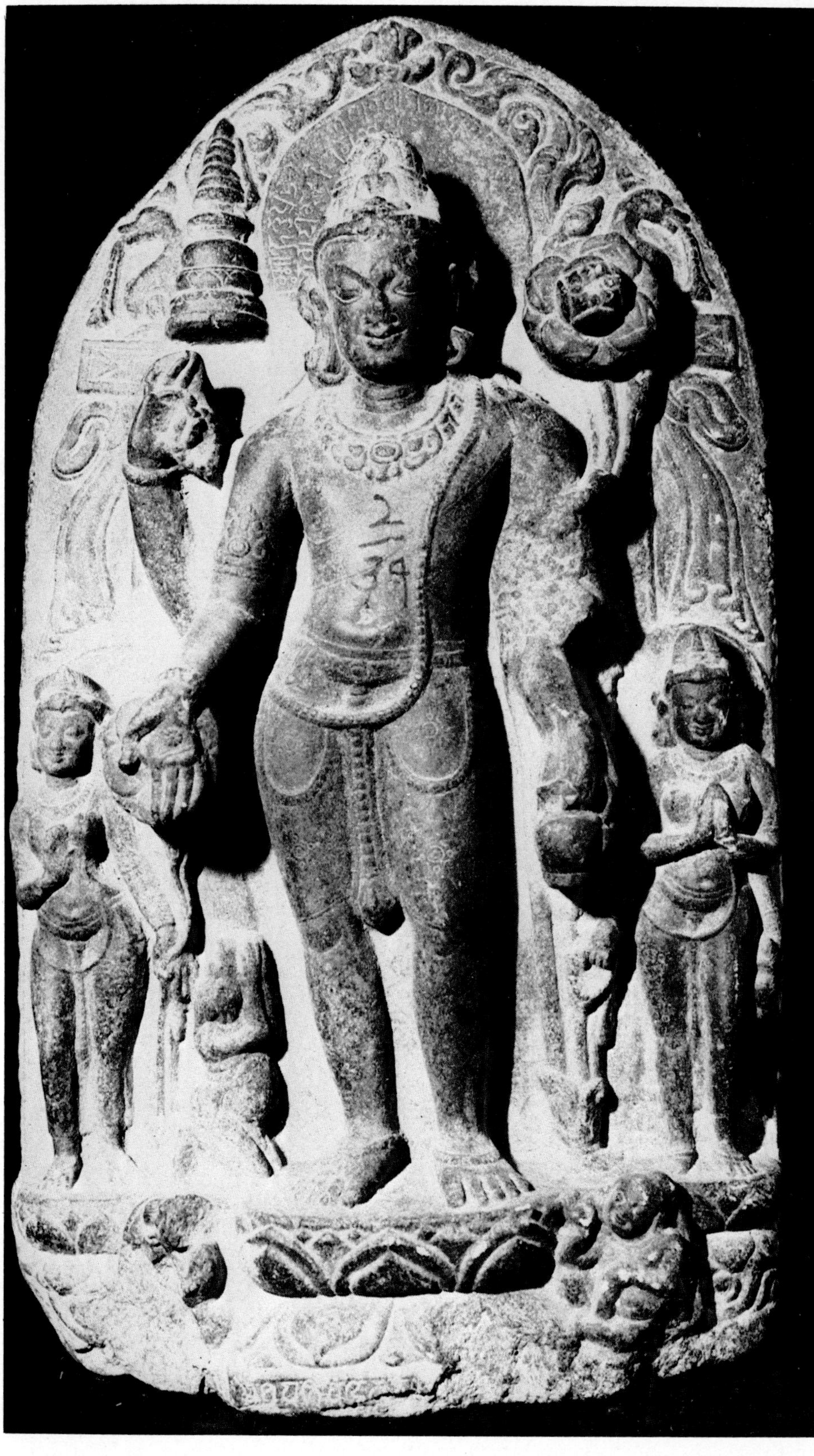

Standing Buddha ( Stone ) Recovered from Jama Masjid Area Delhi in 1987.

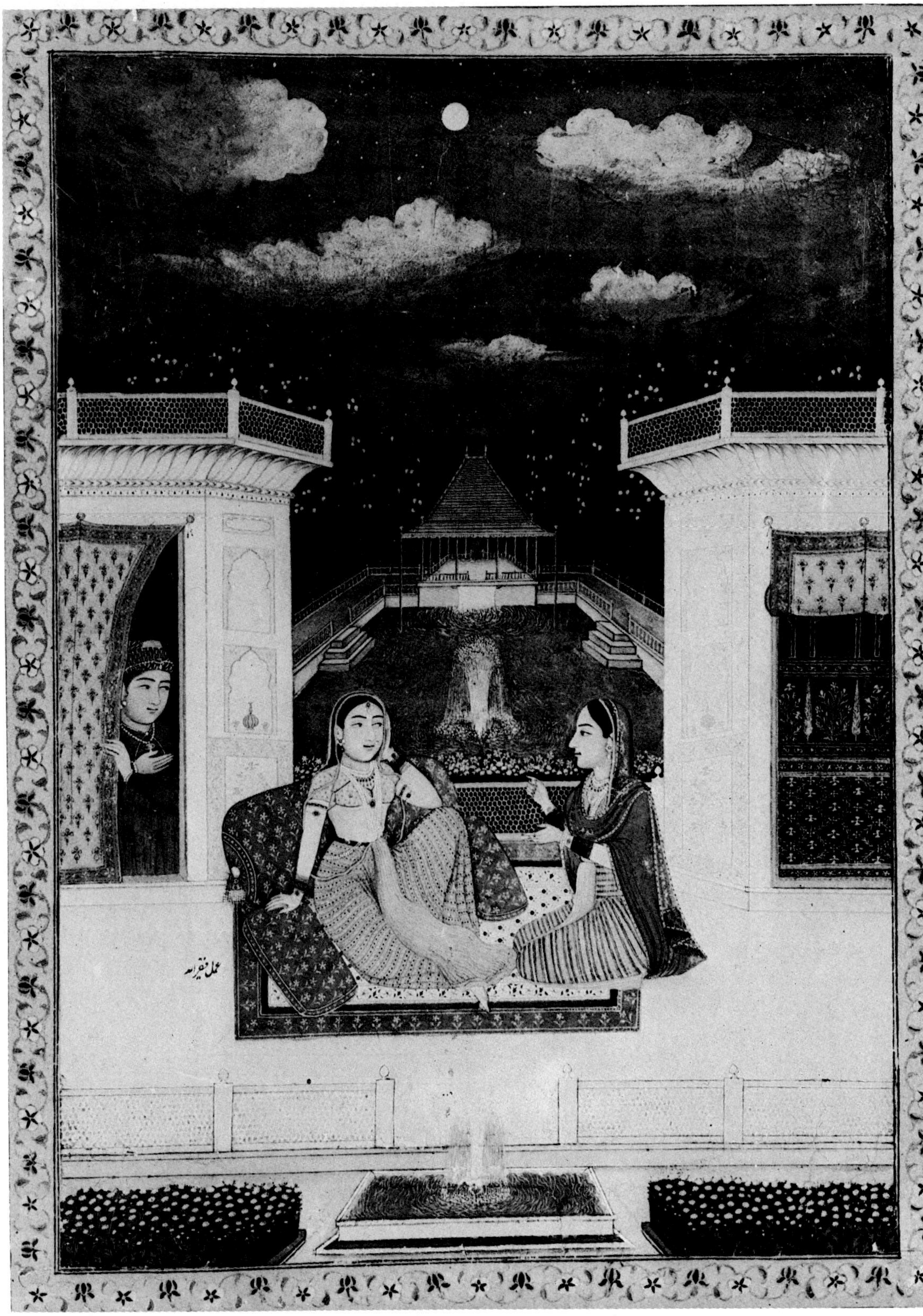

Portrait of ladies on a terrace of post Mughal;
18th century, Jaipur Museum.

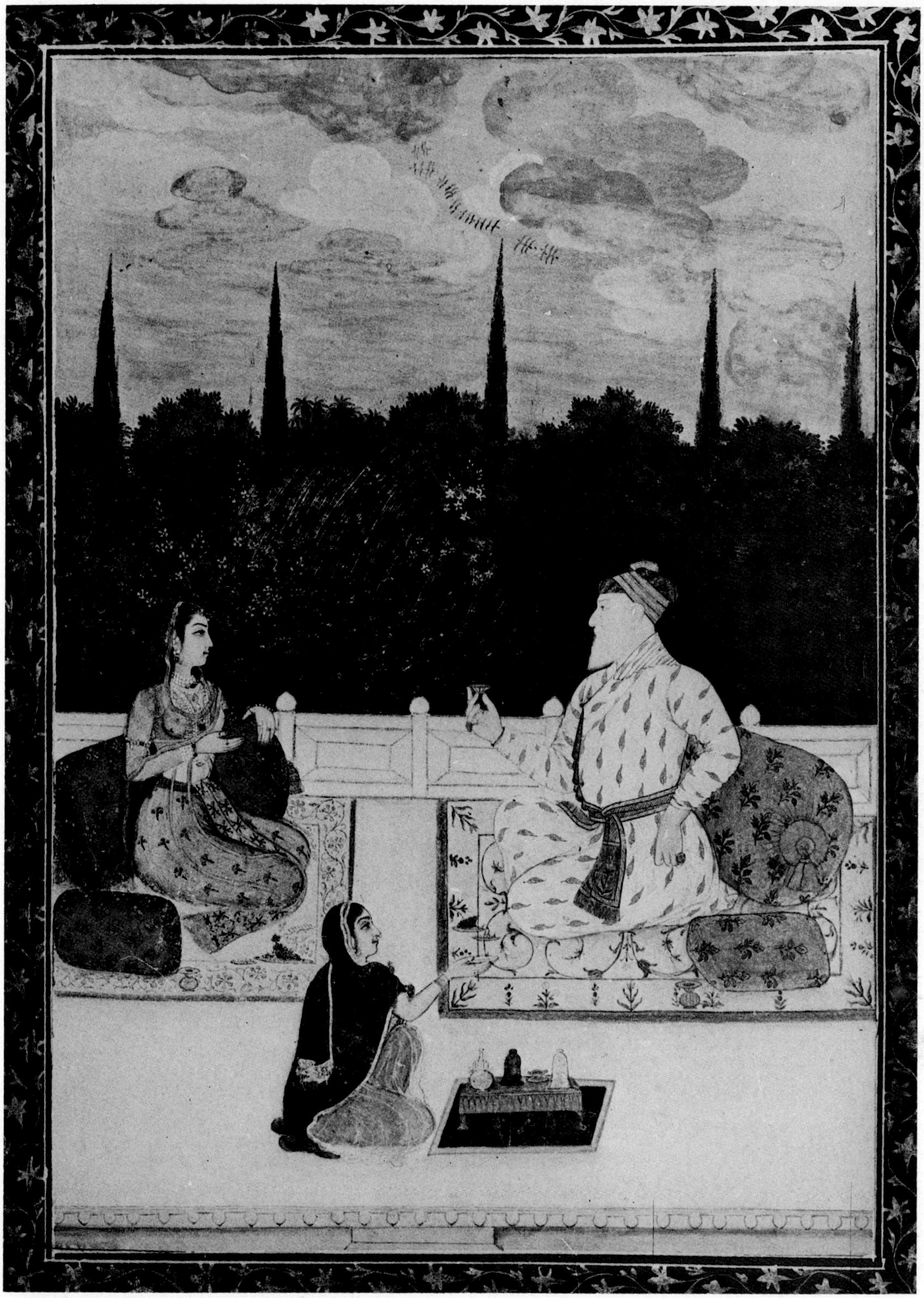

Painting of Darbar of a Nawab Maydu-daulah
Abdul Ahad Khan Bahadur of 18th century,
Delhi Kalam.

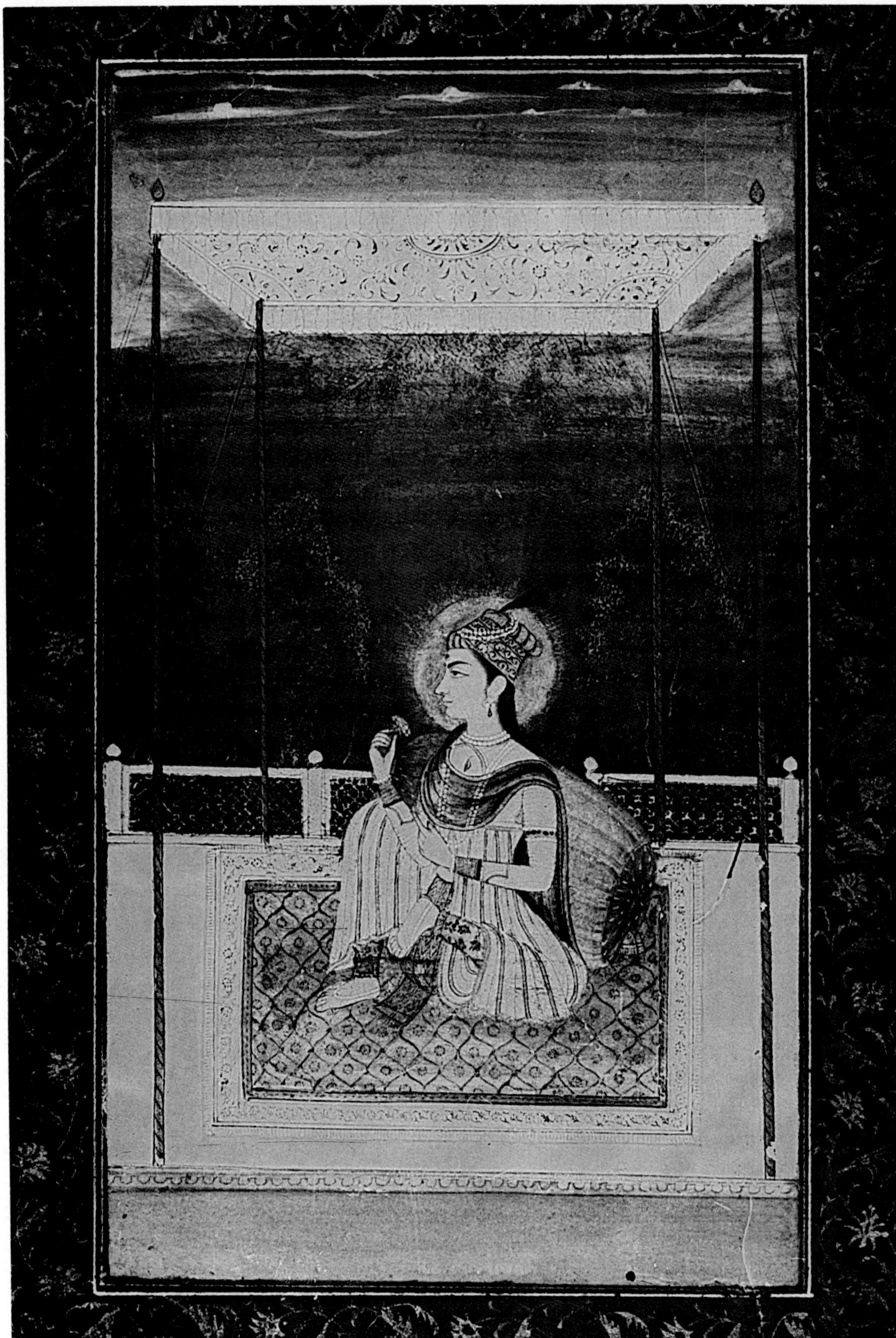

Painting of Zaibun Nissa of late 17th century.

the country. It was only after 1947 that the Indian art objects were appreciated and there was a steady flow to these countries. According to Badar-ud-din Tyabji, 'this late start in the modern world's appreciation of Indian art and antiquities (the ancient world thought highly of them) must be attributed to the vicissitudes of India's political history.' The British took over India at a time when one of her great creative periods was coming to an end. During the colonial period that followed everything that was Indian suffered a drastic devaluation. Though possessions which had rare artistic and historical value were taken away by the British, it did not contribute greatly to the appreciation of Indian art in Britain, still less in Europe. Its owners prized the art objects more out of curiosity and as valuable booty rather than as work of art.

It is only after the independence that a real appreciation of Indian art among a section of the British art-conscious public has begun to grow. It is noteworthy that only in 1947-48 was the first exhibition of Indian art held at Burlington House in London. In a way, it was through that exhibition that Indian art made its first big impact on the British public and thousands of foreign visitors.

Antiques, rare manuscripts, precious miniature paintings and ancient jewellery and idols from various temples worth several hundred crores of rupees have been smuggled since independence. Despite the preventive measures and various checks by the government agencies, smuggling of these treasures has not stopped. Every year priceless idols, ancient objects of art, rare carpets and temple regalia are smuggled out of each state in the country.

Behind this colossal loot of the cultural heritage is the sordid story of international thieves and smugglers, a widespread network of idol runners, shady antique dealers, corrupt officials and an indifferent policy towards preservation of the cultural wealth of the country. According to certain reports only ten per cent of the cases are detected and hardly in one per cent the culprits are booked by the law.

The ancient monuments, museums and places of religious worship are the target of the antique thieves. Temples, churches and mosques often do not report the thefts for two reasons—one, the thefts are mostly committed with the connivance of the temple priests or in collusion with local officials. Secondly, the priests and trustees of the places of worship are afraid of the public criticism. There are also private collectors, the non-poor descendants of the former rich princes and even some members of the staff of the erstwhile princely states make huge profits by clandestinely selling these rare objects to foreigners.

Another factor to be noted is the treatment we give to the foreign experts. The archaeological experts in the garb of study move freely in the monuments and make their special targets to procure the antiques by alluring the officials. An Indian expert while explaining why many rich American individuals were interested in Indian antiques, said that the USA was poor in art and was trying to collect as much as it could from the world over. The wealthy Americans could escape from paying tax, by declaring that the antiques they bought would be presented to the US museums on their death. Thus, they could get their name on a plaque as well as enrich the American museums.

The fascination for beauty and the desire to possess art objects in westerners is considered to be the prime factor behind the smuggling racket having international ramifications. The price offered by the western collectors is fabulous, apart from the fact that even the museums in the West too are ready to pay a handsome money for these pieces. Looking at the market trends it has been observed that during the last two decades, there has been a thousand-fold increase in the selling price of Indian antiques and archaeological pieces of art which makes the smuggling profession a lucrative one.

The channels by which these stolen antiquities reach collectors' homes and the foreign countries are also known. Practically in every antique theft case solved by the police, the linkage of antiques dealer has been established. It is not unreasonable therefore to assume that they form the conduit through which the bulk of the pillaged treasures reach the open market. Similarly, most of the art treasures that are whisked out of the country are passed off as copies or reproduction at the customs and the officials concerned are often in no position to detect a genuine antique from a replica. This problem would continue to remain even if the Government nationalises the domestic trade in antiques. The effective solution to this problem will be to ban even the export of replica of ancient works. Efforts are to be intensified to bring back the stolen antiques either by persuasion or by other channels of law.

The Indian art is now well recognised and appreciated by the art connoisseurs for its workmanship and decorativeness. Further, awareness and acquisition of the Indian art continues to grow in the US as Americans are being exposed to new areas of Indian art. Frequent art exhibitions held in various capitals of Europe and other affluent countries have attracted the Westerners to Indian art and antiques. To judge the value of Indian art, an idea could be formed from the sales held by auction houses in London and New York in 1983. Three big international art dealers, namely Sotheby, Christie and Phillips had a total sale of about Rs. 2 crores worth of art pieces, which proved that the interest in Indian art is on the increase.

During these auctions, an idol from Mathura belonging to the 10-12th century, regarded as the most sensuous Indian sculpture, fetched Rs. 82,500 at Sotheby's sale. A Mughal miniature of 1570 A.D., an illustration of the Hamza-Nama belonging once to Akbar's own copy of Dastan-i-Amir Hamza was sold for Rs. 2.20 lakhs. A gilt copper figure of Durga of 15th century was auctioned for Rs. 7.15 lakhs—which was more than expectation of Christie's. At Sotheby's auctions, a painting of a princess bathing, of 1749 from Bikaner, was sold for Rs. 31,900. Another piece, a Chola bronze piece of Balakrishna of 12th century fetched a fabulous price of Rs. 3.08 lakhs. The high prices are indicative of the interest for Indian art in affluent countries and this has also attracted the notice of art smugglers.

Some connoisseurs have suggested that it is high time that an objective assessment of policies is made with regard to preserving the Indian cultural heritage. The government could undertake a complete documentation of (1) antiques which must remain in the country, (2) objects which could be allowed to be exported only under a licence, and (3) objects which could be freely sent abroad on a mere declaration. Unfortunately, the attitude today is to ban the export of even ersatz objects, merely on the plea that they are antiques which consequently encourages clandestine trade.

So far over three lakh antiques—exquisite sculptures, paintings and manuscripts—have been registered under the antiquities data bank of the Archaeological Survey of India (ASI), New Delhi. Despite the Antiquities Act being in force since 1976, the smuggling activity goes unabated. Still, there may be thousands of antiques buried or lying near old and dilapidated temples and also in the houses of villagers who do not realise their true value. Vandals look for these unregistered antiques and make their profit by approaching the foreign buyers clandestinely. The seized antiques have revealed that they are being bought and sold without the knowledge of the Archaeological Survey of India.

It is a good omen that Archaeological Survey of India wants to prepare a national catalogue of antiques, so that at any given time information, supported with photographs, would be available on India's heritage in sculptures, paintings and manuscripts. This catalogue will go a long way to enable ASI to keep a watch on the valuable treasures of the country and also assist the police sleuths in tracking down stolen antiques.

India's art heritage cannot be evaluated in terms of money; it is priceless and cannot be replaced. It is not enough that the police agencies be vigilant; the people too must be more conscious in the matter and become guardians of the wealth bestowed on them by their great ancestors.

This book on the Plunder of Art is the first attempt of its kind. The antiques of India are not only of decorative value but have a proud heritage behind them, having been created by craftsmen. I shall feel rewarded if it makes the readers aware of some aspects of the continuous loot of our art heritage at the hands of some vandals, so that people are awakened and help the law enforcing agencies to check further plunder.

706, Laxmi Bai Nagar
New Delhi - 110023

H. Bhisham Pal

# THE PLUNDER

How can a man die better
Than facing fearful odds
For the ashes of his father
And the temples of his Gods

THOSE ashes and temples that the bard spoke of today lie in a shambles all over the world. They have fallen a prey to the vandals and profiteers. This phenomenon of clandestine trade in ancient art treasures and objects of heritage has assumed frightening dimensions in the recent past.

Trading and vandalism, often patronised by a country's establishment, is a neo-colonial phenomenon. With the advent of maritime activities and the rise of new powers, any student of history would notice the impact of the emergence of these new colonial powers leading to the decline of some of the most highly evolved peoples and civilisations. The colonial powers, to reinforce their dominance and add a veneer of respectability, collected art objects from the colonies.

Thus, one sees the famous Cleopatra's Needle ending up in London. Even though Sir Mortimer Wheeler was a scholar and archaeologist in his own right, sizeable collection of antiquities from the Indus Valley explorations landed up in the London Museum. So is it with the other Egyptian antiquities. It is no wonder that a sizeable collection of Gandhara art pieces too is today to be found in one of the American museums.

Let us also not forget that it is after viewing the famous Elgin marbles that the famous poet, John Keats, composed his famous 'Ode to the Grecian Urn'. The ancient and splendid Hellenic and Roman civilisations too were not spared by this phenomenon. With the decline of the highly evolved Aztec, Mayan and Incan civilisations, their heritage and artefacts landed in the private collections and museums of their rich neighbour. The Chinese, Japanese and even Tibetan artefacts met the same fate. So has India lost innumerable priceless treasures of centuries. The British Library, even though a late development comparatively, is a glaring example of the recent days.

This 'sickness' has assumed a rather frightening dimension after the two great wars of this century. Added to the political domination, came in another factor—Money. For big money, there are people who are ready to sell their heritage.

There is an interesting story narrated by a close friend, a scholar in his own right, who had gone on a visit to Europe with his new bride. While they were in the Cistine Chapel at the Vatican Museum and admiring Michael Angelo, a bus load of American tourists reached there. In the midst of the camera-totting tourists, an elderly person shouted—and nobody could miss it: 'Oh! what a marvellous replica of our original Gugenheim! So much for ignorance of affluence!

The following pages just delve into that.

Some European scholars took interest in studying the countless rare manuscripts, antiques and valuable objets d'art that were lifted out of India during the last three centuries. It was through their labours that Indology too developed along with Assyriology, Egyptology and Sinology in Europe. The East became aware of the value of its treasures in pragmatic terms when the latter began to adorn the private collections of the elite and affluent families and also the museums of the West.

The temples, whose architectural and artistic splendour have stood the ravages of time and weather, are the target of cultural vandalism.

But, for one sincere connoisseur there are a number of charlatans, faddists and uncultured nouveau rich who do not believe in art for art's sake. To these must be traced the root cause of the plunderers' and the smugglers' raison d'etre. Of course, there are several other motives at work too. Ignorance of the true value and purpose of art, irresponsibility and greed for immediate personal material gains are some of the chief traits of those who, though in charge or in possession of art treasures, fall prey to the robbers. They too must share the blame for the plunder and destruction of our ancient cultural heritage.

The affluent art connoisseurs of the Western countries crave for possessing Indian antiques. These antiques may be in the form of stone idols or an old painting or a rare piece of ancient inscription, they just try to grab in whatever way possible. As a result, a large number of Indian smugglers are thriving and conspiring with them to smuggle out the rich cultural heritage. Westerners do not mind paying high price for these art objects which is a sufficient bait for the petty thieves to indulge in this heinous crime.

Unguarded and unnoticed hundreds of antiques are lying around the ruins of ancient temples and villages in our countryside for many centuries. Their importance and value immediately shoot up, when the eyes of an art connoisseur falls on them. These invaluable antiques are stealthily removed with the help of vandals for monetary consideration. They are brought to the metropolitan cities where deals are struck with foreign buyers. At this point, the Enforcement Agencies sometimes get information and are able to prevent them from smuggling. Sometimes they meet with success in thwarting the plans of the smugglers while many a time they fail with the result that these cultural objects become the property of the foreigners adorning their art galleries or houses.

Last two decades have witnessed a phenomenal increase in this crime. The people in India were shocked at the disappearance of a stucco panel from the Nalanda site and the discovery of a priceless Shivapuram Nataraja of the Chola period in one of the museums in United States of America.

Between 1970 and 1988 no less than 3500 art objects were stolen from various parts of the country. Cultural vandalism though had its root as far back as 1936 but was on a low scale, the spurt came only after 1950. In the same year some members of Parliament discussed the ways and means to check the erosion of cultural property. The public too expressed its annoyance through different communication channels specially through the press. Smuggling of antiques was first detected in 1936 when Dr. Durdainse, a French national from Pondicherry, was found sending out antiques to France with the help of two local men. Another French national, Miss Pierre Gustan, was found exporting art objects in 1937.

According to the conservative estimate of an archaeological expert, antiques, rare manuscripts, precious miniature paintings and ancient jewellery and idols from temples worth over Rs. 200 crores have been smuggled out of India during the last two decades. Many thefts are not even reported to the police as sometimes they occur with the connivance of the temple priests and concerned officials. Behind this colossal loot of the cultural property is the sordid story of international thieves and smugglers, a widespread network of idol runners, shady antique dealers and corrupt officials. There are also private collectors and owners of heirlooms among some taluqdars, the now poor families belonging to erstwhile princely families and even the staff members of the erstwhile princely states who make rich profits through clandestine sales of rare ancient objects to foreigners.

A special target of antique thieves has been temples of Jammu and Kashmir, Himachal Pradesh, Uttar Pradesh, Rajasthan, Madhya Pradesh, Tamil Nadu, Orissa and Andhra Pradesh. The famous temples of Khajuraho, Guna and Shivpuri in Madhya Pradesh and Chamba and Kulu have suffered regularly at the hands of these thieves. From Khajuraho alone over 100 erotic sculptures valued at several million dollars were stolen and smuggled abroad between 1965 and 1970. Most of the figures, carved out in buff colour sandstone with superb artistry of the medieval times, portrayed 'Apsaras' (celestial beauties) in playful moods, nymphs standing beneath the mango trees, couples in loving embrace and female figures arranged in intricate formations. The sculptures, dating back to the 10th and 11th centuries, have been neatly sawed off from the interlocking brackets leaving many gaping holes on the richly carved walls and ceilings which they once adorned. The stolen antiques included five figures from the Ducha Deva temple which were considered as some of the finest pieces in Khajuraho's incomparable treasure-trove noted for their exquisite beauty of form and pose. The stolen sandstone Apsaras, Shalabhanjikas and other figures were valued at several million dollars.

A life-size bronze statue of Lord Vishnu from Hari Rai temple of Chamba was stolen with the connivance of three local men and a foreign antique smuggler. The five-foot tall idol of Vishnu dating back to eighth century is a rare piece of craftsmanship. The idol has four heads and is in a dancing pose. After two months of hectic search and investigation by the police, this priceless Vishnu idol was recovered from a Bombay godown. In January

1969, idols and jewellery were stolen from the Brijweshari temple in Kangra. Around the same time a Manager of a New Delhi hostel, an Englishman, was arrested for stealing a precious idol from Khajuraho. Fourteen valuable miniature paintings of the Kangra, Rajput, Mughal and Deccan styles were stolen from the Salarjung Museum, Hyderabad and were recovered by the Central Bureau of Investigation.

In Orissa, a whole temple was found missing one morning after it had been plundered stone by stone. Thefts of wooden temple chariots with exquisite carvings have also been common. A number of thefts have also taken place from the museums. In a sensational burglary in the Jaipur Palace museum—committed in collusion with some officials of the museum—1,750 rare miniature paintings were removed.

A sensational theft had taken place in the National Museum in New Delhi in 1968 in which 125 pieces of antique jewellery and 32 rare gold coins were missing. In the same year 48 persons had been arrested, on charges of stealing 200 idols from monuments and temples in Rajasthan. Of these, 10 were recovered from Ahmedabad, 10 from Palampur, 152 from Delhi and 2 from Bombay. The recovery of these antiques in Bombay revealed that foreign gangs were involved in these thefts.

The Central Bureau of Investigation (CBI) laid their hands and recovered two truck loads of idols and other antiques with the arrest of a prominent businessman of Rewa. They also recovered from him cheques worth 14 crores in foreign banks. In Rajasthan, a one thousand year old idol of goddess 'Harsidhi Mata' was stolen from Abaneri in Jaipur district. The three-feet high black stone statue of the goddess was chopped off from the ankles by the thieves and taken away. Inter-state gangs of thieves were at this time operating in the state. The sensational theft of 1,300 miniatures from the City Palace Museum, Jaipur was detected when some parcels addressed to a person in the United States were intercepted by the authorities. During the investigation of the case the police came to know that many statues stolen from temples and palaces in Rajasthan had already reached the foreign countries.

In May 1969 historic relics, including a 300 year-old copper plate and a replica of a gold and gem studded Mughal-style turban, were stolen from the Asifi Imambara in Lucknow. Next month a beautiful dancing figure was hacked away from its perch at the world famous Sun temple of Konarak in Orissa. The daredevil culprit was attempting to steal the stone carving from the temple in broad daylight in the presence of tourists. Goa was bereft of 200 idols between 1960 and 1969. A golden replica of the mausoleum of the grandson of the Prophet, Imam Hussain, was also stolen during this period from one of the palaces of the Nizam of Hyderabad. In September 1969, excavated idols, valuable pottery and age-old documents valued at several lakhs were reported to have been missing from the museum of Sanskrit University, Benaras. In the same month, 2208 rare miniature paintings, 200 stone idols and sculpture pieces and several brass and bronze curios were seized by the police in a raid conducted at the residence of a member of a princely family. Another theft of 48 precious idols from the Parasnath temple at Ahore, Rajasthan, preceded the assassination of a 95-year old Jain saint residing at the shrine. During raids in Varanasi, police recovered 50 precious idols including some priceless idols of Rama, Krishna and Buddha.

The year 1970 heralded with the recovery of 15 rare antiques and erotic miniature paintings stolen from different places in Aligarh district during a police raid in New Delhi. The three raids carried out by the Delhi Police in various localities led to the recovery of 148 antiques. It included idols and other precious antiques removed from some famous temples and monuments. Then followed a theft of six Buddha statues of 2nd century A.D. from the Central Museum at Nagpur. An idol of Goddess Parvati was stolen on 25th January from the Meenakshi temple in Madurai. Next month two historical idols were stolen from the Dauji temple in Mathura. Another theft of some icons from a Maratha Fort near Jhansi was also reported.

The thefts and their seizures by the police during raids were the salient features of the year 1970. A diamond idol of Lord Parswanath was stolen from a private temple in Varanasi in May. A week later the customs authorities in Bombay seized a precious consignment of marble and stone antiques stolen from Rajasthan and Gujarat. A Tibetan and an Indian art dealer were arrested when they were trying to smuggle them outside the country. Around the same time a theft of 102 paintings belonging to the Mughal, Basohli, Rajasthani and Kangra schools was reported from the Chandigarh Museum.

During raids organised by the police, statues, ivory carvings and 150 paintings belonging to the 18th century, depicting erotic themes and worship were seized. In another raid, 225 antique pieces were recovered from a godown in Bombay. While several seizures were taking place in northern states, six precious idols from the Bobor temples in Jammu were reported missing. There may have been other thefts of antiques which have gone unnoticed or not reported to the police.

An idol of Lord Mahavira was stolen in 1971 from Etawah belonging to the Gandharva school which flourished during the tenth and eleventh centuries in the area between Allahabad in the east and Delhi in the west. A Durga idol belonging to the Gupta period measuring 1.20 metres high and 0.75 metre wide and carved in black sandstone was also stolen in the same year from a temple in Itora village. The exquisite statue had been attracting devotees for centuries.

In September 1975 police recovered 50 stolen idols from godowns of antique dealers in Delhi's Sunder Nagar, Karol Bagh and South Extension areas and also in Chattarpur near Mehrauli. The haul included a bronze statue of Edward VII, larger than life-size; a statue of Ganesh in a dance pose, which was stolen from Ghazipur in 1969; another Ganesh statue in bronze and two stone idols of Shiva and Uma, dating back to the 11th century. In another theft, two 12th century stone idols of Parvati-Shiva and Nagalingam weighing nearly 200 kgs each were stolen from Shri Loknath temple in Orissa. Fifty-five idols made of bronze, brass and stone worth more than six lakhs were seized from a foreigner in 1973 at the Raxaul police check-post.

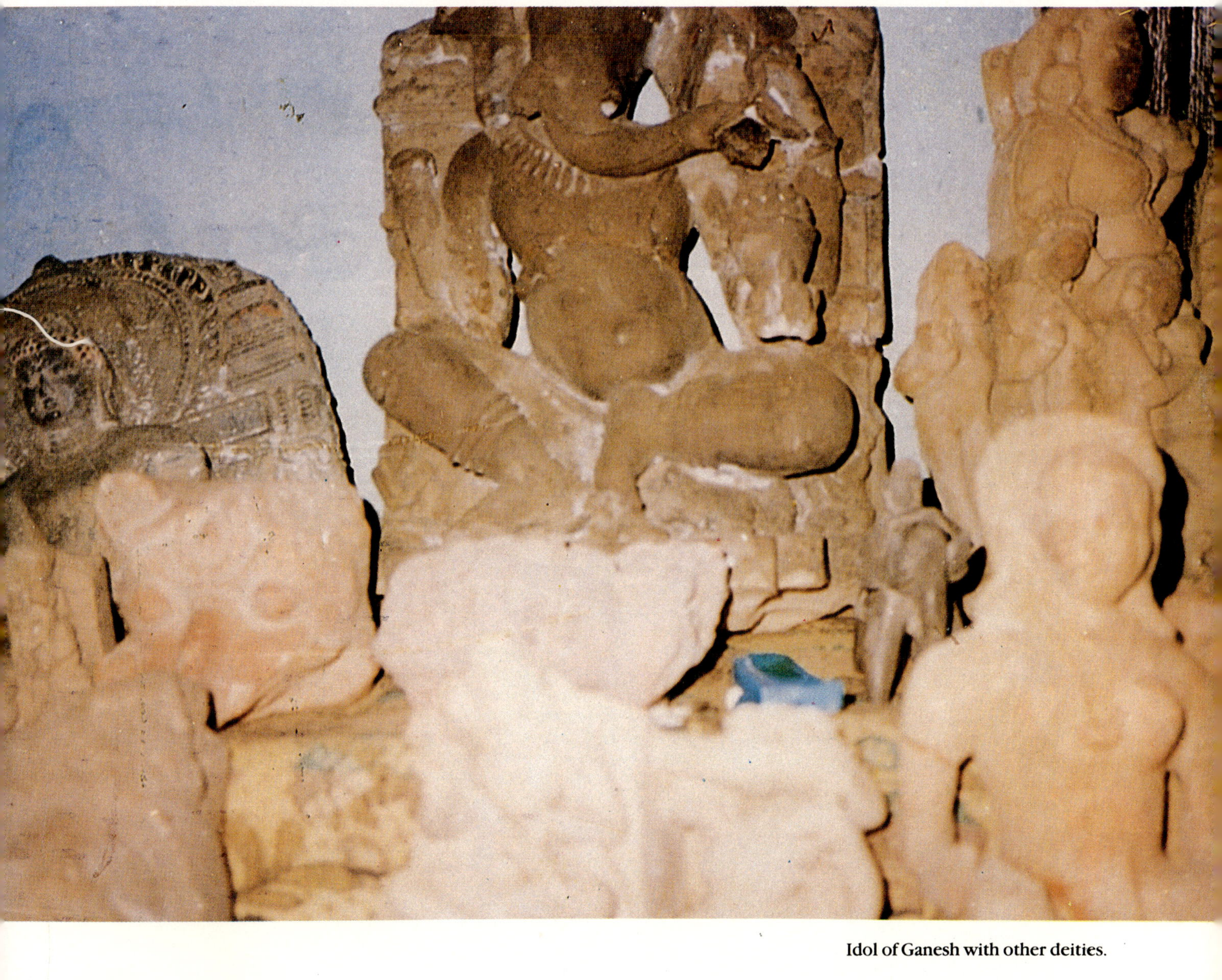

Idol of Ganesh with other deities.

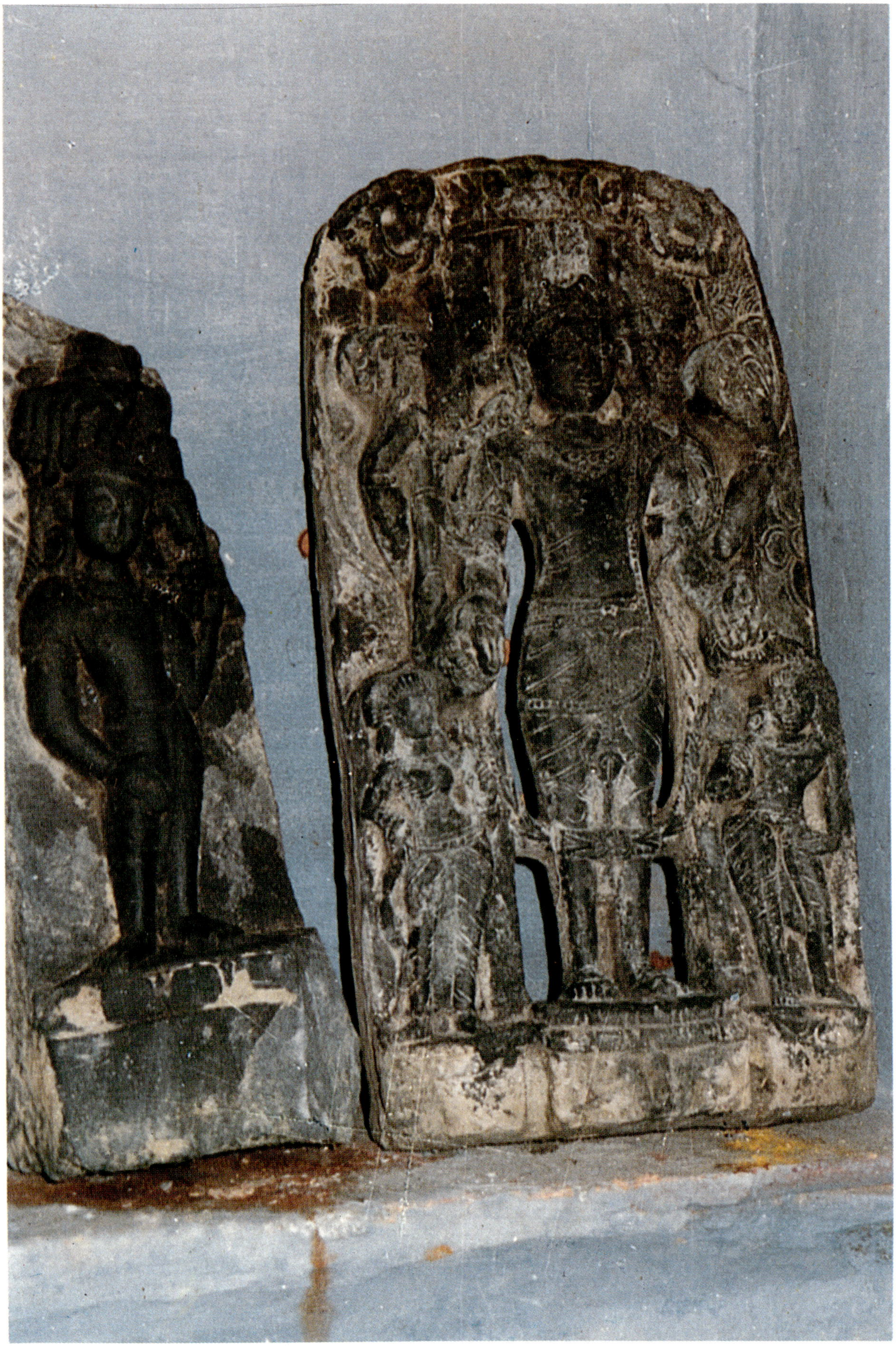

Stone idol of a Goddess.

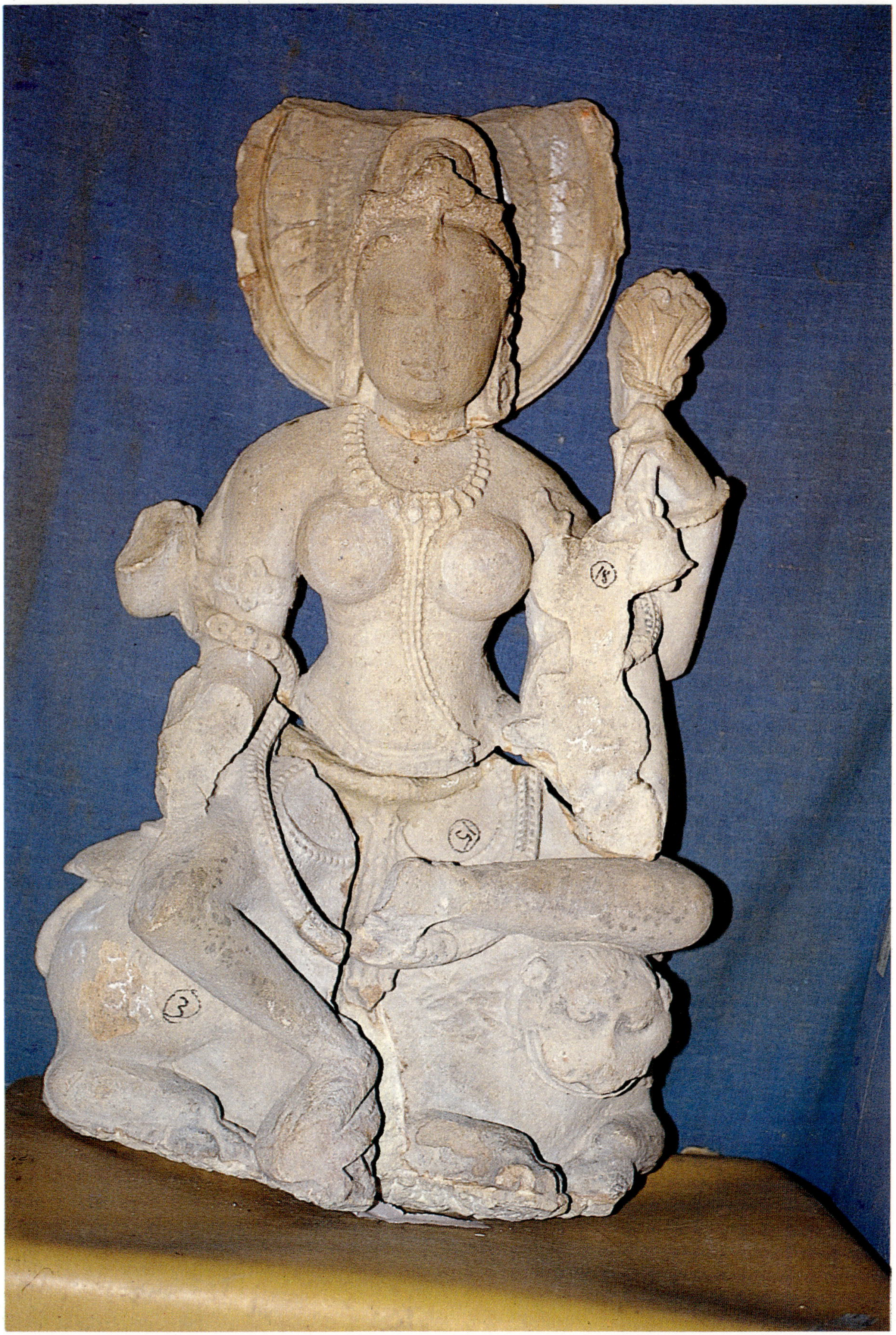

Idol of Goddess Chamundeswari.

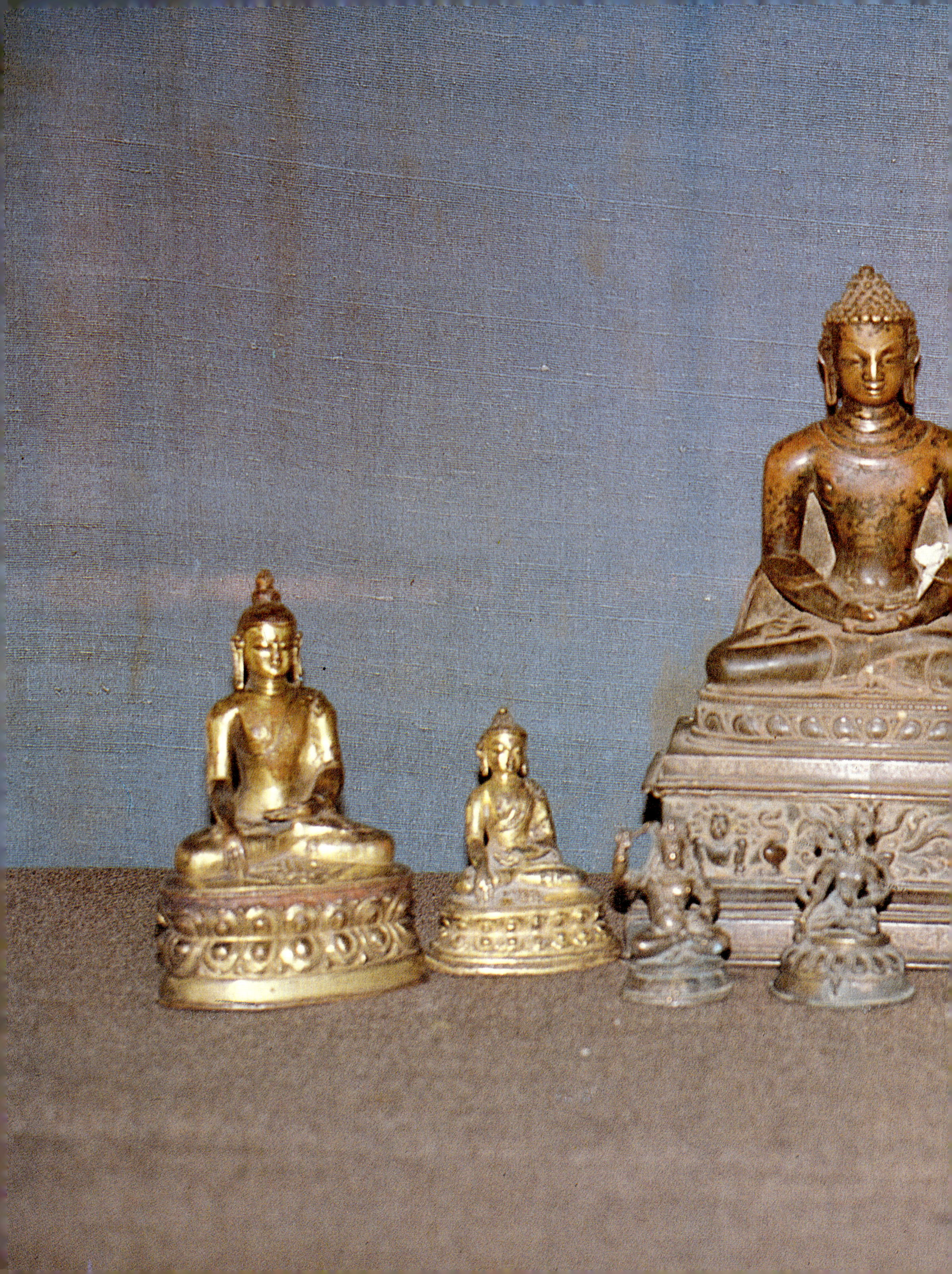

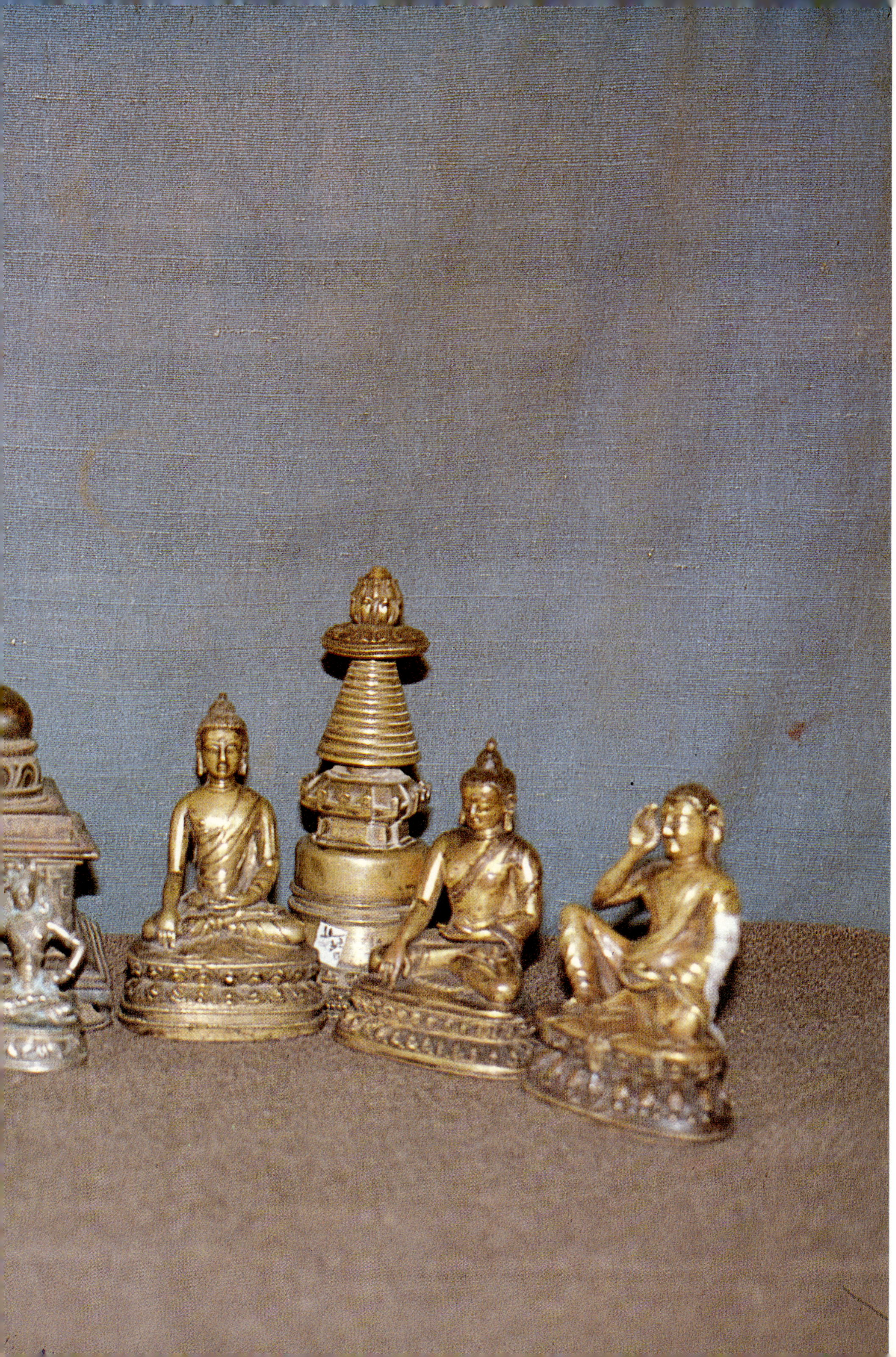

Bronze idols of Lord Buddha.

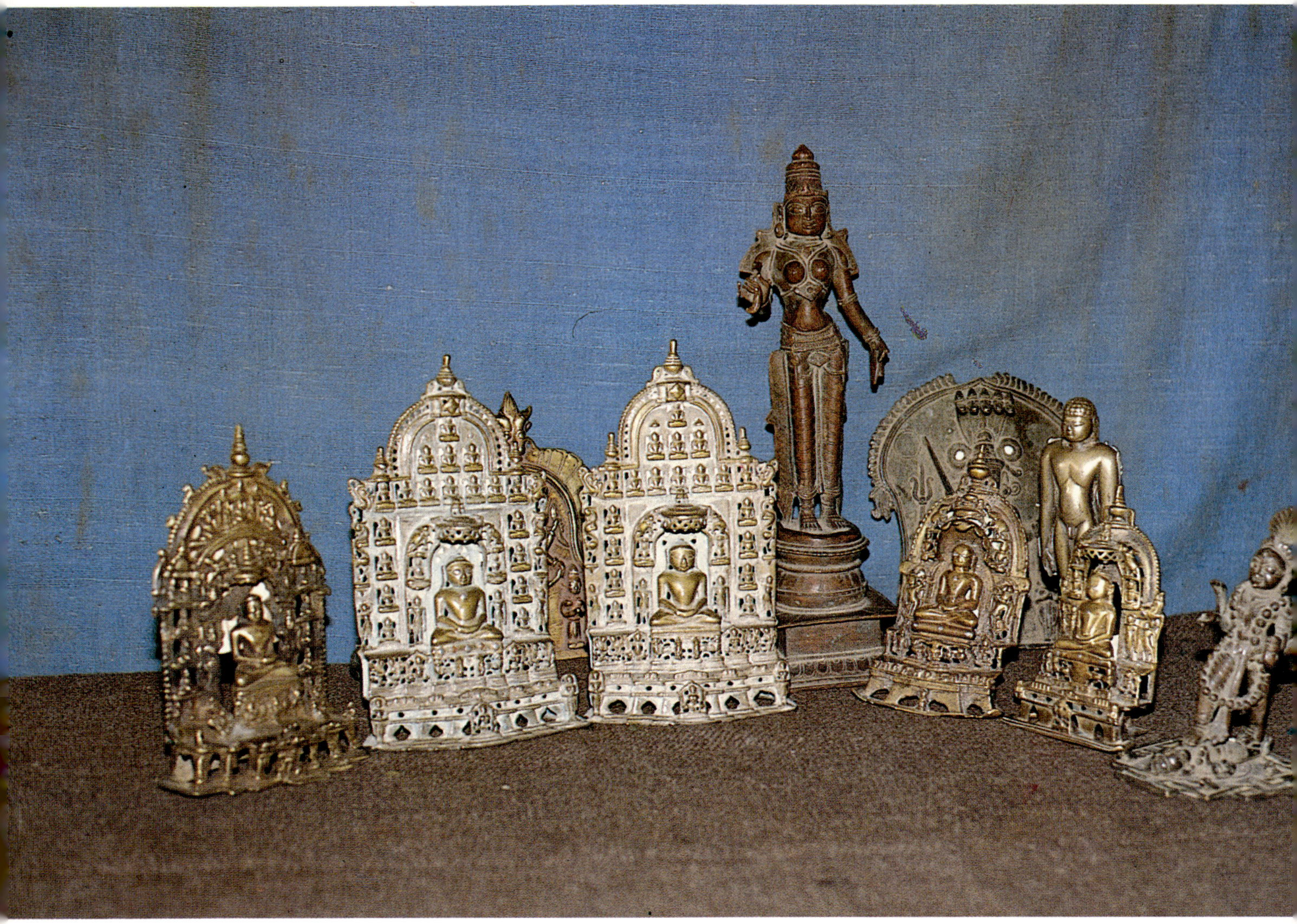

Bronze Idols.

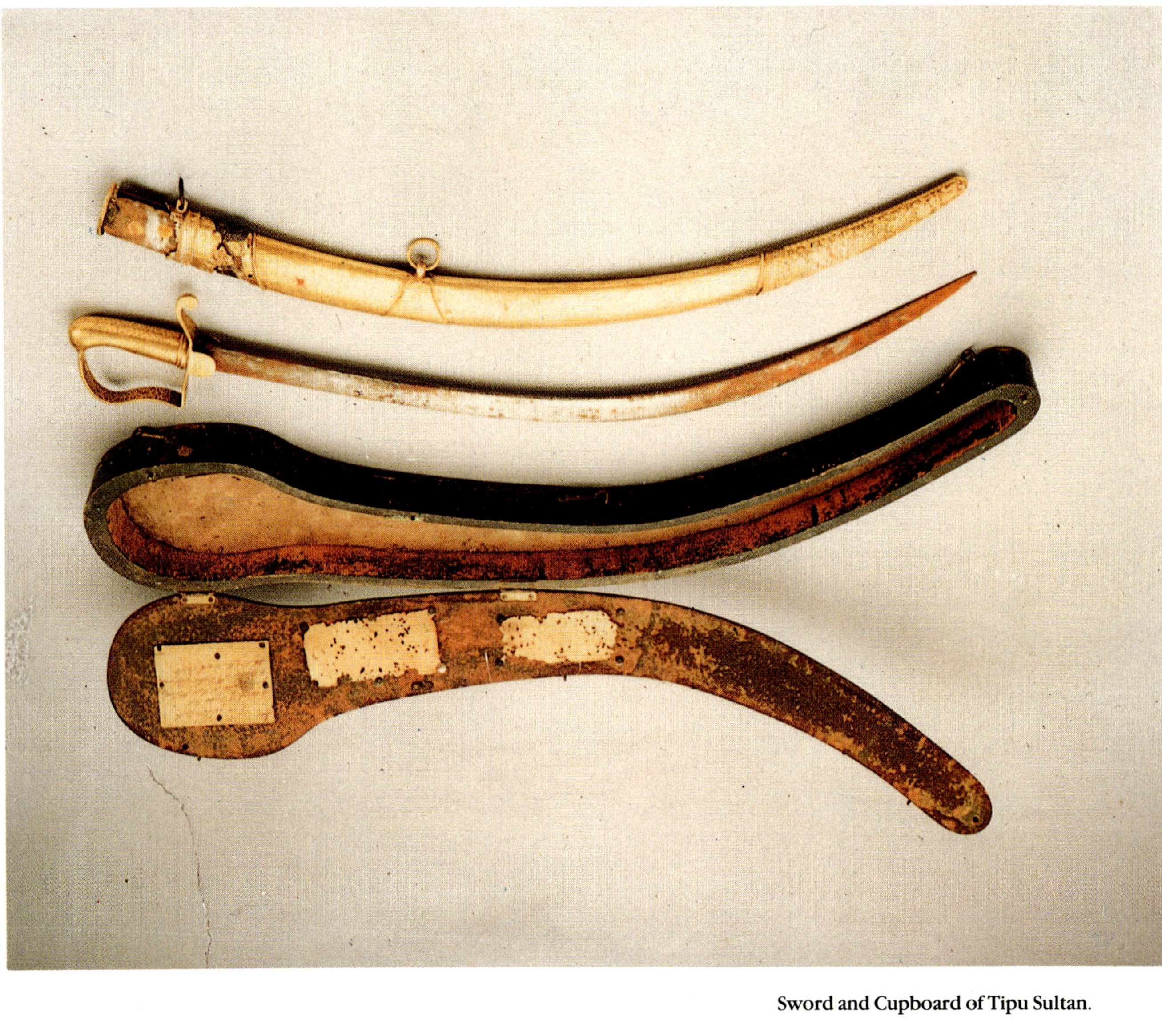

Sword and Cupboard of Tipu Sultan.

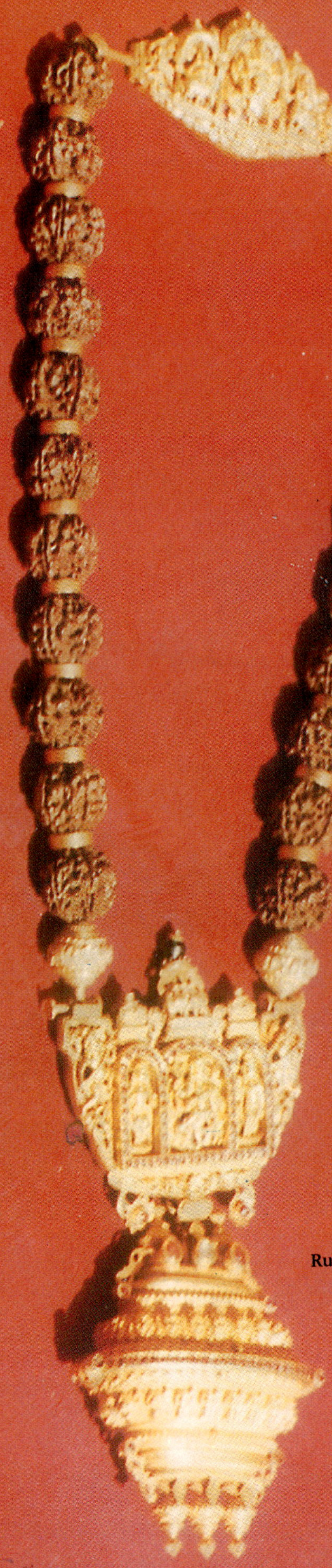

Rudraksha Mala.

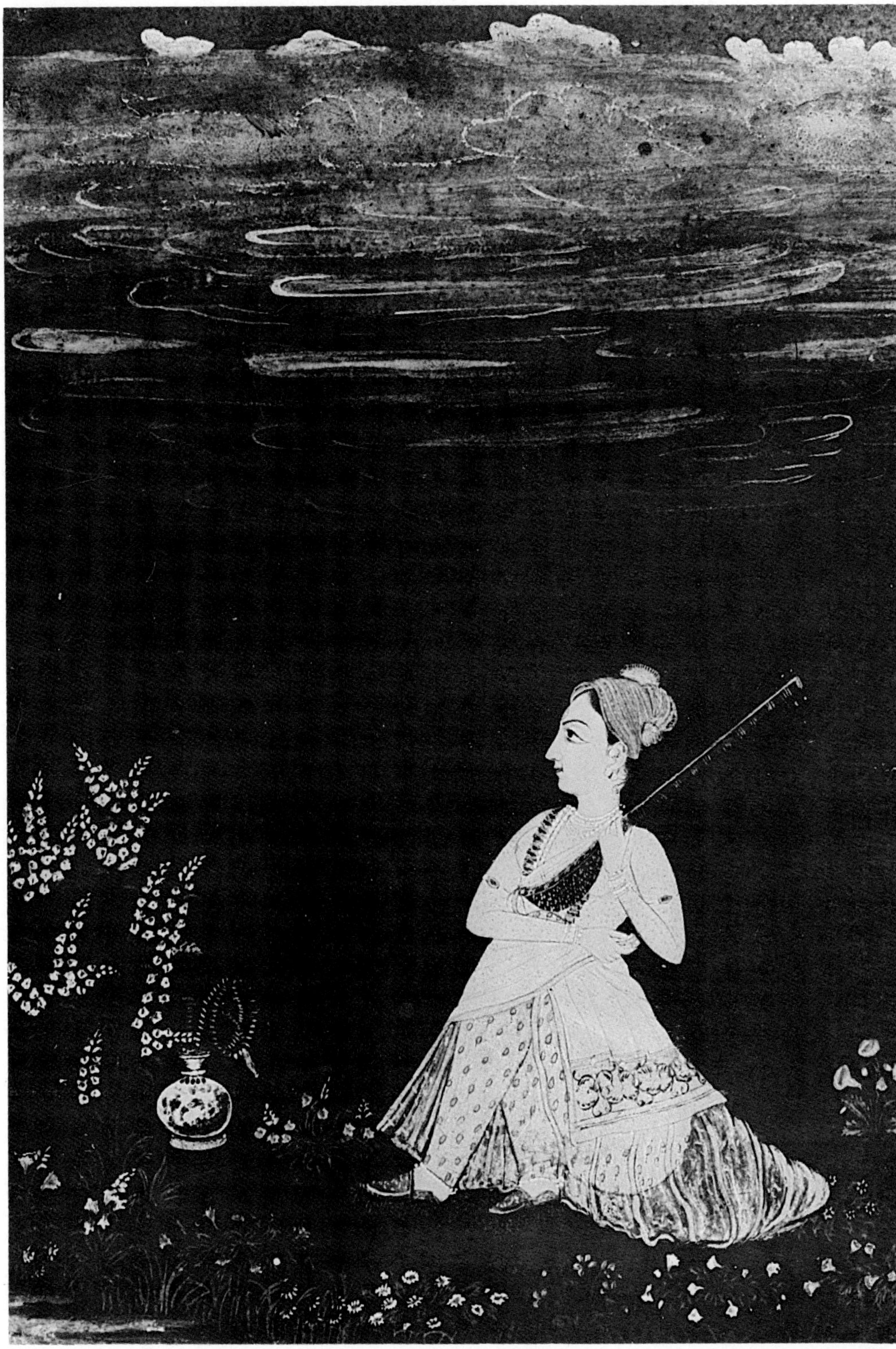

Painting of a lady on the bank of a river holding the musical instrument—Ektara—17th century.

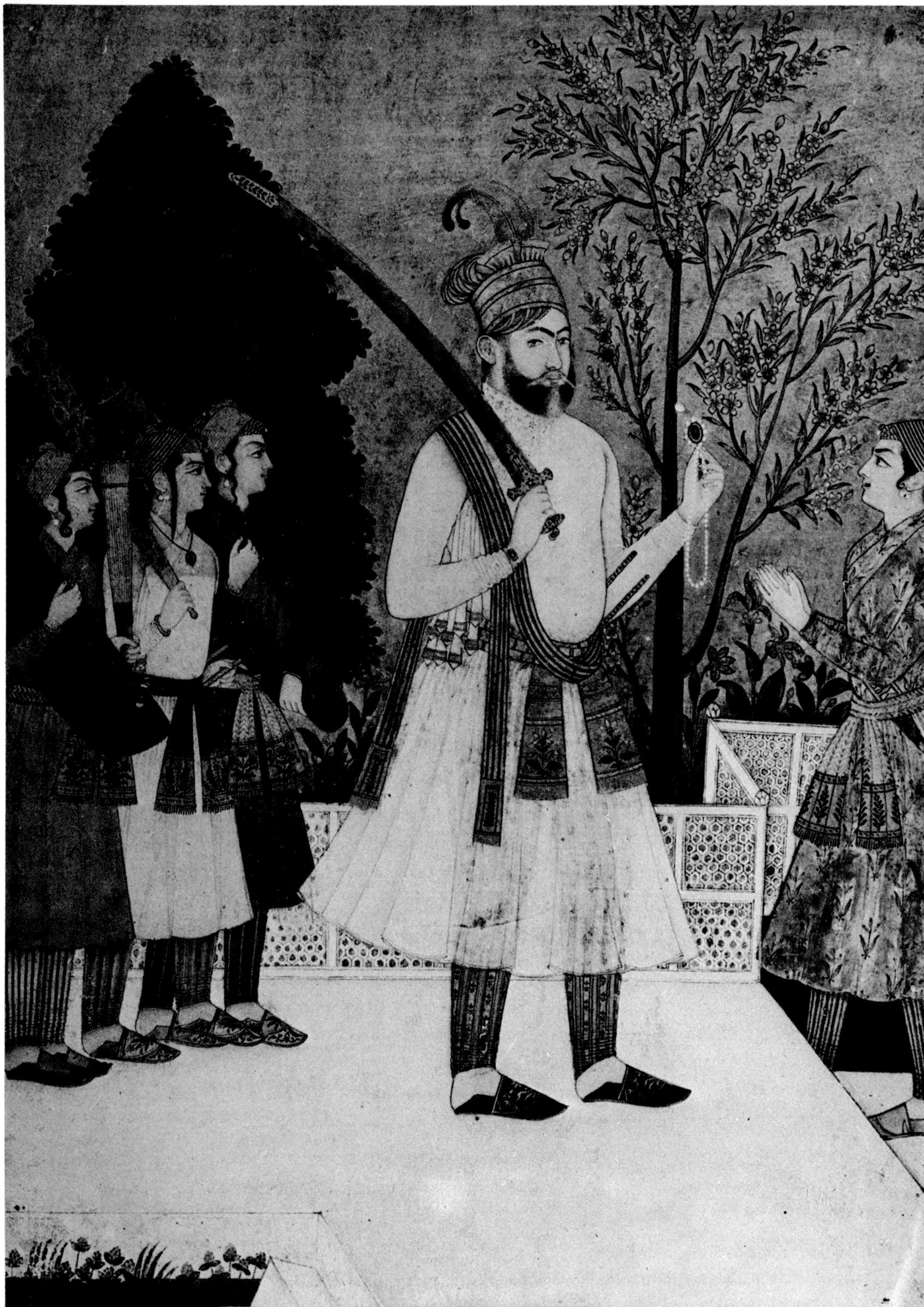

Painting of Shah Hasan-dhoula founder of Bengal dynasty of Afghan rulers of late 17th century.

Painting of Ameer Khan Rohilla, the founder of Ramnagar dynasty—16th century.

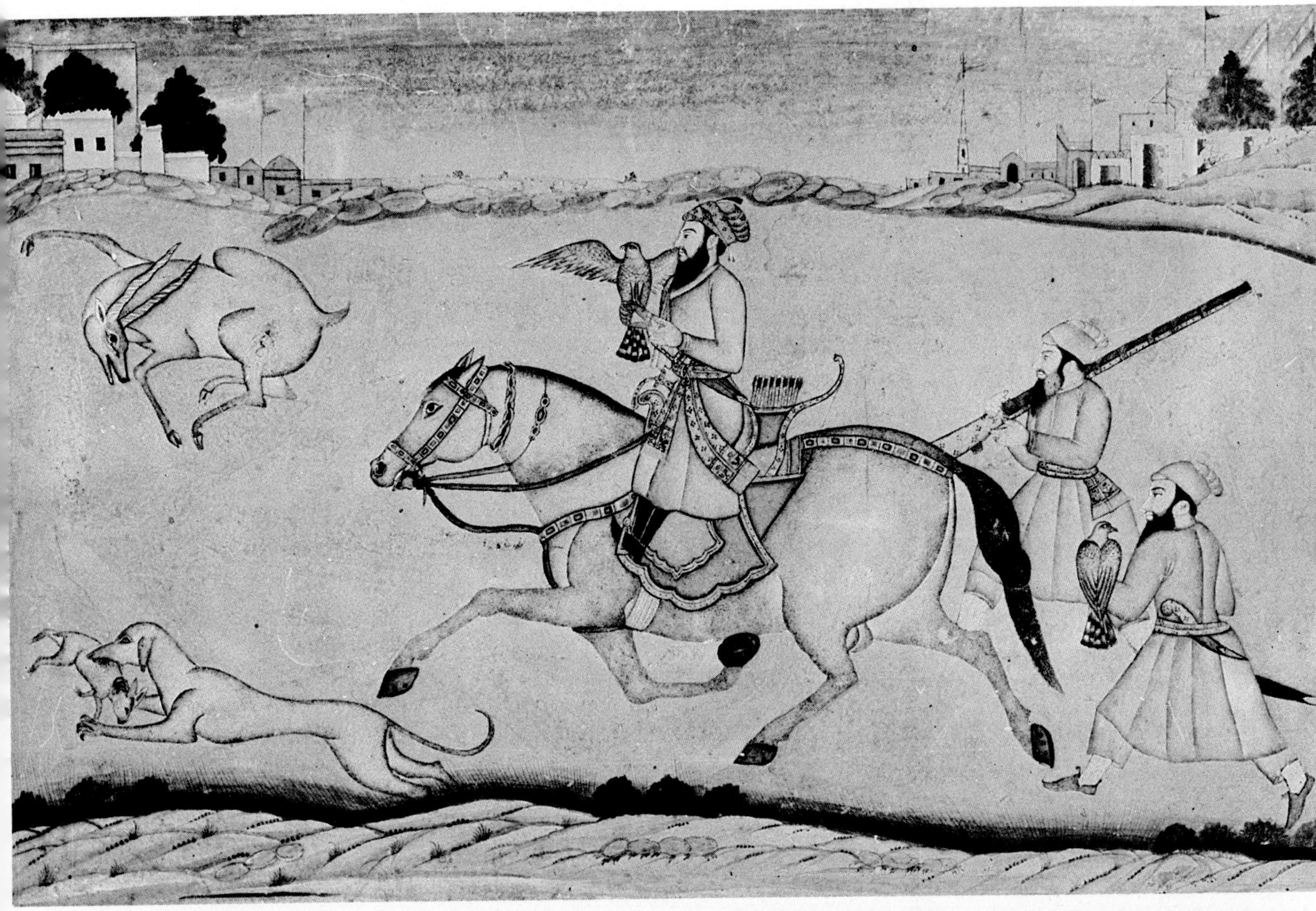

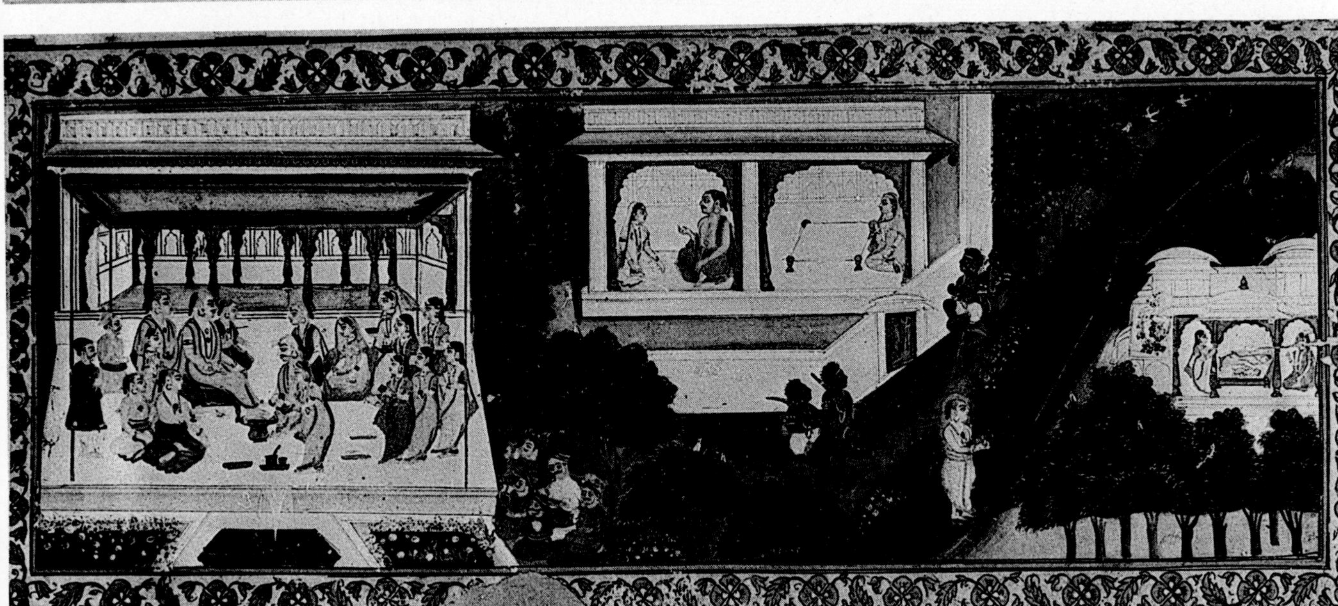

Painting of Rajputana School.

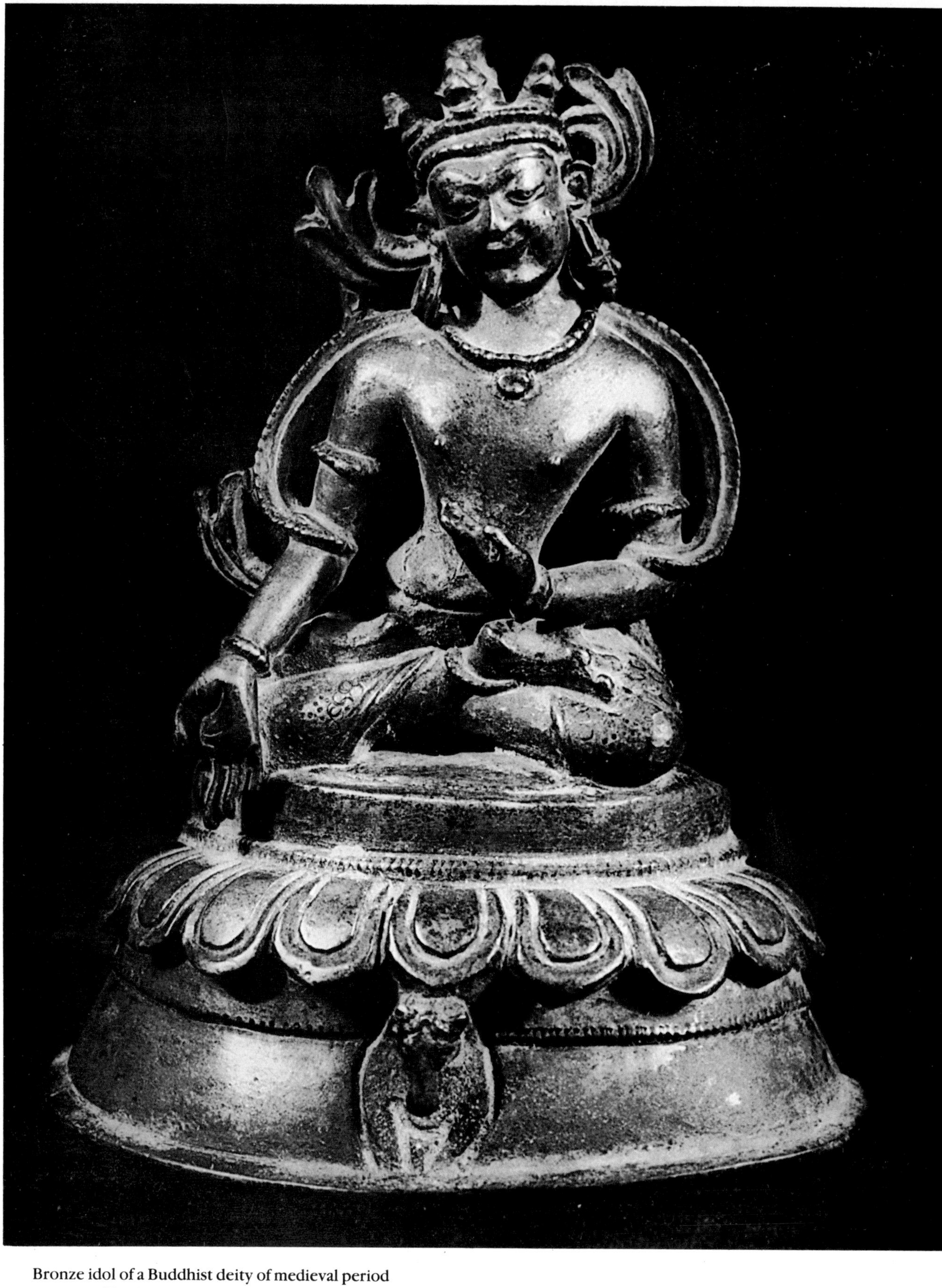

Bronze idol of a Buddhist deity of medieval period recovered by CBI.

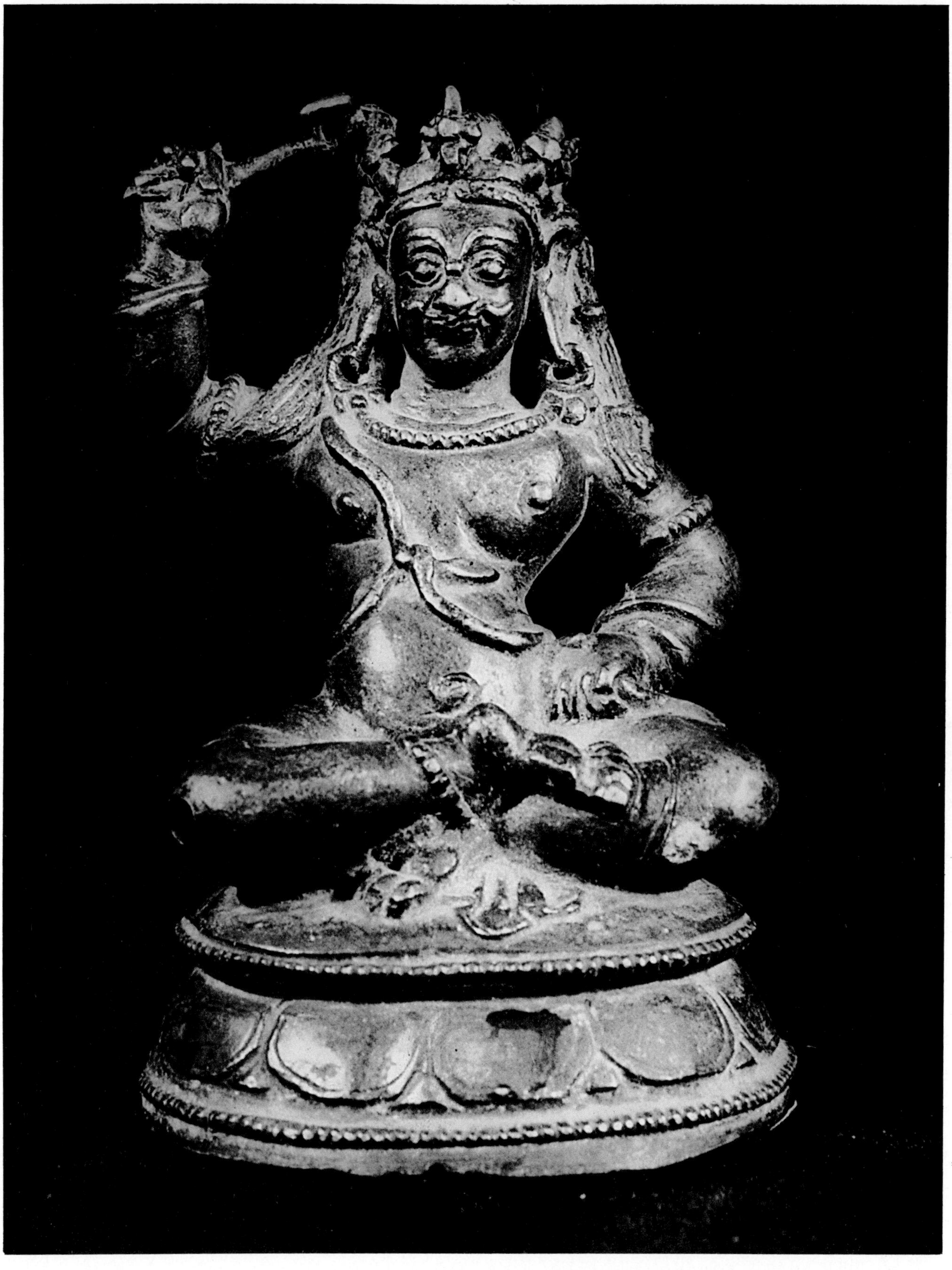

Bronze idol of a warrior deity of medieval period recovered by CBI.

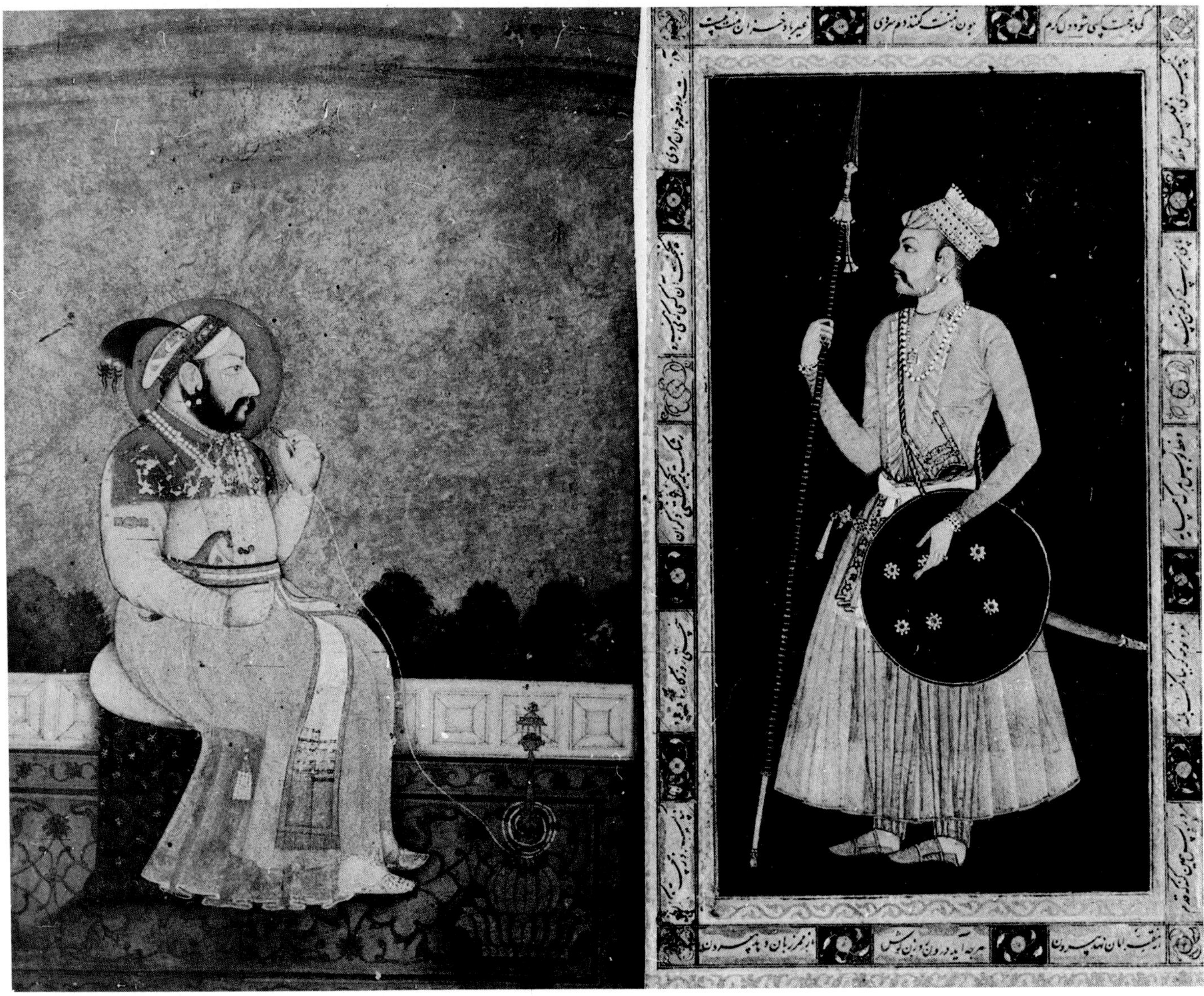

Miniatures stolen from Salarjang Museum.

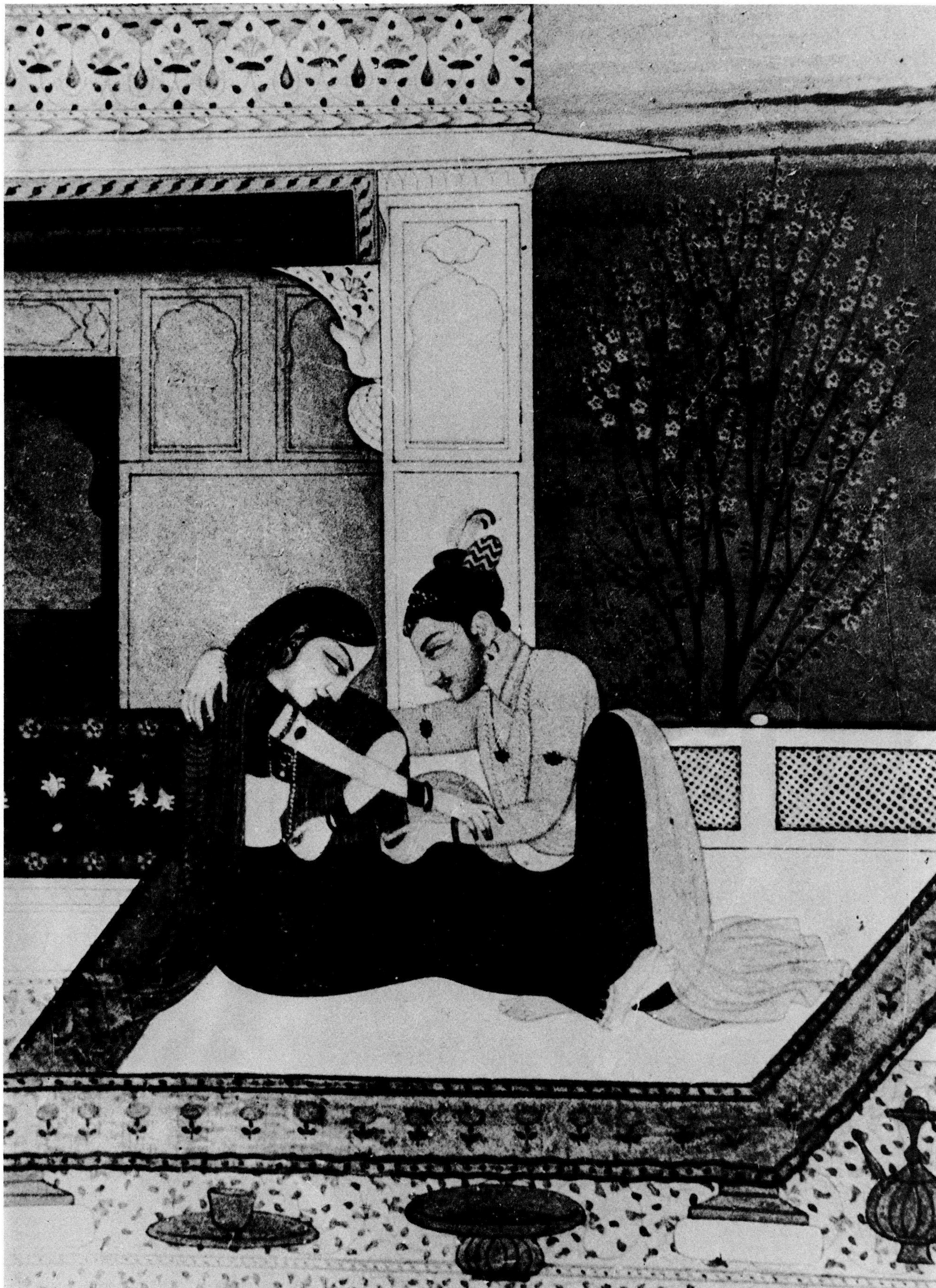

Picture Nayak-Nayika, 17th Century stolen from
Jaipur Mahal Museum.

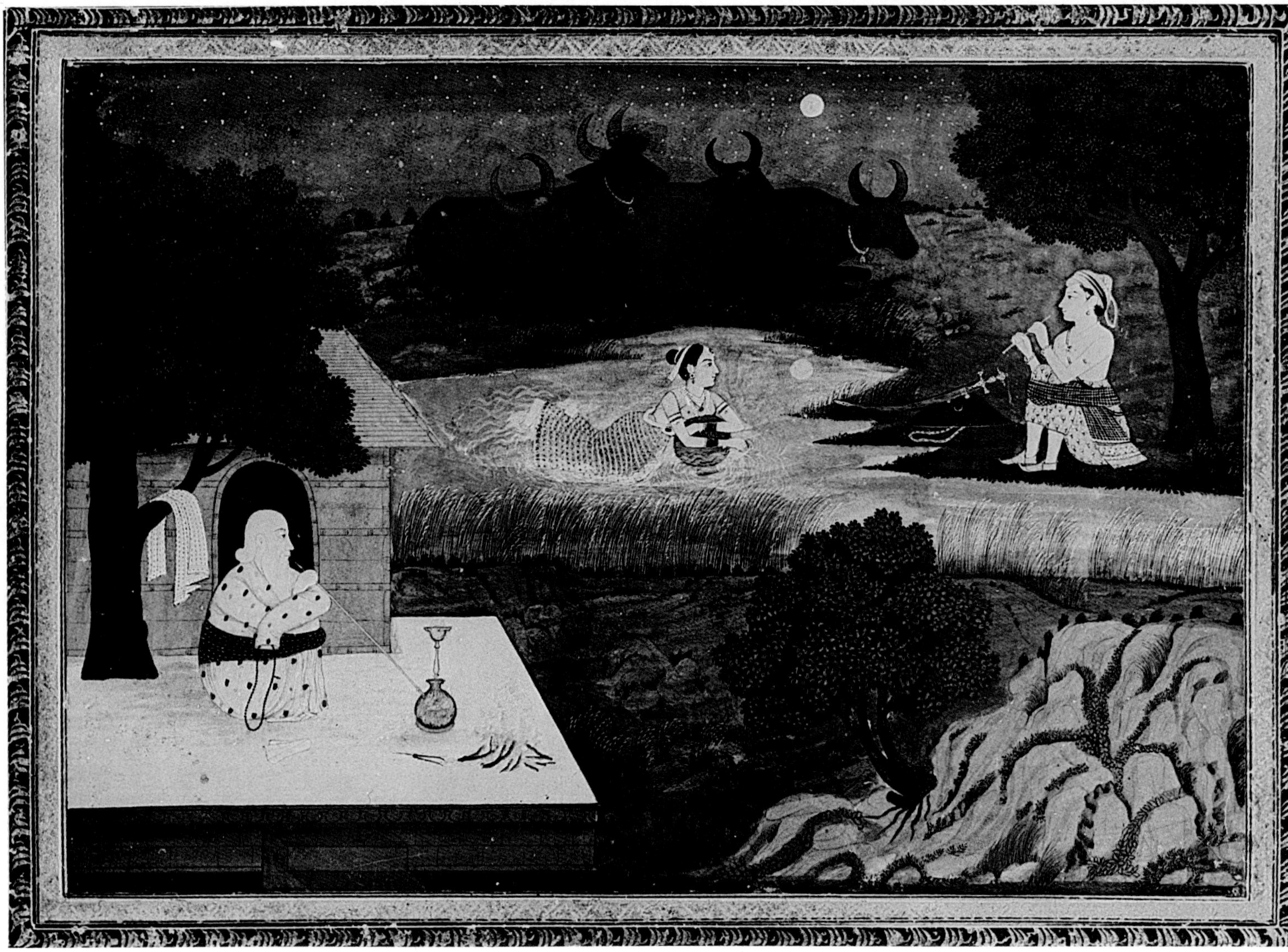

Painting of Heer-Ranjah of 18th century.

In 1972 the CBI caught a senior Government officer red handed at Palam Airport and recovered from him antiques and paintings worth several lakhs. The police at Dindigol seized 46 idols of Hindu deities made of bronze which were worth over Rs. 5 lakhs. In 1973 police made a haul of 27 stolen idols, worth Rs. 1 crore from a receiver of such articles at Tuticorin. The idols, stolen from different temples in South India, included a large Nataraja, Shiva and Parvati, Vishnu and Bhudevi and Lord Krishna on a serpent hood. Most of them were made from the alloy of five metals and some in bronze.

In a major seizure of antiques in a week-long raids conducted by Delhi Police and the CBI in July 1988, 1500 objects which included idols, miniature paintings, swords and coins were recovered. Many of these valuable items belonged to the 17th and the 18th centuries. Two big antique dealers were arrested after raids were conducted at several art galleries in New Delhi. A number of priceless items which were buried underground were recovered at the instance of these two accused. Of the items seized, the blackstone idol of 'Jamuna-Suraj', two Vishnu idols, a marble idol of Govardhandhari Krishna and a sandstone idol of Ganesh were recovered. The idols belonged to a geographical zone covering the states of Bihar, Uttar Pradesh, Madhya Pradesh, Rajasthan, Gujarat and Karnataka. Wood carvings and paintings nearly 200 to 300 years old were also recovered. Twenty-four terracotta items, 40 swords and kirpans and 120 miniature paintings and 23 eroticas were among the booty seized by the police sleuths. Over 400 coins bearing inscriptions in languages resembling Arabic and Tibetan and a muzzle-loading pistol with silver linings were other interesting 'finds'. Ancient manuscripts of the Gita, Quran and Nanak Prakash were among the other items seized. A case under the Antiquities and Art Treasures Act, 1972 and Sections 411 and 292 of the Indian Penal Code was registered against the accused.

The modern technique of plundering, bribery and corruption is a 'civilised' extension of the old hectoring spirit of the colonial powers of the 18th century. According to Fredrick Engelo: 'The old plundering and buccaneering spirit which distinguished our common ancestors of the 16th and 17th centuries.' It is this spirit that made Colin Mackenzie in the 18th century to take away the best pieces of Amaravati sculpture to the British Museum. Lord Hastings gave orders to remove the marble bath in Shahjehan's Palace to be given to King George IV as a gift. Later it was sold by public auction under Lord Bentinck's orders. Kohinoor, the precious diamond, was also taken away by the Britishers.

Theft of art objects and their illegal export is a lucrative trade. The miscreants have a wide range of scattered sites to choose from. The Archaeological Survey of India is now responsible for the protection and preservation of all centrally protected monuments. State Governments having their own Archaeological Departments look after those falling within their sites, while a number of structures and complexes lying in wilderness are open to the culture vandals. Effective prevention of thefts from monuments cannot be fully assured since the archaeological departments and the security personnel stationed in far away places are often the solitary custodians of the cultural treasures, whose real value they may not be fully aware of.

# VANDALISM

THE tremendous demand and the fancy prices that the antiques fetch in the global market have given rise to smuggling from their countries of origin. However, a big step taken forward today is that India alongwith most other developing countries has passed stringent laws banning the export of culturally significant art and craft. In spite of the strict legislations and checkings, vandals are still active in this illicit trade, playing their role in plundering the country's heritage.

The incidence of cultural vandalism—theft of art objects of antique value from archaeological sites, museums and temples—is continuing. Are the priceless treasures adequately protected in India from unscrupulous vandals and money-makers? Are we making enough efforts to conserve these magnificent treasures?

The problem of conservation remains a staggering one, specially in a country like India where almost every inch of space has a link with some chapter in history. The climatic conditions and the varying nature of the structures and objects to be preserved add to the problem. The difficulties of conservation have been highlighted by Dr. M.N. Deshpande in one of his articles. In his words, "In a country of the size of India with a variety of geophysical features and climatic variations, the problem of conservation naturally differs from one part of the country to the other. Added to this environmental factor is the problem of the differences in building material used in different periods of its long history." There are rock-cut monuments in western India and parts of Orissa, Bihar, Tamil Nadu and Andhra Pradesh and stone monuments literally in every part of the country; then there are the purely wooden structures found in the foot-hills of Himalayas and also in some areas of Kerala and the brick and timber monuments of the Indo-Gangetic plains.

The cultural heritage of India is slowly being robbed of its past. Its richness is being wafted away in the dark to grace the drawing rooms and museums of the newly rich millionaires. The vandals resort to bribing or even to the extent of murdering the custodians to get to these objects to sell them for petty sums. The neglected monuments of India are the easy prey to these notorious people. But now, with the Press reporting these incidents, the government and the people have become aware of this and are expressing their anger at this loot. The selected brand of dedicated detectives and archaeologists are now utilising computers and magnifying glasses to project the relics of yesteryears.

A crime of this nature was detected after India attained independence. In the U.S.A., some unscrupulous men had become millionaires out of their war industries, and they let it to be known that they were in the market in a big way for cultural antiques. These millionaires tried to buy or even steal from countries like Mexico and India. The easy money in the sellers' market has sparked off a number of gangs in the country who specialise in such activities.

## TYPES OF VANDALS

The idol runners and antique thieves operating in India are classified into four categories. In the first category are included the ex-rulers of the erstwhile princely States. Sculptures scattered in the areas under these erstwhile States are claimed by the ex-rulers as their own property over the years. Much of this wealth has been disposed of by them to private collectors, curio and antique dealers and smugglers. Many a Maharaja sold for a pittance a cultural stock of their forefathers, who had taken great pains to amass that wealth for generations.

The second category includes those with personal and religious interest, who have been appropriating ancient images and idols claiming to belong to their faith from authentic archaeological sites.

The third such category is of spurious archaeologists and archaeological associations who claim to preserve or prsemote cultural heritage. On many occasions they have even been found removing objects from sites on the pretext of their being transferred to museums for safe custody. These pieces are taken by them for invariably passing on to the hands of unscrupulous persons to be smuggled out of the country. Influential and resourceful persons like politicians, businessmen and even bureaucrats who adorn their homes with these antiques to satisfy their egos, form the last category. They too sometimes indulge in selling these to the foreign buyers for some easy and quick money. Few years back, an officer of the All India Service was intercepted for smuggling some old paintings as part of his baggage on his foreign visit.

In the past, museums in India have been the main targets of theft of antiques. Studies revealed that two types of criminals have been operating in the museums. Firstly, those who are interested in the intrinsic or face value of the objects and secondly, those who are interested in their antique value. The first category of thieves look for valuable articles such as coins, ornaments, gems etc., which can be quickly disposed of through ordinary local receivers. The criminals of the second category always pounce on objects of antique value which in return give them rich dividends. An international seminar organised by Interpol in 1962 made their observations that most of the art thieves had been attracted towards museums and art galleries. They also develop close links with museum employees to achieve their object. The thefts that took place at the Indian Museum, Calcutta in 1962, National Museum, New Delhi in 1968, City Palace Museum, Jaipur in 1971 and the Salarjung Museum, Hyderabad in 1966, revealed that the thieves were hand in glove with the museum employees, local criminals and jewellers.

The United States of America and the European countries offer the most lucrative and readily available markets to the exporters of Indian antiques. The reason is the affluence of the purchasers and a virtual absence of any kind of legal restrictions. In the U.S.A. there are hardly any restrictions on the import of art objects nor is there any duty imposed on them. It may be of interest to note that of the 15 items smuggled out of India in the late seventies, 13 were found to be in the U.S.A. and the two items—one a 1100-old Sun god idol from Baroda museum and one miniature of the Basohli School stolen from Chandigarh were reported to be in West Germany and Holland, respectively.

Alarmed by the increase in theft of antiques in 1970, the National Committee for International Council of Museums commented, "In some of the Western countries particularly America, art collecting in all its ramifications has developed into a mania. The Director of the National Gallery, London, has already warned that Britain can no longer safeguard her art treasures against depletion by American wealth and that the only remedy is an embargo on exports. The position of India is no better than that of Britain. Indian art objects, both metal and stone, have always evoked world-wide admiration because of their aesthetic appeal. The Americans vie with one another in acquiring precious art pieces. This has made objects in our museums unsafe and vulnerable."

Lack of effective legislation and inadequate facilities for documentation have given the antique thieves an easy way to commit the plunder. The Antiquities Export Control Act of 1947 did not provide effective safeguard or any control on trade, or sufficient deterrent punishment to culprits, nor for compulsory acquisition. Even if an antique was recovered the police had difficulty in tracing its origin for lack of proper documentation. Out of the 86 recoveries made in Delhi alone in 1970 only six could be linked and restored to their original owners.

The Interpol meet held at Ottawa in 1971 underlined the gravity of the problem posed by the theft of art objects and their sale on an international level. It pointed out that there were continuous reports of thefts from museums, ancient monuments and even churches and temples. In Italy this had become such a big national scandal that the Government had given the problem urgent attention and instituted new and more stringent regulations to prevent any cultural thefts. The value of a Titian stolen from Italy was estimated at £ 1 million at the least. In England too there had been several thefts from exhibitions. Big museums and art exhibitions could not make themselves foolproof from the crafty thieves. In India too, effective protection of ancient monuments has not been possible. Neither the agents nor the collectors are interested in finding out the source. To the former these acquisitions represent a very good investment and to the latter, ownership of invaluable rarities brings special personal triumph and pride. It is for this reason that the purchasers do not mind paying fabulous prices for age-old paintings, sculptures and other art objects of guaranteed quality. Art exhibitions and museums, not to speak of ancient monuments and religious places, are still not safe against the well organised and well financed determined crafty burglars.

# MODUS OPERANDI

THE antiquity wealth of the nation has been systematically plundered by the smugglers and vandals. Various methods have been adopted by them to remove the antiques from temples, museums and archaeological sites. They have also applied dubious means for their transportation, sale and smuggling to foreign countries.

The modus operandi of committing thefts of cultural property is evidenced from the Uttar Pradesh Report. With regard to thefts (principally of statues other than gold and silver idols) committed by organized gangs, the sculptures to be stolen are generally identified by persons familiar with their artistic value and potential marketability; the desirable items are photographed, dated and their location is sketched. At this point information is passed on to the gang of thieves and a resale agent is contacted; often the resale price to the latter is determined in advance. The actual theft is committed by just a few members of the gang, generally with some local support; appropriate tools are used either to remove the entire sculpture, or just those parts considered to be valuable and easily marketable. The piece is then taken away and often buried underground until it can be safely transported by suitable vehicles, generally by lorries or even by trains to big cities like Delhi, Bombay or Calcutta for the final sale, often to foreign visitors or by exporting to foreign countries. The antique thieves have inter-state and even international ramifications.

A stolen antique is generally kept in a secret place till the heat is off. Then the purchasers are contacted and the art object is put on sale in underground market or even openly depending on its quality. If the buyer is a foreigner then arrangements are also assured to smuggle out the pieces in the garb of engineering or other goods for legitimate export. They are usually sent either by air or by ship from Bombay or Calcutta depending on the size, destination and the cost involved.

Uttar Pradesh, Madhya Pradesh, Rajasthan, Tamil Nadu, Orissa, Gujarat, Karnataka and Kerala have proved to be the vulnerable haunts for thieves. Most of them act as agents of big-time smugglers and antique racketeers. States like Andhra Pradesh, Haryana, Himachal Pradesh and Assam have also not been spared by antique lifters. Despite various measures adopted by the enforcement agencies to check the menace of antique smuggling, theft cases have been on the rise. According to these agencies, every year nearly 350 to 400 sculptures and art pieces of significant value are stolen from neglected monuments and temples located in unguarded and isolated areas. The main cause for these thefts is the huge return received for a small investment. The recovery rate of stolen antiques is hardly ten per cent.

The culprits in most cases are local people who are engaged by some middlemen, while the mastermind behind all the activities like scouting for identification, photography, engaging intermediaries and details regarding transportation etc. remains unknown in most of the cases. To trace the actual beneficiary is often a hard task and this is best illustrated by the theft of a Buddha-head from the Government Museum at Mathura in Uttar Pradesh. Sometime after September 1961 the exhibit disappeared from the gallery only to reappear in Switzerland. The reconstructed story gave the details of the operation, carried out with a great deal of planning and preparation. It is reported that an art dealer from Switzerland engaged an agent to acquire Indian sculptures from various historical sites. That agent after arriving in India stayed in a hotel in New Delhi and he established a contact with an Indian, who helped him in acquiring the Buddha-head. An antique dealer with his shop located near the hotel finalised the transaction. It was fairly certain that the Buddha-head from Mathura was despatched from Bombay by ship. The theft came to the notice of officials only when the Swiss art dealer tried to sell it to the Indian Department of the Museum of Ethnology in West Berlin.

The art objects are often removed by local thieves who are familiar with the surroundings and are well-equipped. After stealing they generally go to a neighbouring state before handing them over to the person who has commissioned them. At times gangs send their own 'experts' to the site and 'assess' the targets on the basis of artistic value, labour and time required to remove them. They even use photographs for identification. These are also shown to prospective buyers. There is a network of antique dealers in all the major cities and tourist centres. Delhi, Bombay, Calcutta, Madras and Jaipur are the major transit points for export. There have even been cases where temple priests have been persuaded by smugglers to sell original idols and replace them with fake ones.

In the sensational case of theft of 2,492 medieval period paintings from the City Palace Museum in Jaipur, it was revealed that the criminals were familiar with the place and their planning was perfect. On the fateful day the criminals climbed on to the roof of an adjacent building. Through the ventilator on the outside of the room they made their entry into the storeroom. From a particular almirah they picked up the required paintings and left the place unnoticed by even the guards of the museum.

A theft in the National Museum at New Delhi in 1968 gave a filmic scene enacted by the accused Yadugiri. Influenced by films, Yadugiri planned to burgle the National Museum single-handedly. He reached the roof of the museum building by climbing up a drain-pipe and entered the gallery on the second floor through a skylight after climbing down from the roof by means of a rope. He cut open the rods of the grilled door by a saw and entered the jewellery room. He broke open the bullet-proof covers of the show cases in the room. He picked up the coins and some other valuables, put them into a bag and effected his exit by climbing down the electric cables which he had earlier removed from the fans and tied to the skylight. His meticulous planning could be judged from the fact that he stayed for seven hours in the room without being noticed by anybody. On interrogation he revealed that he had visited the museum several times before launching on this venture.

The lapse in the security at the museum and the modus operandi of a burglar was revealed when he managed to hide himself in the Prince of Wales Museum in Bombay in 1968 and removed some silver articles. The burglar had hidden himself in the museum at the closing hour and after successfully removing the valuables he made his exit through a window and climbed down with the help of a rope.

Deposing in the Court of the Special Judge, Patna on 18th June, 1976, while trying Baqar Hassan Bilgrami, the 'Nawab', Vazir Haider, T.R. Khan and three others on the charge of stealing four rare Mughal period manuscripts from the Bharatpura Library on the night of January 8-9, 1973, Mr. Suraj Deo Pandey narrated the sequence of theft. According to him Khan accompanied by a Patna jeweller had visited Bharatpura and met the mother of Mr. Dhrupad Narain Singh, Secretary of the Library. Mr. Singh was not present. He said that he knew from the mother of Mr. Singh later that Khan and others had offered Rs. 10,000 for some manuscripts but she refused to sell them since they were her ancestral property. Mr. Pandey further stated that he heard the cries of 'Chor Chor' about midnight of January 8-9, 1973 and rushed towards the fort and found the gate closed. He said, "We entered the fort when Jhalak Lal opened it." He knew from Jhalak Lal that five thieves had come. One of them was trying to strangle Jhalak Lal and when Pradeep, the night guard, attacked them with a lathi he was stabbed in his back. After the search for the thieves was over, Mr. Drupad Singh's mother accompanied by Prakash came to the western room of the library and found one of the desks open. She said that the manuscripts including Sikandernama and Shahnama had been taken away.

A new modus operandi of smuggling was revealed in a theft case of Durga idol on 18th April, 1981 from an ancient temple of Lord 'Takshkeshwar Mahadev' of "Pauranik" importance in Allahabad. The thieves booked the stolen idol as 'motor part consignment' through a transport company of Allahabad and brought it to New Delhi where it was sold to a dealer. Later, this idol was broken into four parts which were kept along with 14 other antique idols and terracottas in 5 VIP suitcases. These suitcases had been booked by an Air India flight from New Delhi to New York.

During the theft of the image of Lord Mahavira dated eleventh century A.D. at Etawah, antique thieves adopted the modus operandi of threatening the chowkidar of the temple at gun-point. In this case, the chowkidar was pinned down to the ground by the gunmen while six others grabbed the image weighing five maunds.

In another instance, a villager, who was held earlier on smuggling charges, was among those engaged by the gang to steal the Durga idol—1.20 metres high and 0.75 metre wide, belonging to the Gupta period, after a Delhi firm offered Rs. 60,000 for it. Ten per cent of the amount was given as advance to the gang by this firm. Members of the gang entered the temple one night after breaking open the steel door and stole the idol. The idol was first hidden in a pond and later buried in a field. For a few days only the temple authorities knew about the theft. The priest, perhaps fearing that the importance of the shrine might be reduced, put up another idol and wrapped it in cloth in such a way that no one could notice the difference. Later, on filing a report, the police swooped into action and arrested five persons including a lawyer and a relation of a former MLA.

In a major seizure of antiques on 14th July, 1988, the Delhi Police and the C.B.I. seized 1500 objects—idols, miniature paintings, swords and coins. Investigation revealed that 'pickers' moved around in different villages and purchased these items for pittance. They also procured items from excavation sites all over the country. Following the 'pick-up', photographs of the art treasures were sent to 'dealers' who approved them and purchased the items in question. These priceless items were bought by art lovers in the country, but some pieces were also sent abroad, especially to European countries. The modus operandi used in this case was to take permission from the authorities to make a replica of a particular piece for export purposes. After obtaining the permission, instead of exporting the replica, the unscrupulous dealers sent the original abroad.

An example of the modus operandi used by the culprits from a case of an antique theft in 1981 investigated by CBI is given below:

Central Bureau of Investigation, Antiquities Branch received an information that the accused Shreekant Jain, Ramesh, Kashinath, Jhanna Lal, Ashgar and Dulal Chakravarthy committed theft and attempted to smuggle out 18 antique stone sculptures and terracottas during 1981. CBI registered the case and put its machinery in gear to book the culprits.

Kashi Nath, an antique broker of Delhi had instructed the co-conspirator Ramesh alias Chhedi Lal resident of Varanasi to supply him such antique objects which could be taken from ancient temples or historical monuments at Allahabad. Ramesh alias Chhedi with the help of Jhanna Lal, Dulal Chakravarthy alias Dinesh and Ashgar, a rickshaw puller, stole the idol of Goddess Durga, installed in an old temple of Takshkeshwar Mahadev in Mohalla Dariyabad, Allahabad during the intervening night of April 1981. Shri Ram Chandra Pathak, the priest of the temple, lodged a complaint at the Police Station, Attar Suiya, about the theft of the aforesaid idol of Goddess Durga. A case was registered by the local police under Section 380 IPC but the investigation did not reveal any fruitful result and the case was closed.

The investigation made by the CBI revealed that after committing the theft, the accused Ramesh alias Chhedi with the assistance of the co-accused Jhanna Lal and Dulal Chakravarthy transported the idol to Delhi and sold it to accused Shreekant Jain through another accused Kashi Nath. The investigation also established that Shreekant Jain got the idol of Goddess Durga broken/cut into 4 pieces by one artisan Natwar Lal and as stated earlier, these 4 pieces along with 14 other antique pieces were concealed in 5 suitcases to be sent abroad.

In order to smuggle out the aforesaid antiques Shreekant Jain, the accused holding an Indian Passport No. Q-240868 dt. 17.10.1980 issued at New York, purchased an air-ticket and also 2 excess baggage tickets on May 30, 1981 for Air India flight No. 101 leaving Delhi on June 1. Shreekant Jain however did not proceed abroad by the Air India flight. Instead on the 7th morning, he reached Palam Airport alongwith the 5 VIP suitcases containing the stolen antiques. He managed to get a berth by Air India Flight No. 115 and booked all the 5 suitcases. When he entered the International Departure Lounge at the Delhi

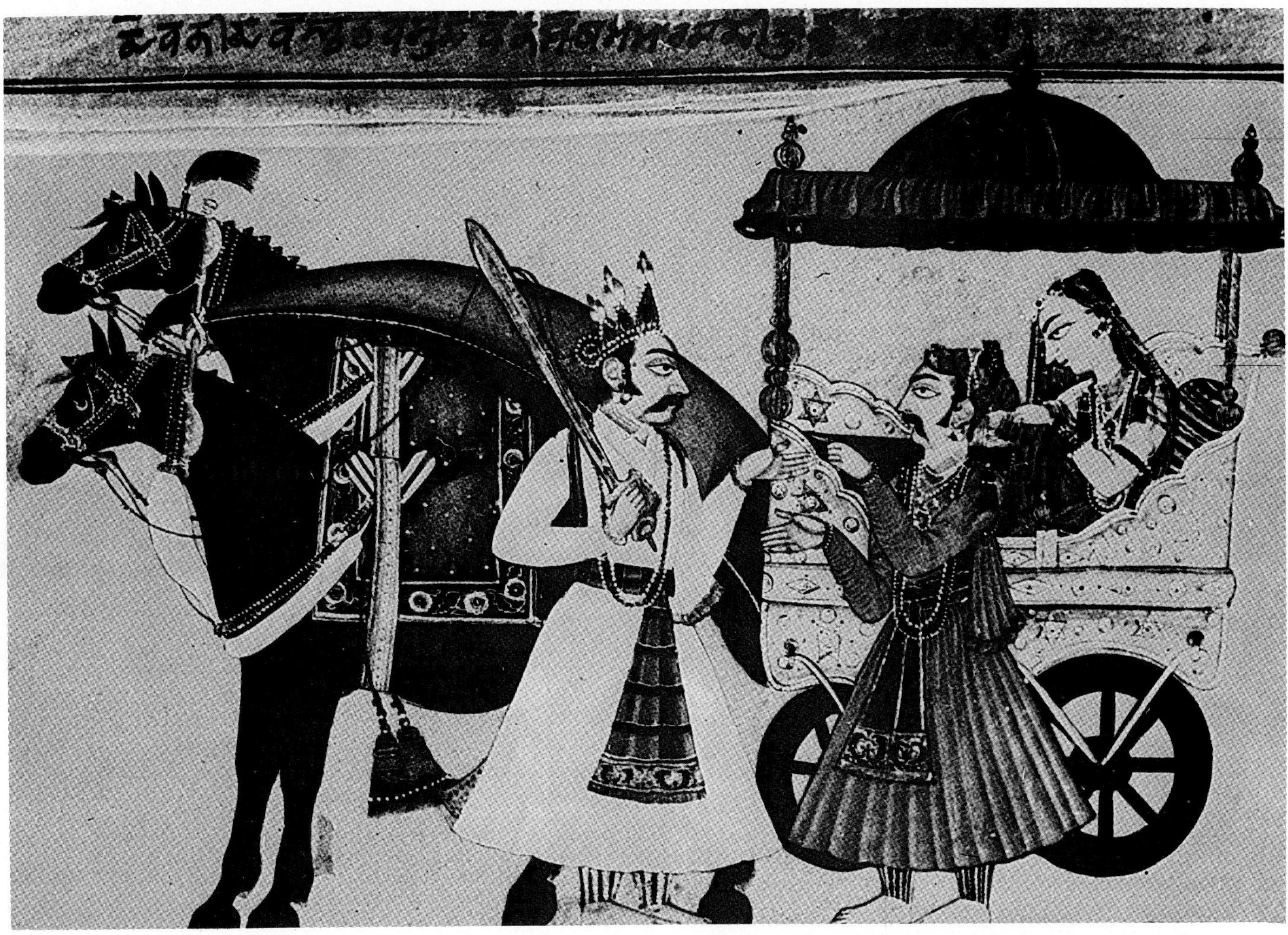

A Miniature Stolen from Jaipur Palace Museum.

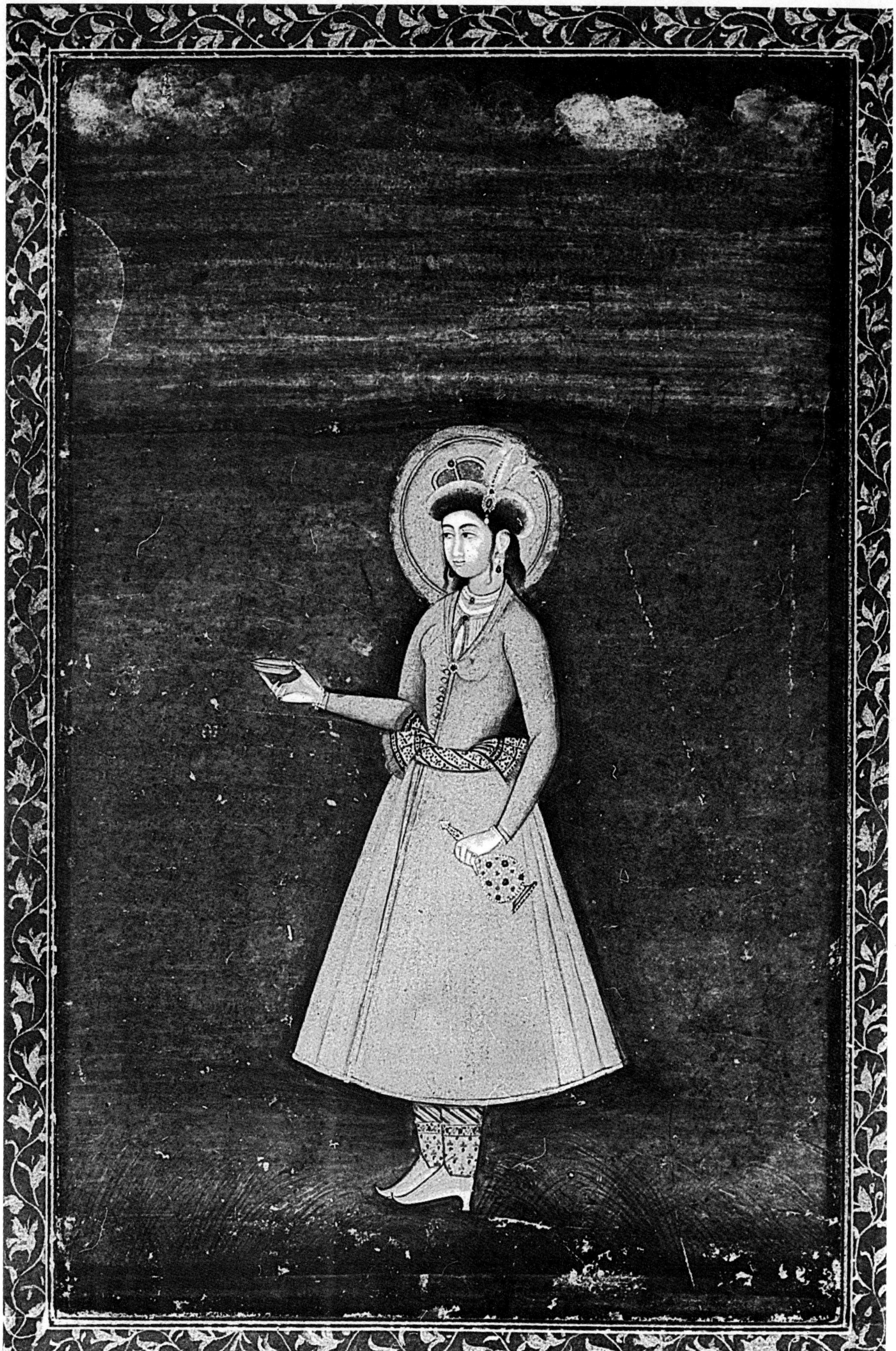

Painting of a lady of early 17th century, Persian Style.

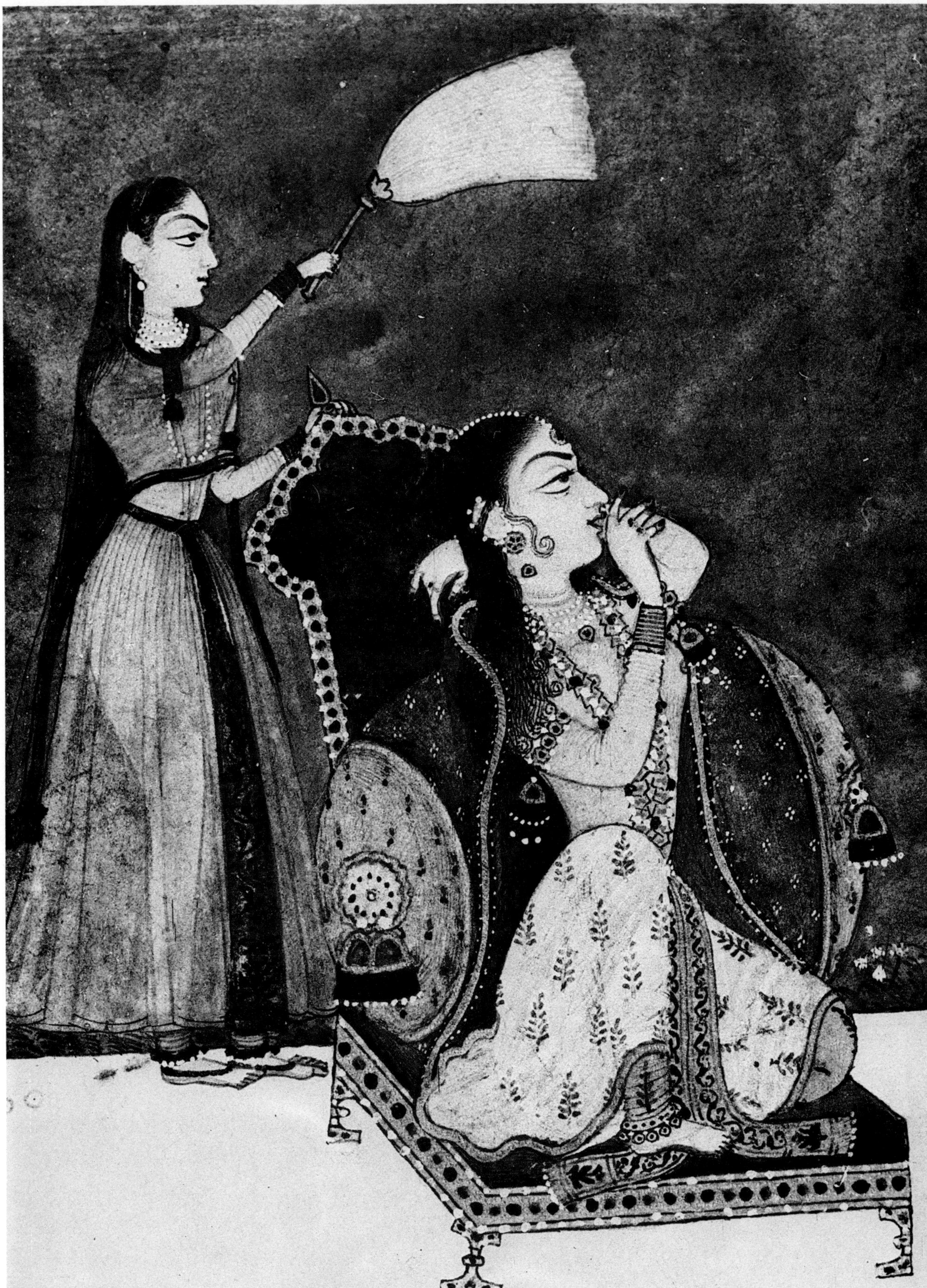

A Miniature painting of 17th Century from Salarjang Museum.

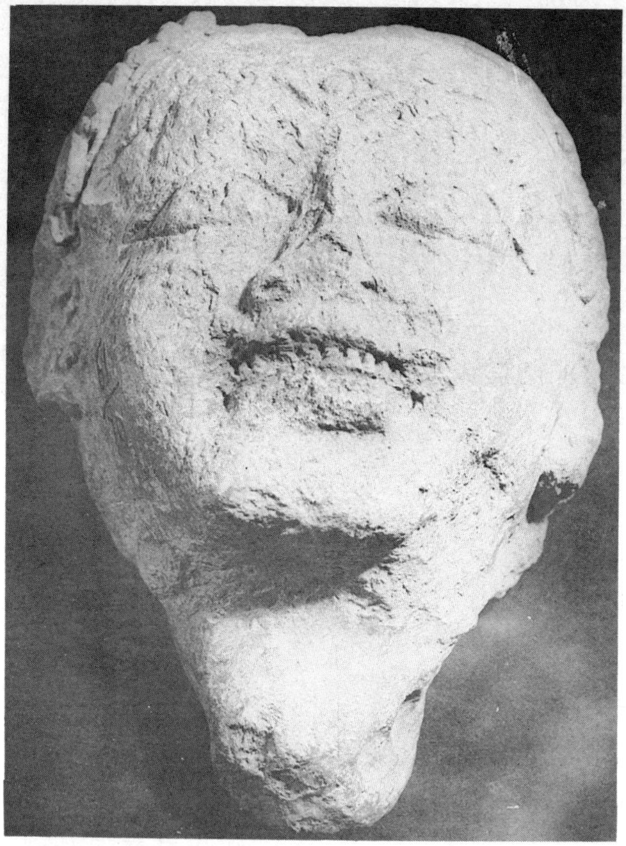

Terracotta human head.

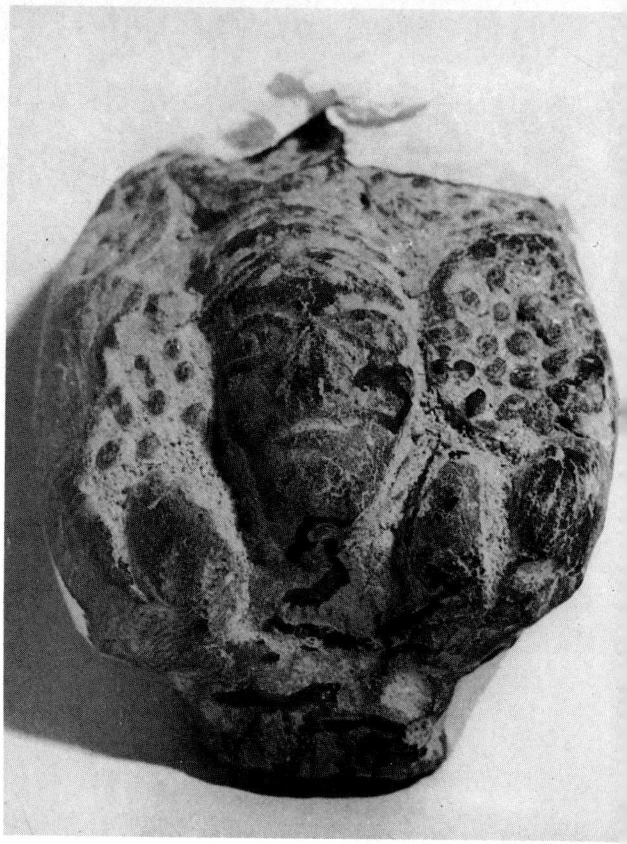

Terracotta female head.

Terracotta Kirtimukh broken into Three pieces.

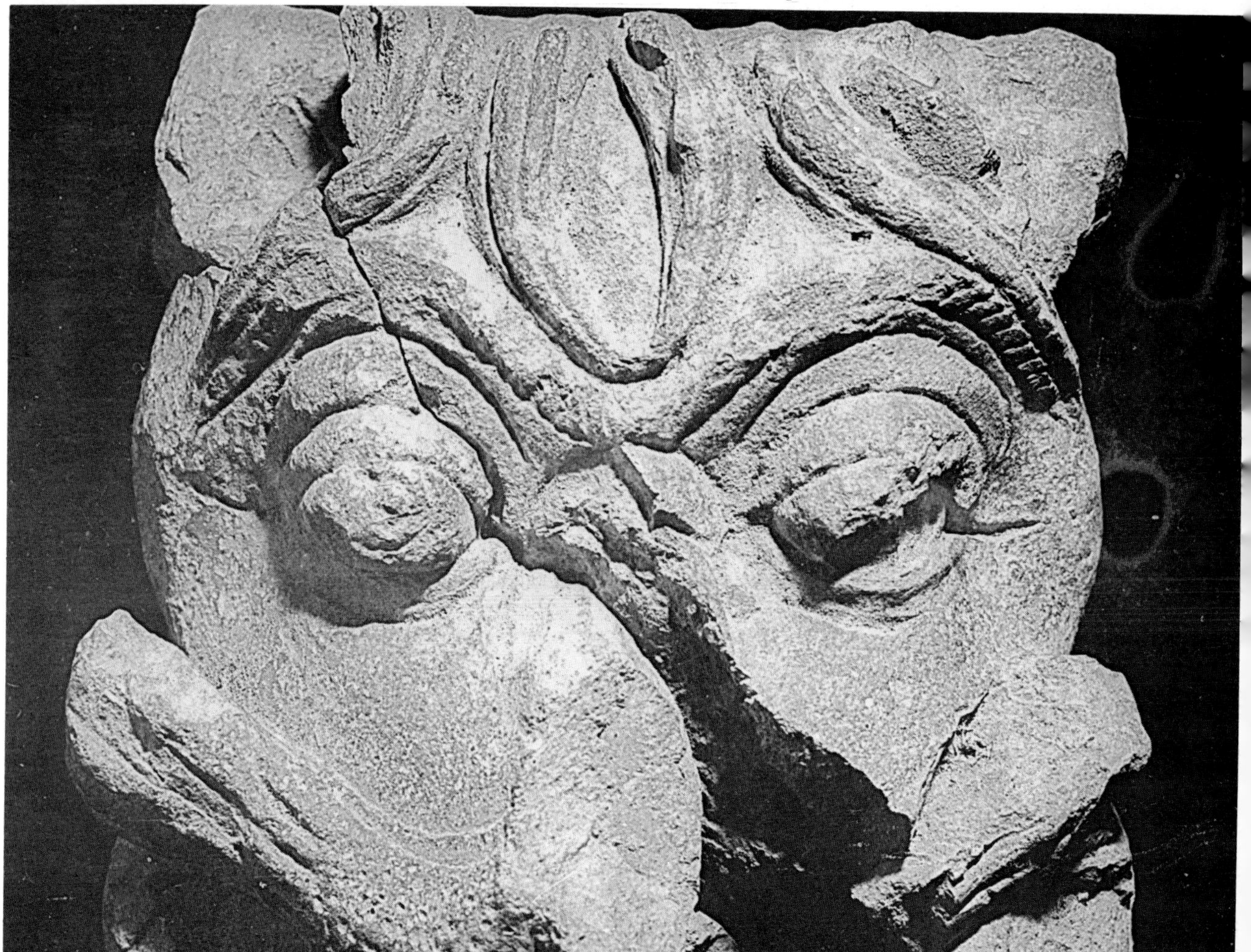

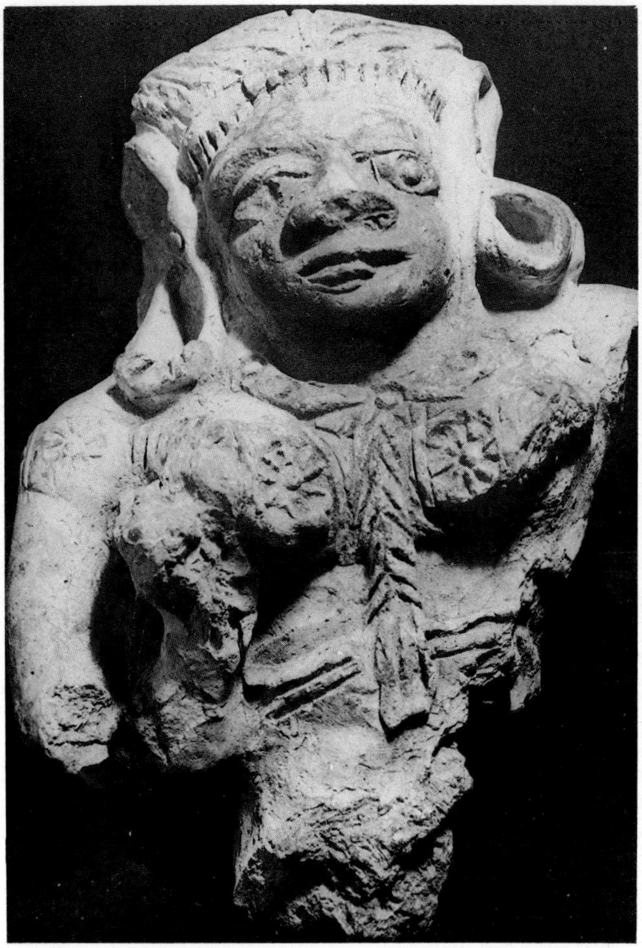

Terracotta female bust.

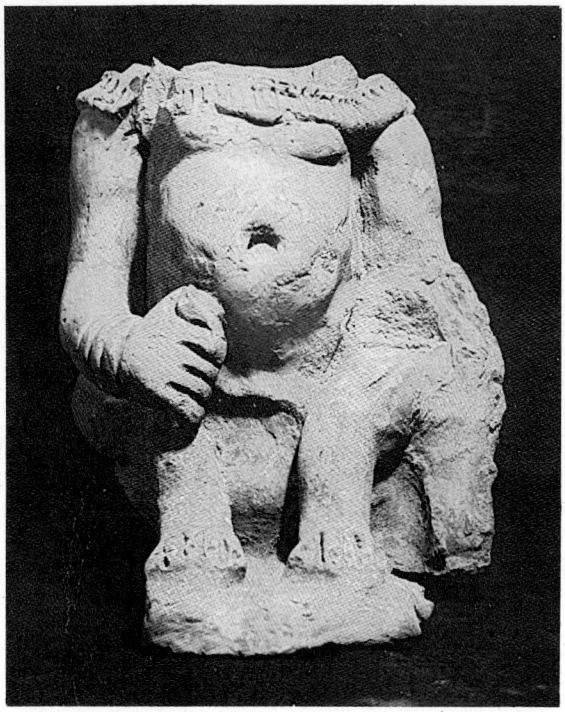

Pot bathed headless figure left arm broken.

Urdu inscriptions on a slab.

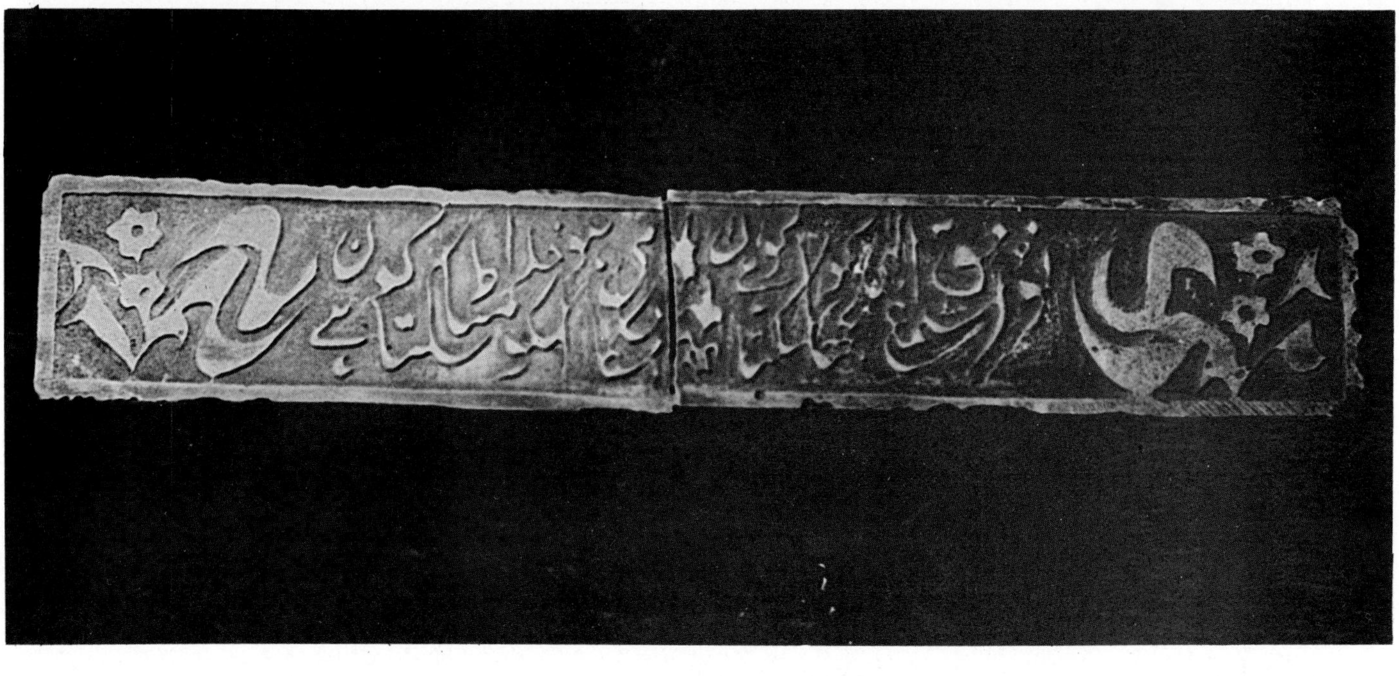

Raillery showing some symbol.

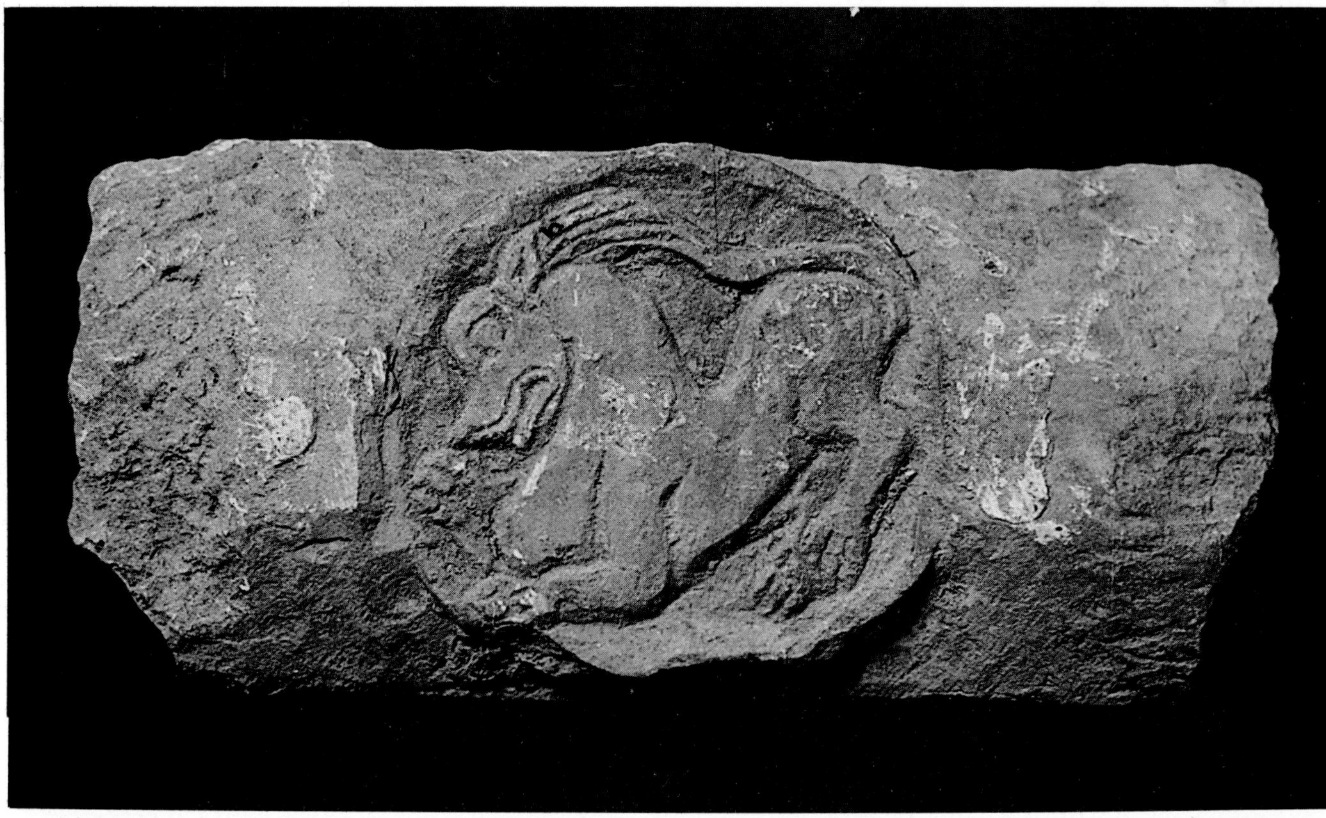

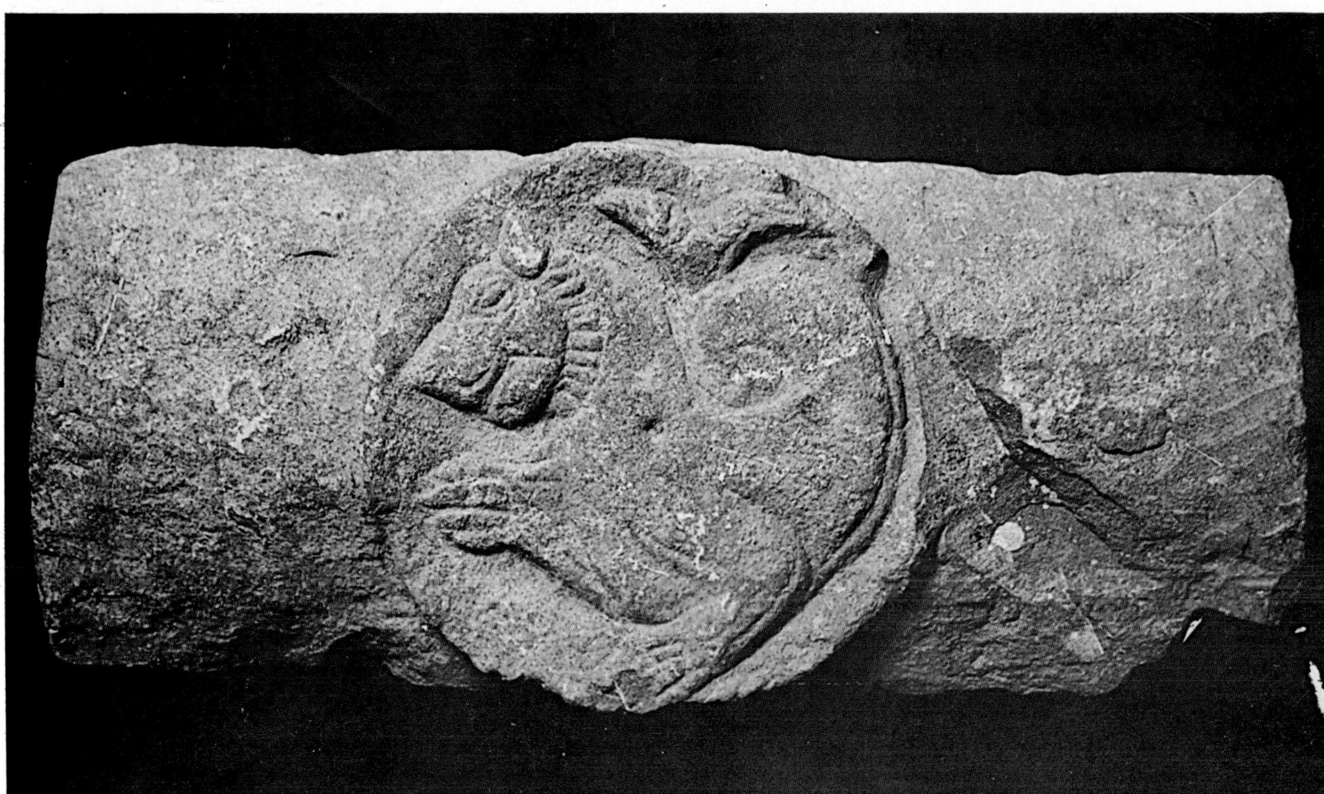

Raillery fragment depicting animal figure.

Shardula.

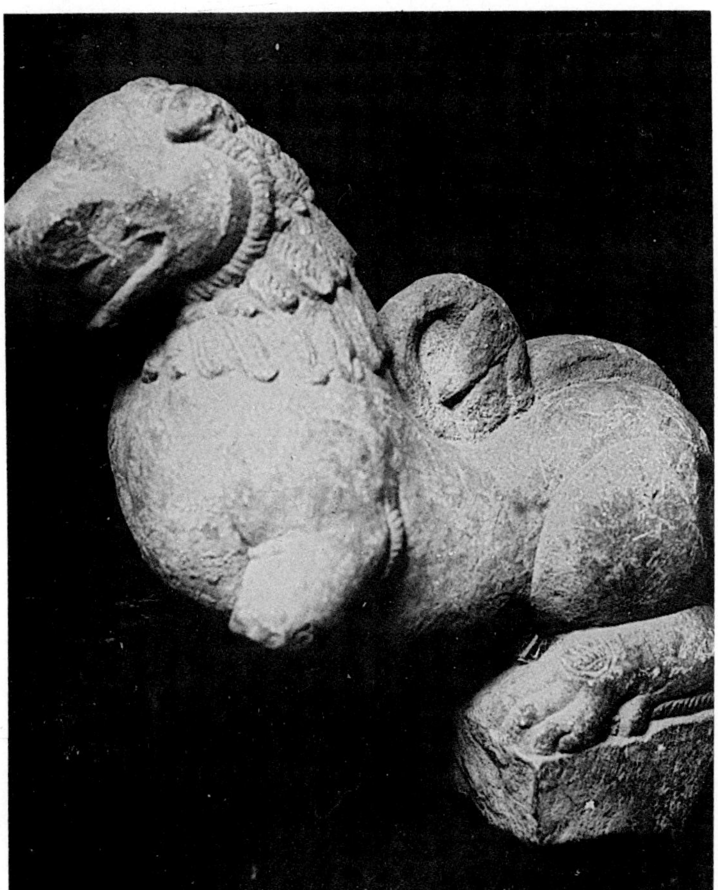

Shardula.

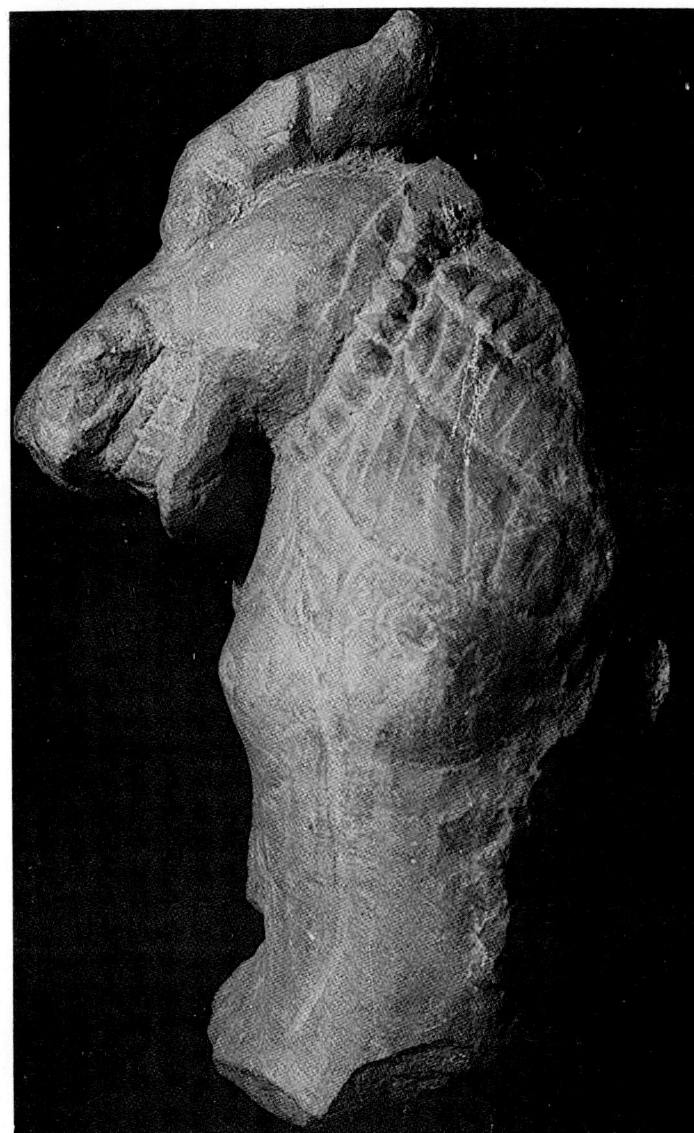

Fragment of a male gana figure.

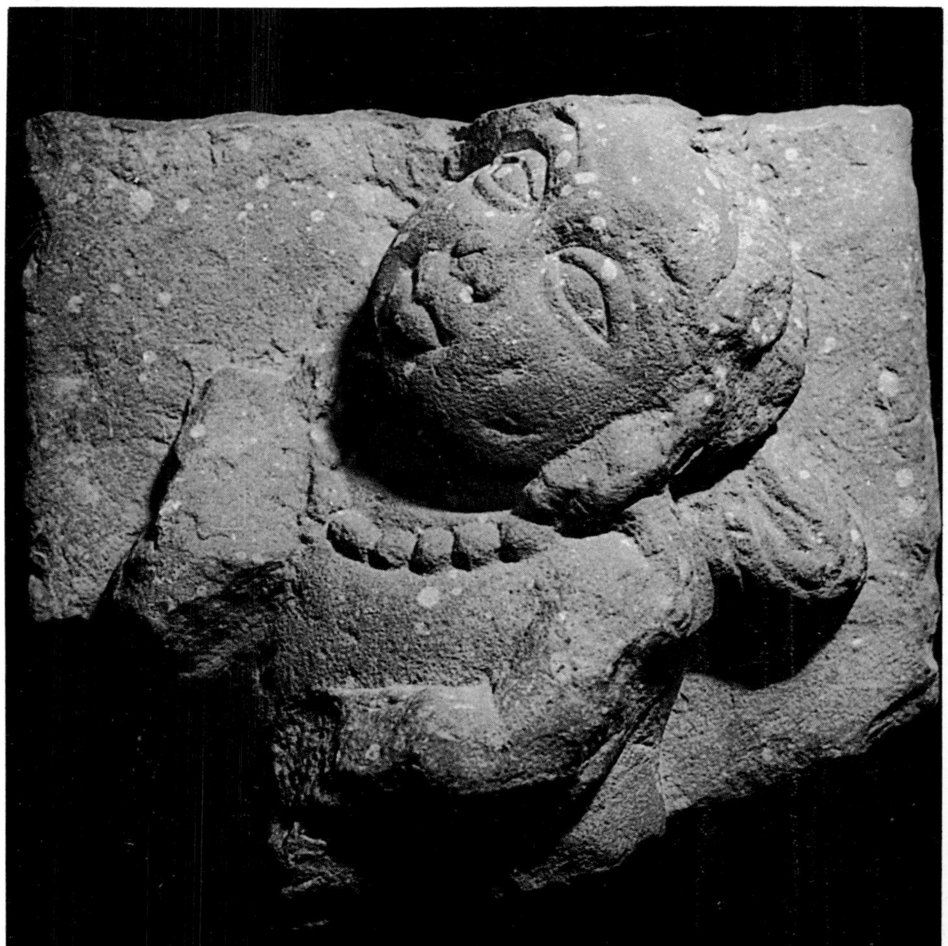

Fragment of a seated Buddha with two attendants.

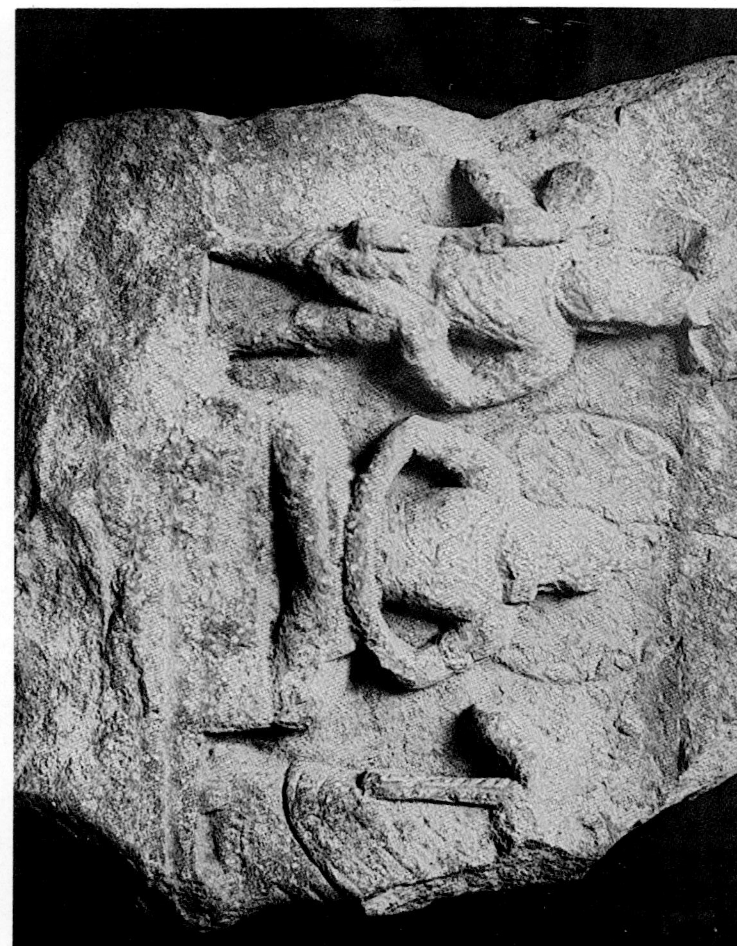

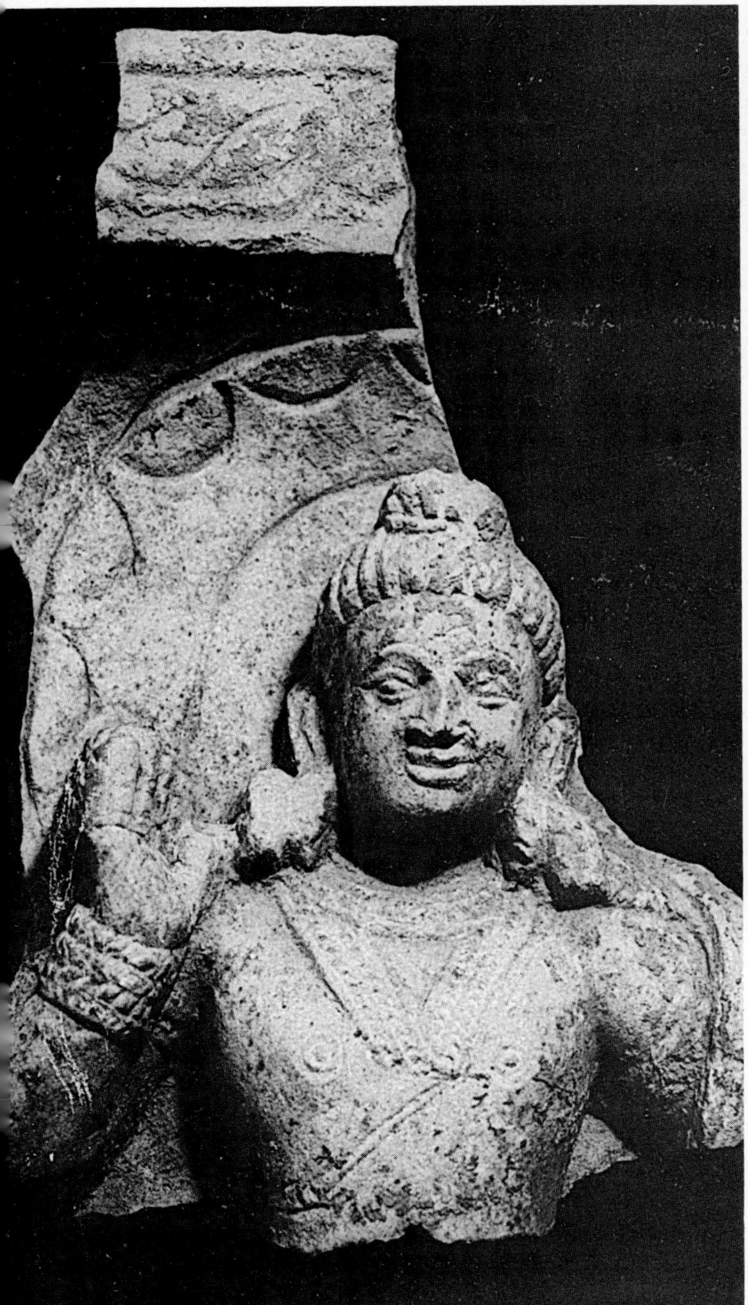

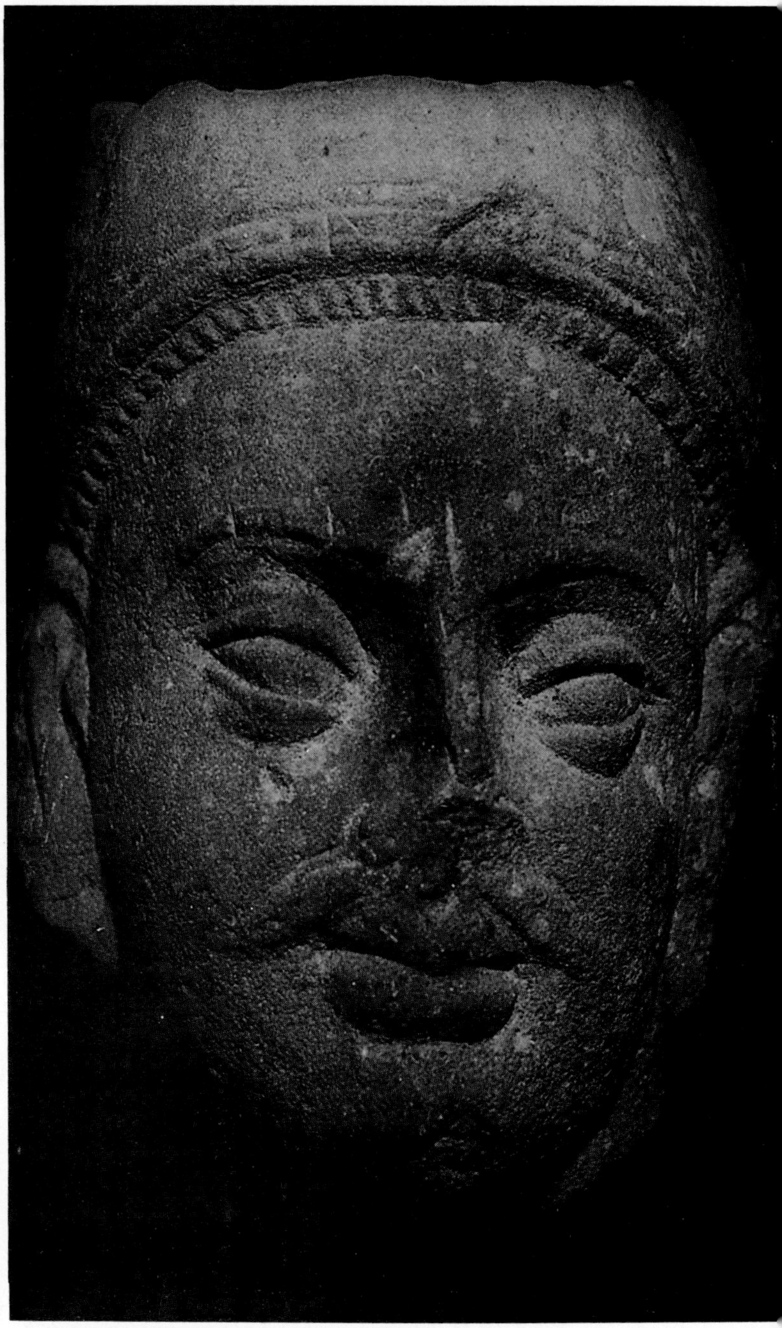

Bust of Buddha.

Fragment of a male head with moustaches.

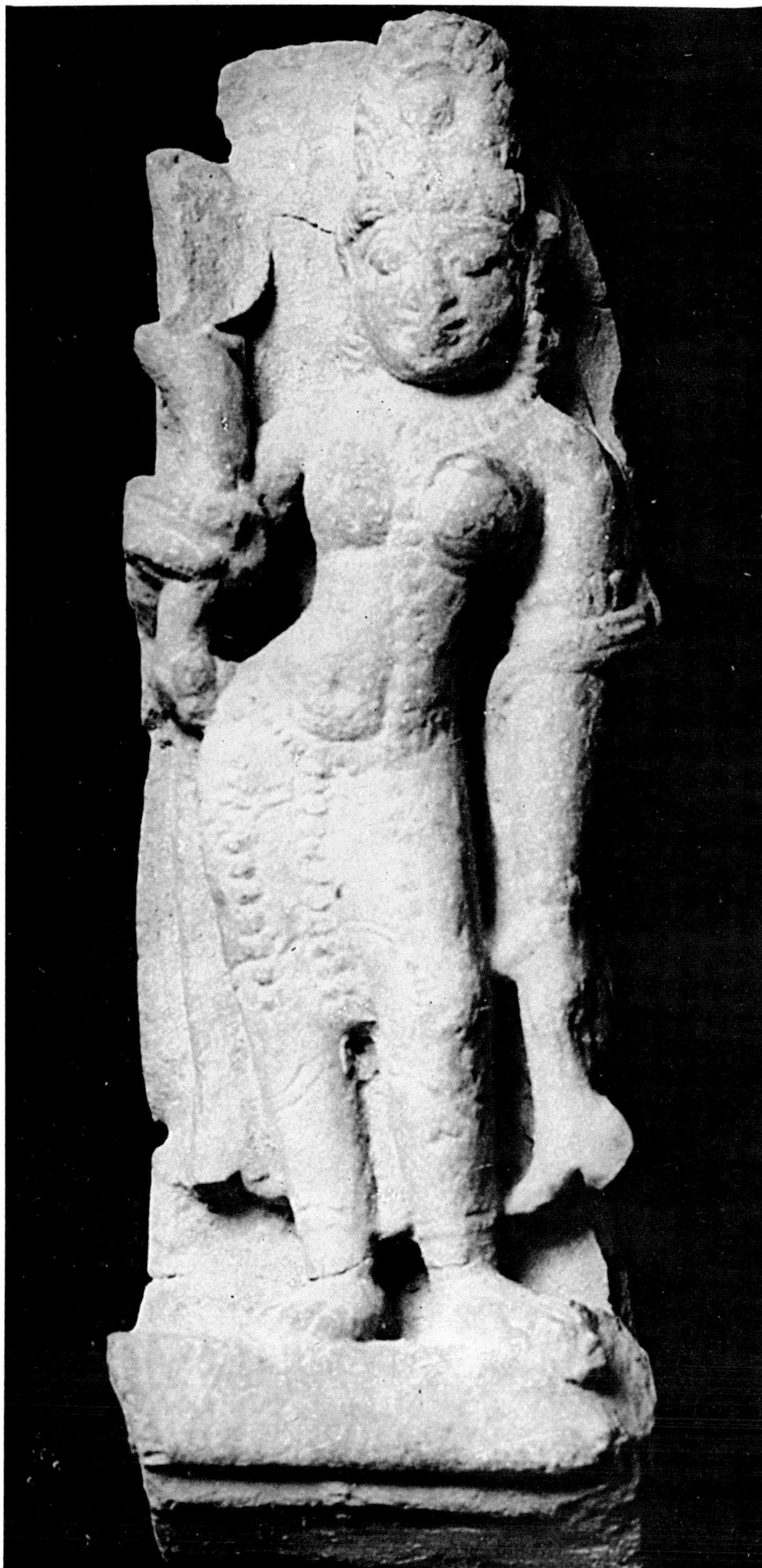

Standing female figure holding stalk of lotus in her hand.

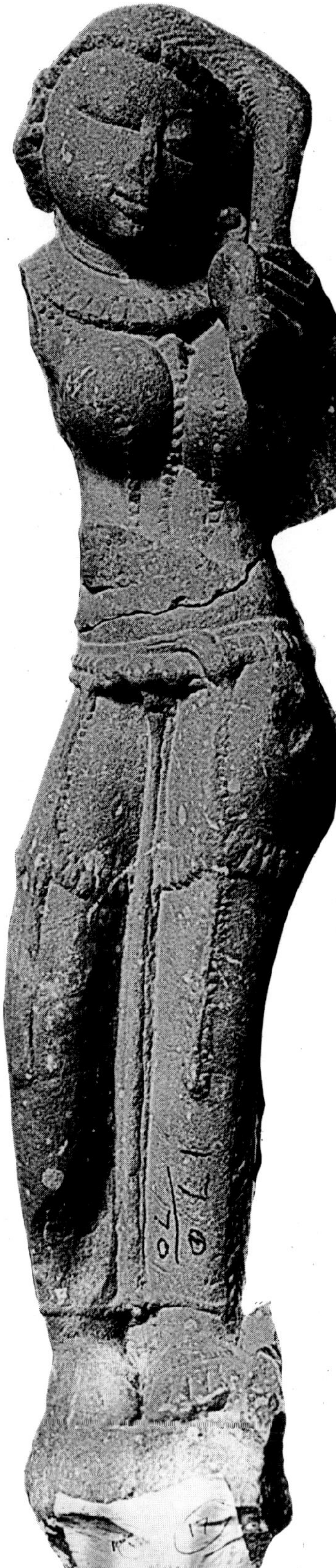

Fragment of female figure doing her hair (broken into two pieces).

Bust of male figure.

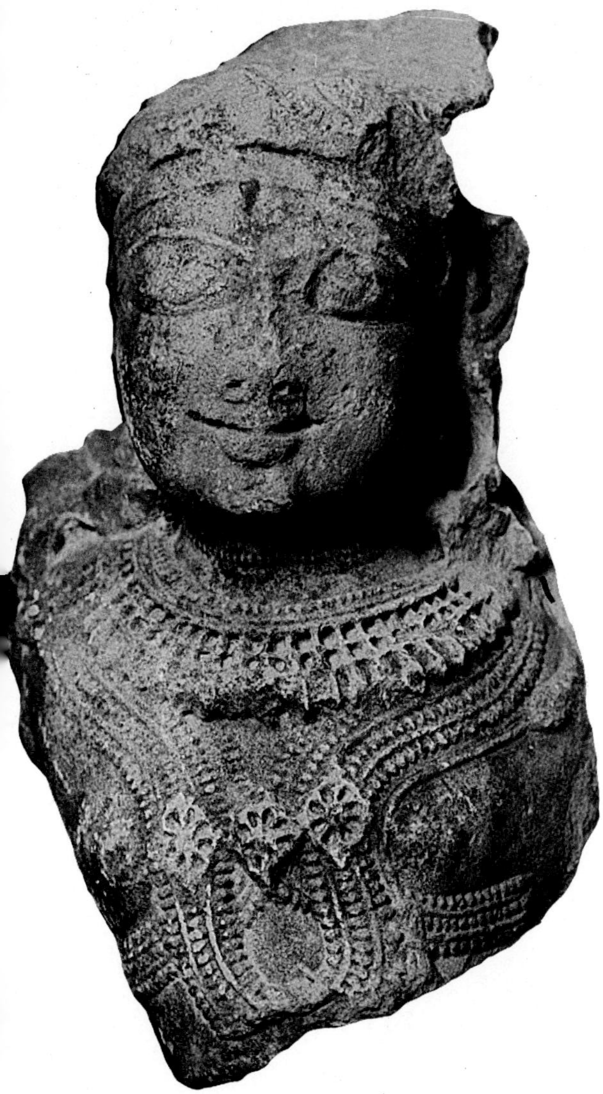

Fragment of female head.

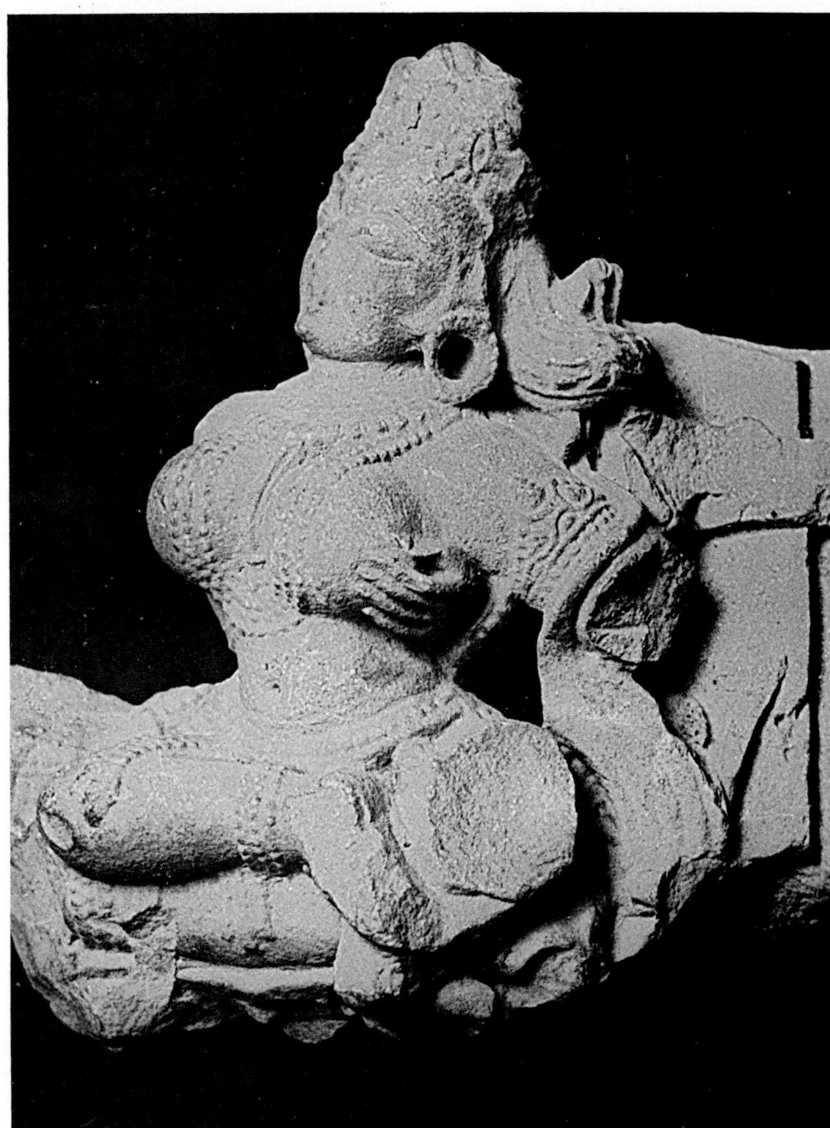

Fragment of male figure.

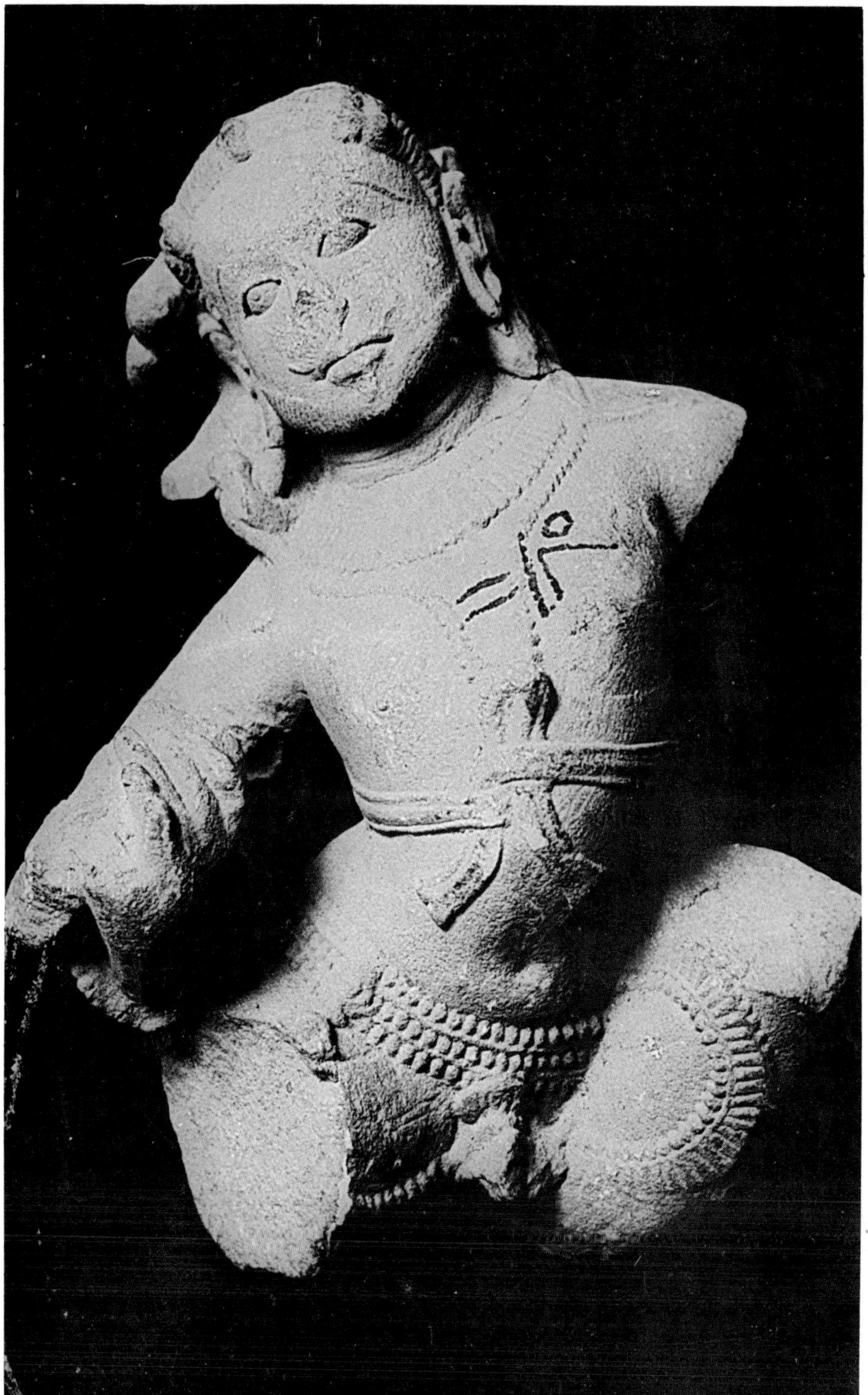

Standing female figure.

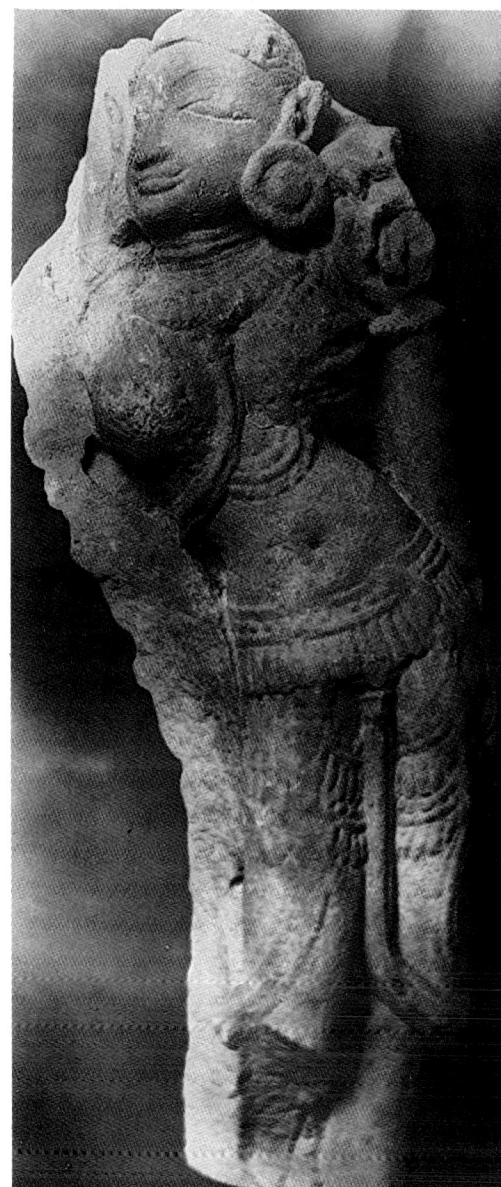

Female figure doing her hair.

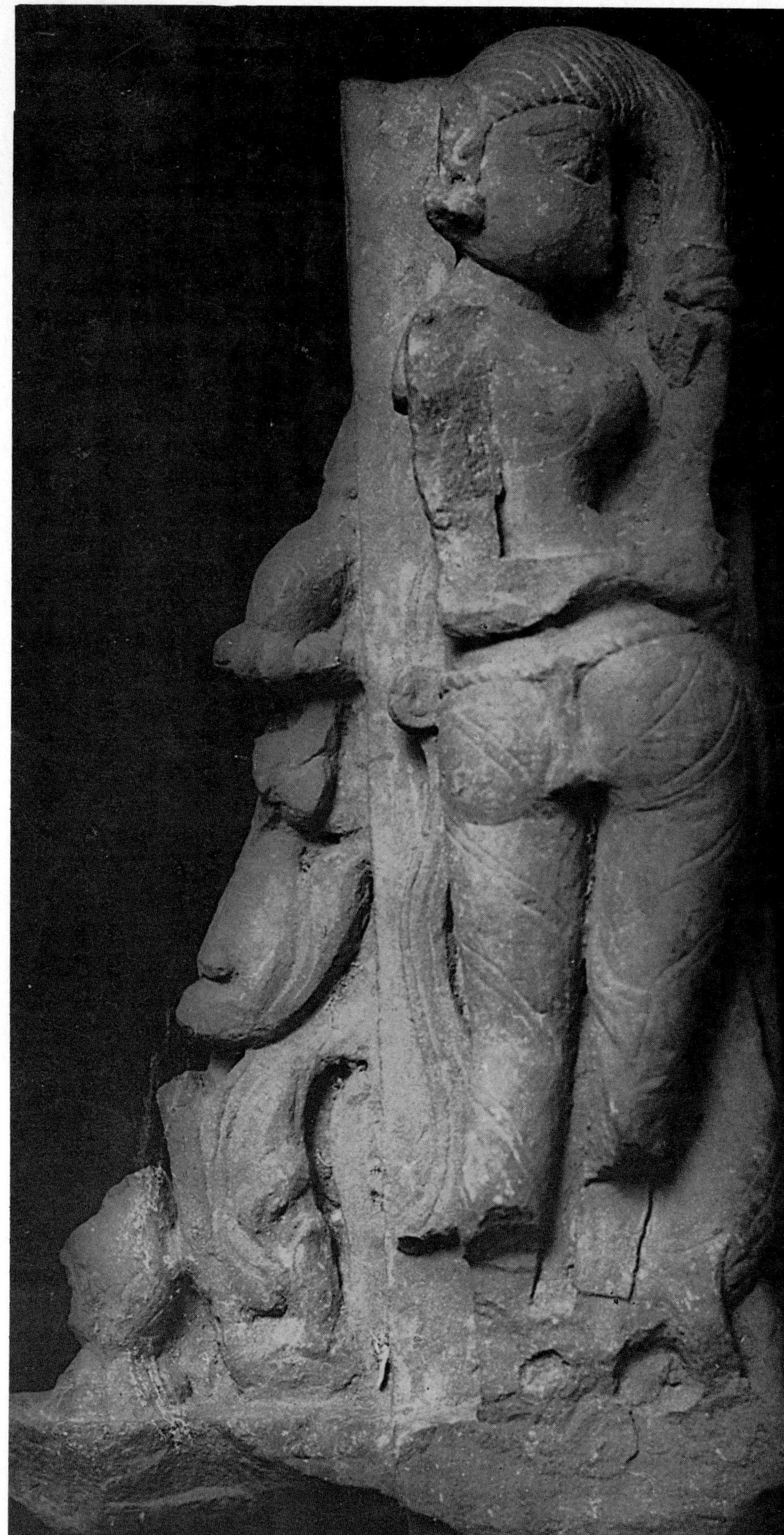

Garuda asana female deity with two chakras in both the arms.

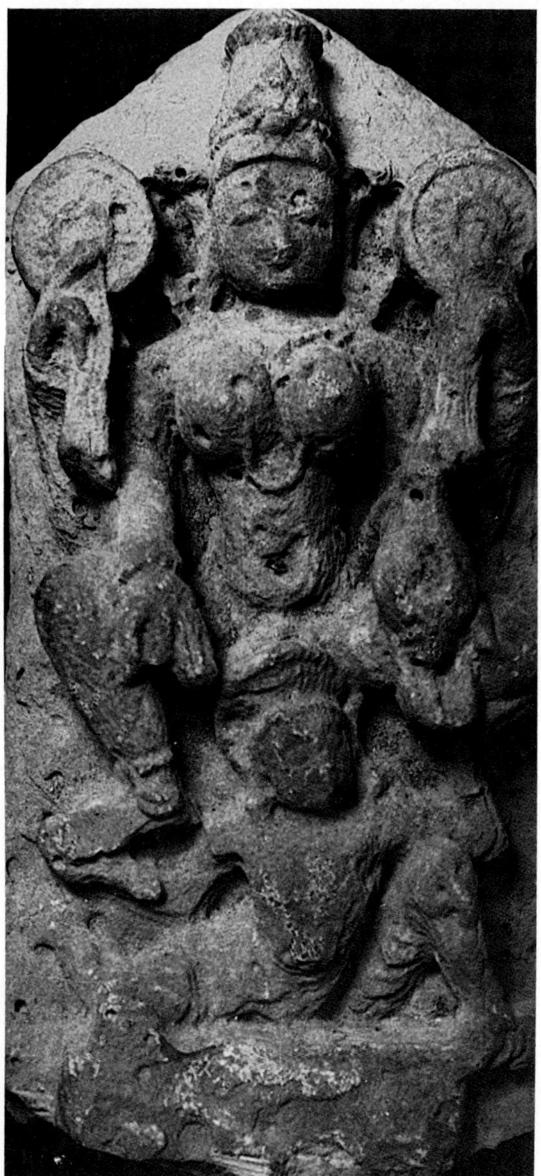

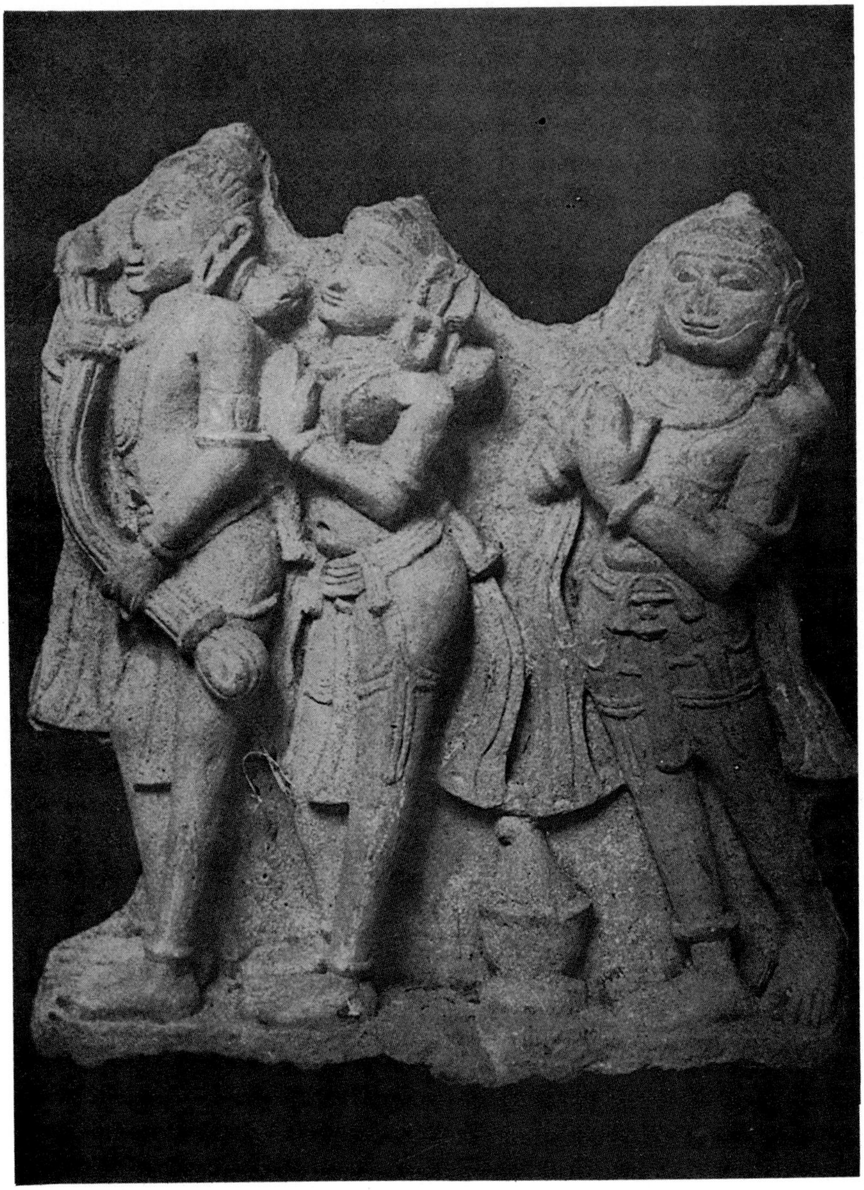

Stone panel showing Ram, Laxman & Sita.

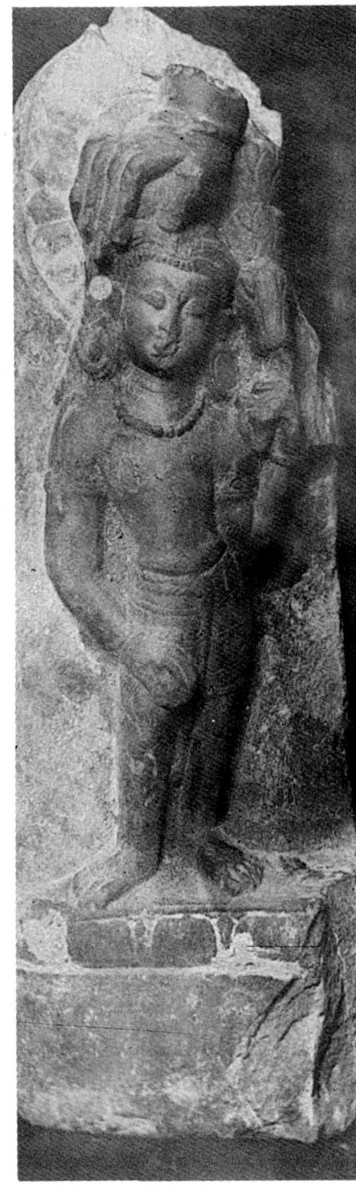

Fragmentary image showing an attendant on whon
rests a hand.

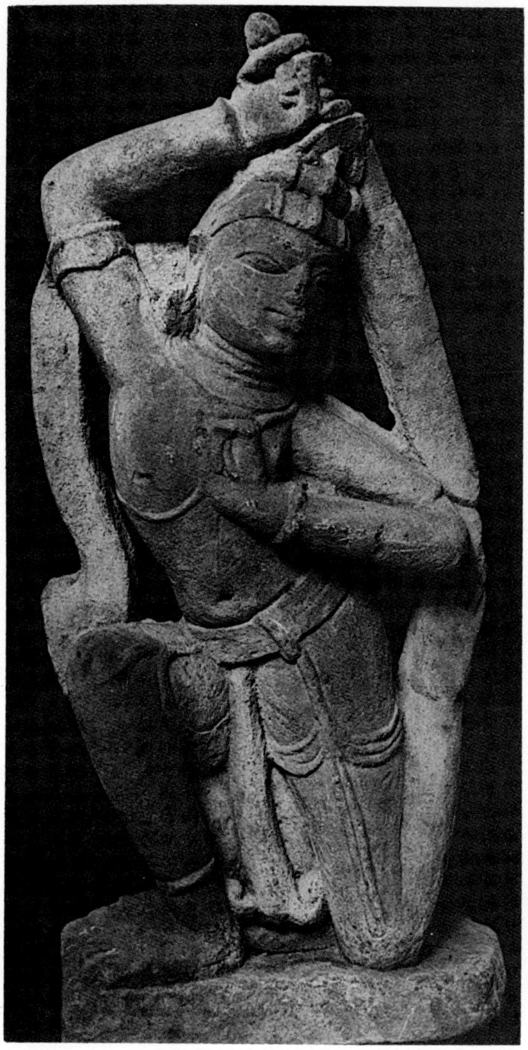

Stone Male figure.

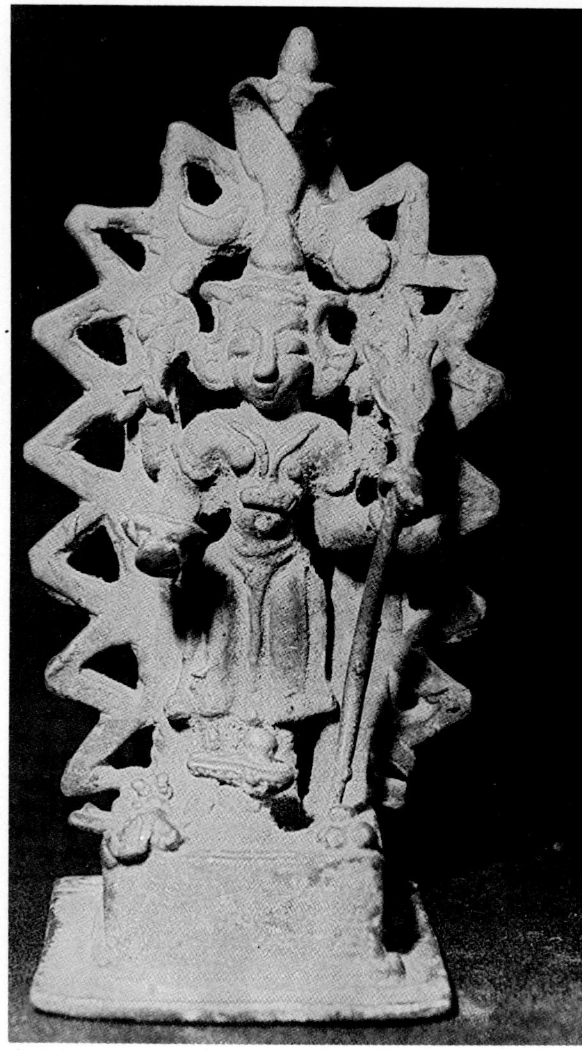

Standing Deity (Bronze).

Standing Krishna playing flute (Bronze).

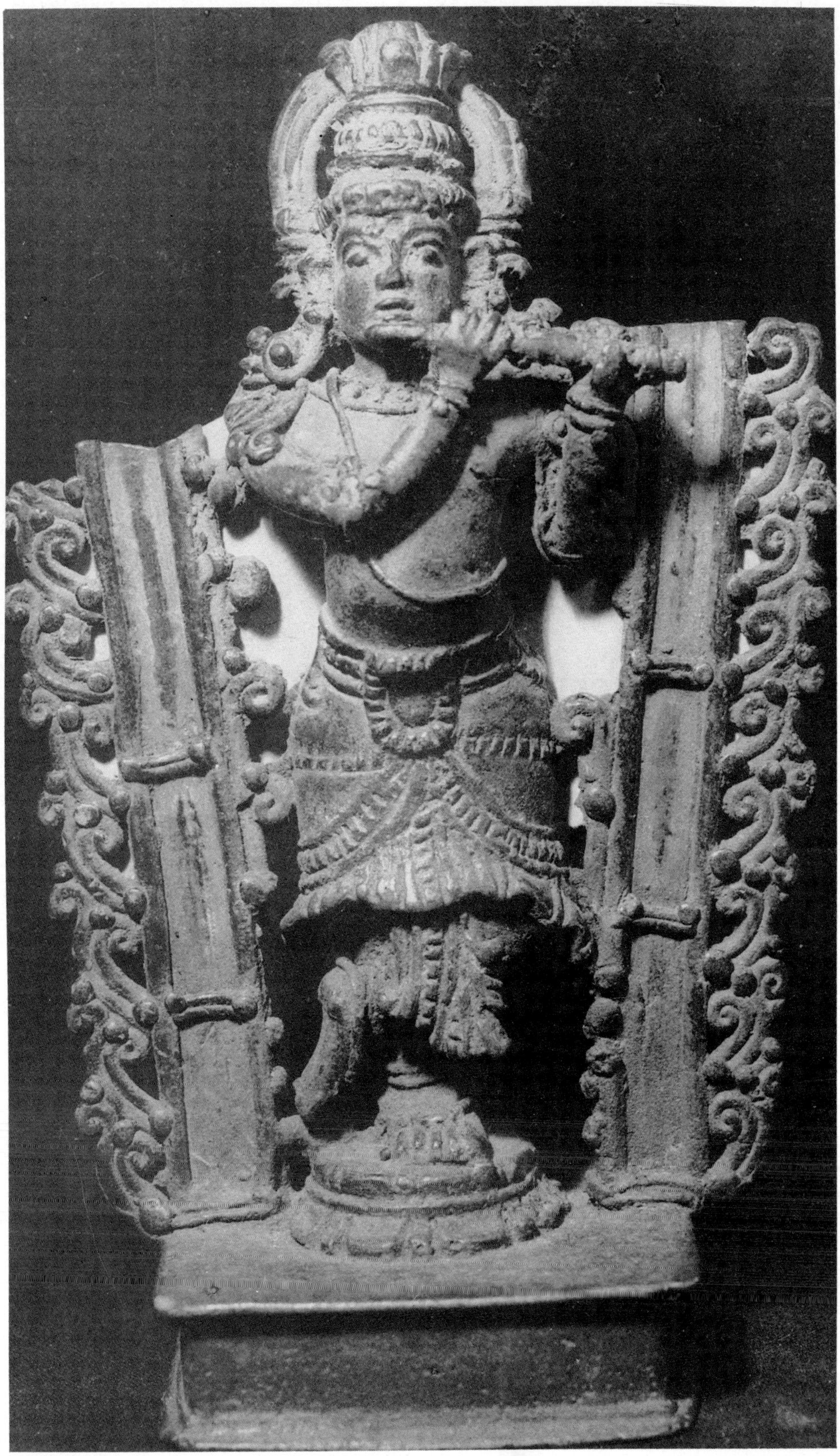

Copper Implement.

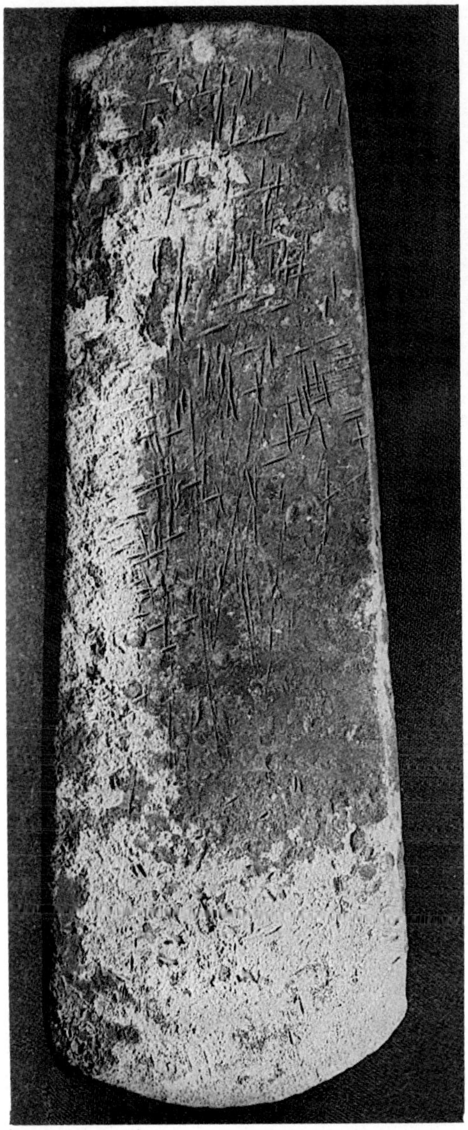

Airport, he noticed the Air Customs Officers standing near his 5 suitcases. Apprehending his arrest by the Customs Authorities, he left the place quietly and managed to proceed to New York subsequently and has since been absconding.

The aforesaid 5 VIP suitcases were opened by the Air Customs Officers in the presence of independent witnesses and the 18 concealed antique objects were seized by them. Subsequently, these 18 objects including the idol of Goddess Durga were produced before the Director General, Archaeological Survey of India, for examination and expert opinion. On examination, the seized 18 objects were certified as antiques by the ASI.

On completion of the investigation, it was decided to prosecute the accused in the court of law, after obtaining the sanction from the Archaeological Survey of India. On receipt of the sanction from the ASI, a charge-sheet under Section 120 BPC, r/w Section 380, 411, 414 IPC and Sec. 25(1) of the Antiquities and Art Treasures Act, 1972 had been filed in the Court of the Chief Metropolitan Magistrate, Delhi on 28.2.1983.

A large number of antiques and idols stolen from India usually find their way into antique markets of United Kingdom, Switzerland and the United States of America. Indian antiques are a craze in foreign markets. Even for a second-rate bronze statue or antiquity from India, a foreign collector may be ready to pay as much as rupees one lakh. A four-to-five feet high metal idol of a Hindu god and if it is more than 1000 years old may fetch anything from Rs. 20 to Rs. 50 lakhs abroad.

The operators, who mastermind the antique smuggling operations, are usually well-to-do and influential priests or trustees of the temples. Some of them are lured by the huge money, while some others are in league with the smugglers' syndicate.

Transportation is also an important aspect of smuggling activity. The safest way to smuggle stolen antiques is by sea. Because of the rigorous check at airports on baggages and cargoes despatched by air, very few smugglers take this recourse. Sometimes they even go to the extent of sending these items through diplomatic bags either by befriending the staff of the foreign embassy or even making them partners in the trade. There have been many cases when diplomats have misused their diplomatic immunity and smuggled priceless antiques out of the country. The safest way to smuggle them is by sea, in the garb of some commodity neatly packed in wooden crates although it is a long wait for the other party at that end. The important ports misused for this purpose have been Bombay, Madras and Calcutta.

The operators of this trade take big financial risks if one views their investments from the rupee expenditure angle. A digger, who removes an idol from a monument, gets anything from Rs. 1000 to Rs. 10,000 depending on the worth of the object. Then there are relays of carriers. The first team carries the antique from the place where it is stolen to the first place of hiding. Once the heat is off, it is delivered to the first buyer, usually an antique dealer in a metropolitan city. He gets anything from Rs. 10,000 to Rs. 1,00,000 for the job. Sometimes an entrepreneuring smuggler may cultivate the local officials and take their help for transporting the goods, of course for a price depending upon the status and capability of the officials. Many a time even government vehicles have been used for this purpose. In Rajasthan, a senior Civil Engineer was found involved in this racket. He used to collect antiques from dilapidated temples and bring them to his official residence and decorate his garden and finally passed them on to smugglers at pre-arranged places.

Another team transports these stolen antiques from the first buyer to the second dealer, usually a rich Indian in Bombay or Calcutta. From there the consignment is shipped by generally greasing the palms of certain staff, whose duty is to check accompanied or unaccompanied baggages. The passage for the carrier is often booked a month in advance of the theft so as not to arouse any suspicion. Once the antique reaches its destination abroad the returns are fabulous. With an investment of Rs. 10 to 15 lakhs on the whole smuggling operation, the master-operator can earn as much as Rs. 40-50 lakhs on a single consignment and that too in hard currency, resulting in earning considerable foreign exchange just at one stroke. According to antique valuers, the price of smuggled antiques has gone up by 500 per cent in the last one decade.

# FAKE TECHNIQUES

ONE sinister aspect of the illegal trade in antiques the world over is the replacement of originals by fakes, which even experts are not sometimes able to detect. Suspicion is deep-rooted in the world of art that in several cases the genuine articles have been removed by unscrupulous persons and replaced by replicas and they are so cleverly planted that they can be recovered by the police and passed off as original. A case in point is the famous Nataraj idol which was smuggled to the U.S.A. and in its place a fake idol was installed in the temple. Another case was of the two pillars smuggled from a malkhana of a court in Haryana and replaced by fake ones. There are numerous other cases of fake paintings being sold to foreign buyers as original ones. Many curio shops in the metropolitan cities were suspected to be involved in these illegal acts. The trade in fake antiques was being carried on for a long time unchecked as it was very difficult to prove and hardly any evidence was available to prosecute the culprits.

The difficulties to declare a fake as a fake arise due to the reluctance on the part of all the parties concerned. The police and the other antique smuggling detecting agencies are always keen to declare one more case on record as solved. The owner of the piece is anxious to regain whatever is given back to him and accept it as original. That way the price of the piece also does not go down and in the bargain he does not suffer any financial loss also. In the case of an institution, the head of the institution is always anxious to save its reputation and hence will go to any length to accept the fact that the antique piece recovered is the original one. Sometimes even government agencies get involved because of the sentimental and emotional unrest that accompany the theft of an antique of religious or historical value. Their action reflects the religious reputation and also the mood of the people. In such cases even the recovery of a fake is announced as original, since it helps in pacifying the anxiety of the people aroused on this issue.

Many antique dealers pointed out that the replacement of the genuine antique with fake ones was being carried on for a long time. But, the dealers would not go to the extent of identifying the fake images. One antique dealer cited the example of a 'Nataraj' from a temple in the South. When this was put to a police officer, who was in knowledge of the case, he agreed that the original Nataraj was no more in its place.

Antique fakers are the backbone of idol smugglers in India. Fake antiques are used as decoys to smuggle out. The modus operandi used by the idol and antique runners is to order consignments of fakes. According to an artisan, an expert faker presents a dozen of bronze Buddhas, exact replicas for the famous 4th century piece, for sale. The layman and even an antique buyer is unable to differentiate between the fake and the genuine piece. The operator then obtains permission to export these newly fashioned bronzes. With the connivance of those in the consignment section, one genuine piece is substituted for the fake one. The irony is that the operators of this underground trade in idols and antiques are better archaeologists and appraisers of fabulous pieces of antiques. In some instances they have proved to be better than experts.

Important centres of fake trade in antiques are located in India and Nepal. Most fake bronze Buddha pieces are fashioned by skilled craftsmen in Nepal, then brought to India and from here they are exported alongwith the genuine pieces. For making fake idols of stone and paintings of traditional sculptures, the smugglers look to artisans and painters from Rajasthan and the Southern States. These artisans are employed by the unscrupulous traders for furthering their nefarious activities.

According to an antique dealer, to produce a clever replica of a 5 ft image the artisan may need only 24 to 48 hours for preparing two sets of moulds from which a bronze statue could be casted. To sculpt a stone image the time required is much more, depending upon the size of the piece and the intrinsic workmanship needed. Wooden pieces and paintings do not require much time. The art dealer always emphasises on quality and craftsmanship from the artisan. With the pathetic economic condition of our craftsmen, the unscrupulous dealers do not find any difficulty in securing the services of competent craftsmen as the remuneration they (artisans) get in such cases is much higher as compared to their ordinary earnings. The other factor which lures them to the clutches of such dealers is the benefit of being anonymous and thus living comfortably.

To check this fake trade in antiques, it has been suggested that an official agency may be established for reproducing replicas of most of the famous antiques using the same medium so as to satisfy the rich antique-hungry foreigners. This will have two-pronged effect—one, it would check smuggling of antiques and two, earn foreign exchange, which otherwise the government exchequer is being denied. This step, apart from putting a stop to thefts, will take Indian culture to more homes in the West and also provide employment to many artisans at home.

As stated earlier, perhaps the most bizarre case was the replacement of the mammoth Nataraj idol in the Shivapuram temple in Tamil Nadu by a fake one. The beautiful bronze idol was being worshipped by thousands of devotees. The notorious antique smugglers cast their evil eye on the idol and they lured the artisans who succumbed to their greed for money. The method adopted was interesting. The trustees of the temple had given the idol for restoration to an expert artisan. But, he being a part of the gang had other ideas, and instead took a plaster cast of the original Nataraj and then made a bronze replica. He gave acid treatment to the replica and stained it with natural dyes, which transformed it to such an extent that even the experts could have least suspected. He returned the fake idol to the trustees, which was installed after a great ceremony. The original idol was packed in a gunny bag and put in a wooden case and transported to a middleman who shipped it to the U.S.A.

The Indian government moved the local courts, which ruled that the statue ought to be restored to its home in India. The Nataraj's story sparked off a comment from prominent American collectors and museum directors who quipped that if all artefacts were to be shipped back to India from them their show windows would be empty.

Skilful techniques adopted in making the replicas of original antiques are sometimes quite difficult to detect. Besides art, where modern chemical methods are used for forgery, innumerable takes have been detected with ceramics, glass, motifs, metal work and pottery.

Critical visual examination yields a lot of information and clues. Forgeries are obvious because of tone, texture, even joints in repairs and additions. Perhaps, one sure-fire way of detecting fakes is from the consistency of patina. The normal handling of an antique over a period of time produces signs of wear. Environmental factors also might produce colour changes or even cracks and splits. What might have taken centuries to form, could be removed in a few minutes and all their antique quality could be erased. On the other hand, repatination can also be achieved by clever forgers. Every genuine antique possesses a mysterious silence, a concrete reminder of the bygone times. Some of them were probably instrumental at one period of time or another in shaping the history of the country.

# LEGISLATIVE MEASURES

ARTICLE 49 of the Constitution of India lays down that "It shall be the obligation of the State to protect every monument or place or object of artistic or historic interest, declared by or under law made by Parliament, to be of national importance, from spoliation, disfigurement, destruction, removal, disposal or export, as the case may be."

In 1861 the British Government in India established the department of Archaeological Survey of India to centralise the collection of exhibits in the museums from site explorations and ancient monuments. The Central and State museums acted as store-house and protector of the antiquities recovered in the course of scientific excavations and from ancient monuments. They were also subjected to study by the researchers at the museums as they possessed the authentic data and the evolution of styles of the antiquities.

With the enactment of the Indian Treasure-Trove Act in 1878, Government was also empowered to acquire ancient and medieval sculptures, coins, seals, copper plates and other art objects. As this Act was handicapped to provide foolproof protection to the art heritage the Government of India enacted another Act in 1904, termed as Ancient Monuments Preservation Act. This Act was "to provide for the preservation of ancient monuments, for the exercise of control over traffic in antiquities and over excavation in certain places and for the protection and acquisition in certain cases of ancient monuments and of objects of archaeological, historical or artistic interest." After independence this Act was succeeded and made more broad-based by another Act called Ancient Monuments and Archaeological Sites and Remains Act, 1958.

As a follow-up of Montague-Chelmsford Reforms of 1919, the devolution rules were framed in 1921 which classified Archaeology as a Central subject. All the monuments, declared protected, came under the control of the Centre. Subsequently, the Government of India Act of 1935 made Archaeology a federal subject and all powers relating to ancient and historical monuments were vested with Government of India. This also included archaeological sites and remains which were earlier under the jurisdiction of the provinces.

To further tighten the export of antiquities, Indian Parliament passed the Antiquities (Export Control) Act on 18th April, 1947. Under this Act, no antiquity could be exported without a licence issued by the Director General. According to this Act, antiquity did not include any object which was less than one hundred years old and the Antiquities (Export Control) Rules, 1947 included provision for giving certificate as to whether an object was an antiquity or not antiquity. The Antiquities (Export Control) Amendment Bill of 1965 transferred the power of Director General who was hitherto the final authority to decide the nature of antiquity to a Board called the Antiquities Appellate Board. With this amendment to the Bill, the Board's verdict was to be treated as final.

With the promulgation of the Constitution of India on 26th January, 1950 the responsibilities relating to Archaeology between Centre and the States were defined and the functions allocated as per the Seventh Schedule of the Constitution. These are as follows:

List I (Union List), Item 67: Ancient and historical monuments and records, and archaeological sites and remains declared by or under law made by Parliament to be of national importance.

List II (State List), Item 12: Libraries, museums and other similar institutions controlled or financed by the State; ancient and historical monuments and records other than those declared by or under law made by Parliament to be of national importance.

List III (Concurrent List), Item 40: Archaeological sites and remains other than those declared by or under law made by Parliament to be of national importance.

Since the thirties, the rich western countries have developed a great attraction towards the cultural property of India. As a result, many of the artistic and valuable antiques made their way and adorned the galleries of U.S.A. and other countries in Europe. A band of smugglers surfaced with the prospect of good money in this trade, who had no respect or pride for their country's heritage. They became easy pawn in the hands of the foreign buyers. Innumerable idols and objects from temples and ruins of monuments were stolen and sold for personal monetary gain. Art pieces like paintings and old scriptures were also not spared. When this piracy of cultural property reached a threatening height the matter was deliberated in the General Conference of UNESCO. The convention on the Means of Prohibiting and Preventing Illicit Import, Export and Transfer of Ownership of Cultural Property adopted by the General Conference at the Sixteenth Session of UNESCO at Paris in 1970 defines it as follows:

For the purposes of this convention the term "Cultural Property" means property which, on religious or secular grounds, is specifically designated by each State as being of importance for archaeology, prehistory, history, literature, art or science and which belongs to the following categories: rare collections and specimens of fauna, flora, minerals and objects of palaeontological interest; (b) property relating to history including the history of science and technology and military and social history, to the national leaders, thinkers, scientists and to events of national importance; (c) products of archaeological excavations (including regular and clandestine) or of archaeological discoveries; (d) elements of artistic or historical monuments or archaeological sites which have been dismembered; (e) antiquities more than one hundred year old, such as inscriptions, coins and engraved seals; (f) objects of ethnological interest; (g) property of artistic interest, such as:

(i) pictures, paintings and drawings produced entirely by hand or any support and in any material (excluding industrial designs and manufactured articles decorated by hand);

(ii) original works of statutory art and sculptures in any material;
(iii) original artistic assemblages and montages in any material;
(iv) rare manuscripts and incunabula, old books, documents and publications of special interest (historical, artistic, scientific, literary etc.) singly or in collections;
(v) postage, revenue and similar stamps, singly or in collections;
(vi) archives including sound, photographic and cinematographic archives;
(vii) articles of furniture more than one hundred years old and old musical instruments.

In India, there are three legislations—Ancient Monuments and Archaeological Sites and Remains Act, 1958, Antiquities and Art Treasures Act, 1972 and Wild Life Protection Act, 1972—which partly cover the items categorised under UNESCO's definition of cultural property.

UNESCO has in its subsequent conventions introduced new definition of cultural property. On the International Exchange of cultural property, it defines it as:

Cultural property shall be taken to mean items which are the expression and testimony of human creation and of the evolution of nature which, in the opinion of the competent bodies in individual states, are or may be of historical, artistic, scientific or technical value and interest, including items in the following categories:

(a) zoological, botanical and geological specimens;
(b) archaeological objects;
(c) objects and documentation of ethnological interest;
(d) works of fine art and of the applied arts;
(e) literary, musical, photographic and cinematographic works; and
(f) archives and documents.

At various sessions of the UNESCO and of INTERPOL the subject of smuggling of antiques has been discussed and many recommendations in this regard circulated to the member countries. Many countries in the East have enacted laws to prevent the theft of cultural property. The proliferation of fakes has also posed danger in preserving the cultural property. Pakistan's Antiquities Act of 1968 considers counterfeiting an antiquity as an offence. Iraq has also taken stringent measures by enacting the antiquities law to check forgery and fake business.

The craze for acquiring other nations' cultural property has its roots in the remote past; all conquerors had taken hold of the creations of beauty belonging to the vanquished; in the hey-days of imperialism all colonies suffered immensely from the loss of their artistic and cultural heritage. In those days some amount of outflow through illicit channels must have been going on but the problem did not assume international dimensions. Nevertheless the lure of possessing other nations' patrimony still persists. Man's love and passion for what is beautiful and charming will never die out. Added to all these, in affluent countries, possessing an art piece or an antiquity from distant lands is taken to be a symbol of high social status. Or in the days of fluctuating currencies and high inflation spending money

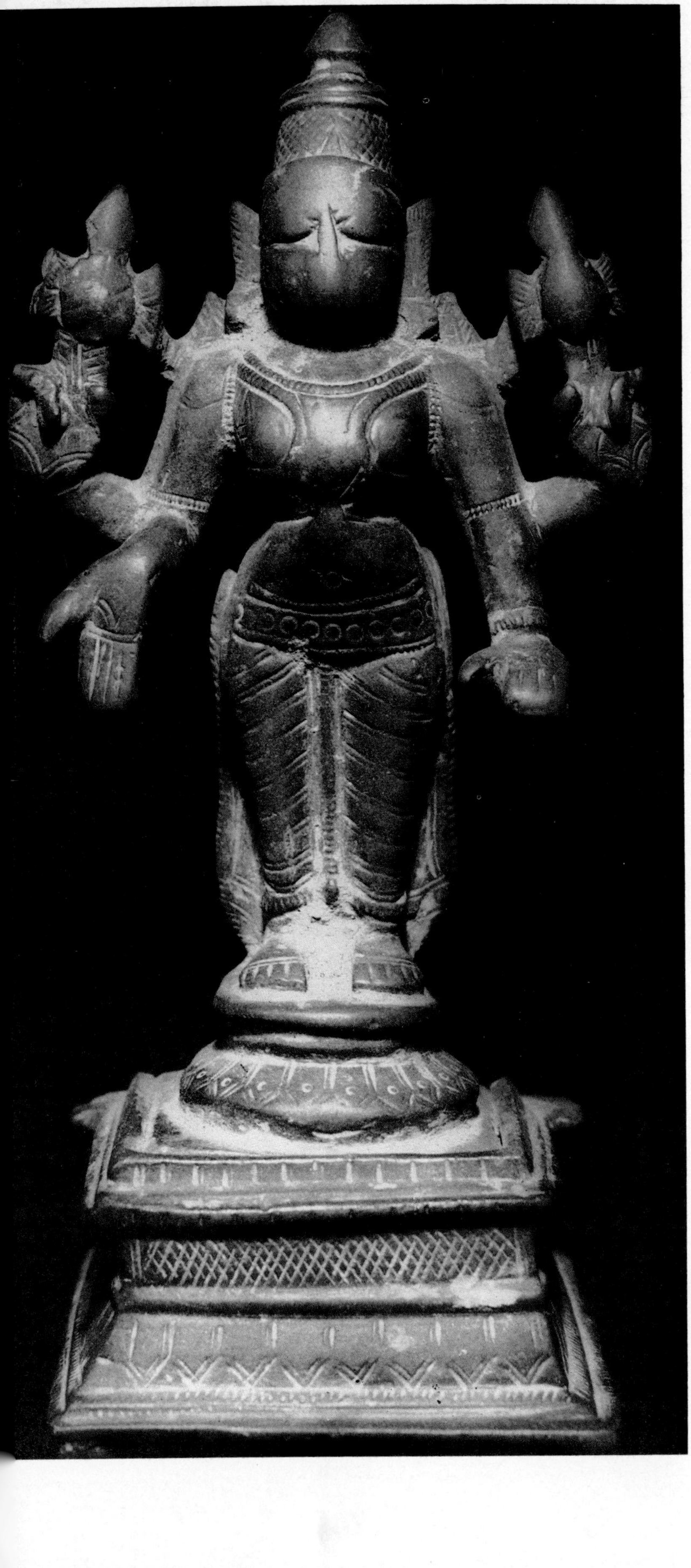

Four-armed standing female deity on pedestal with state showing Snakehood (Bronze).

A piece of Terracotta.

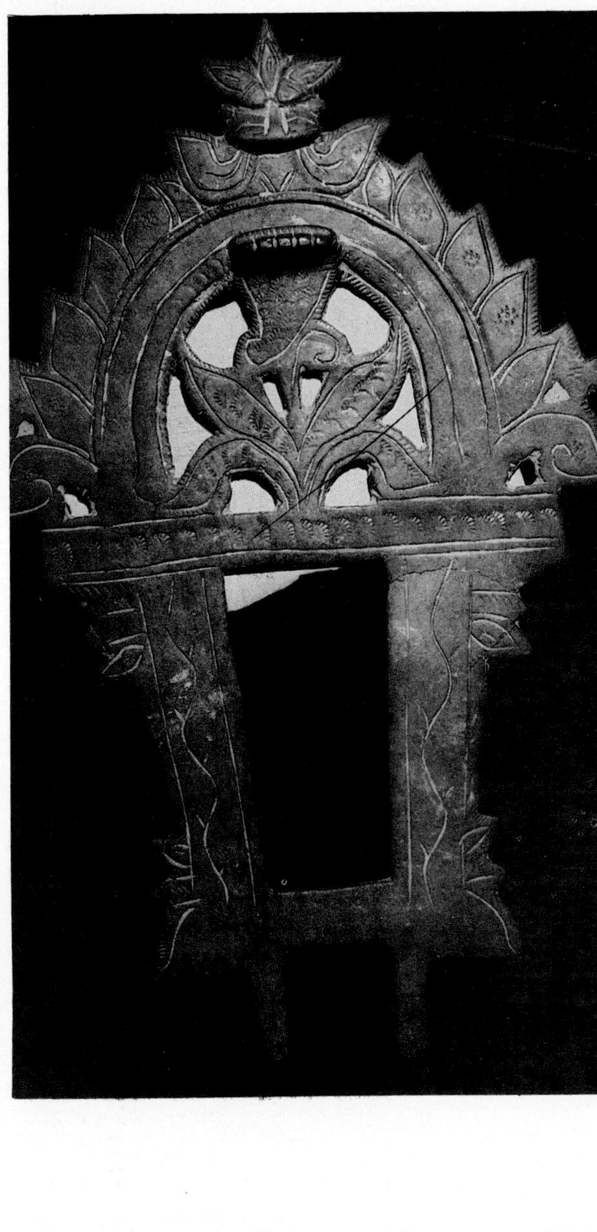

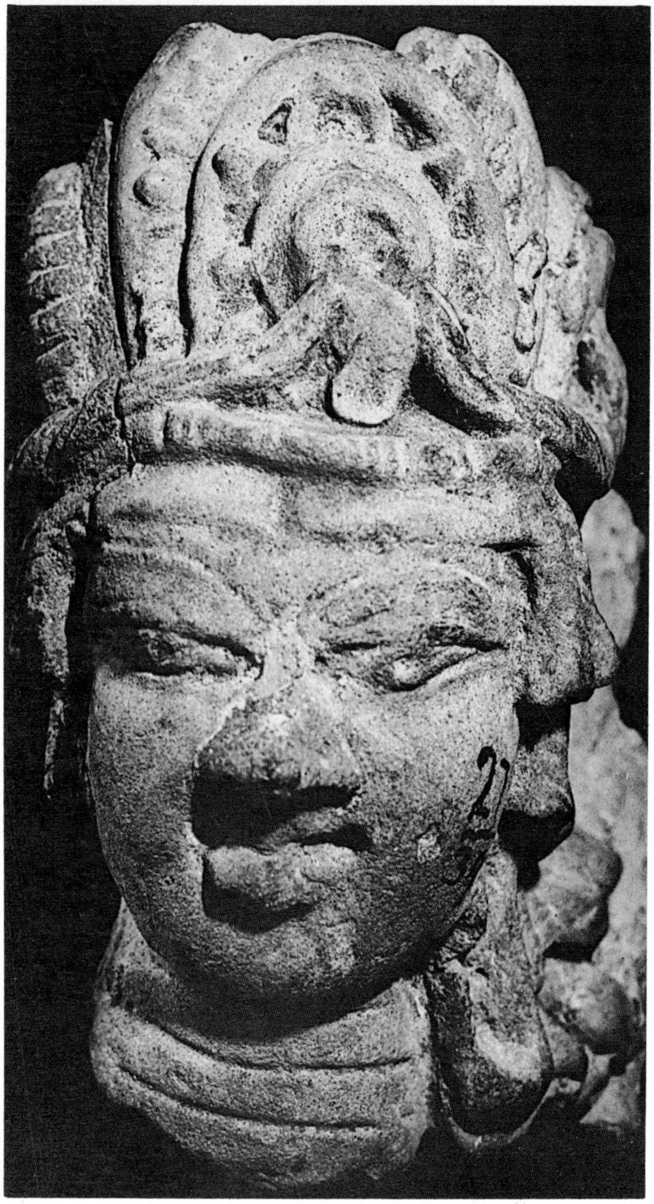

A piece of ornate crowned human head cracked—tip of the nose shows some mending.

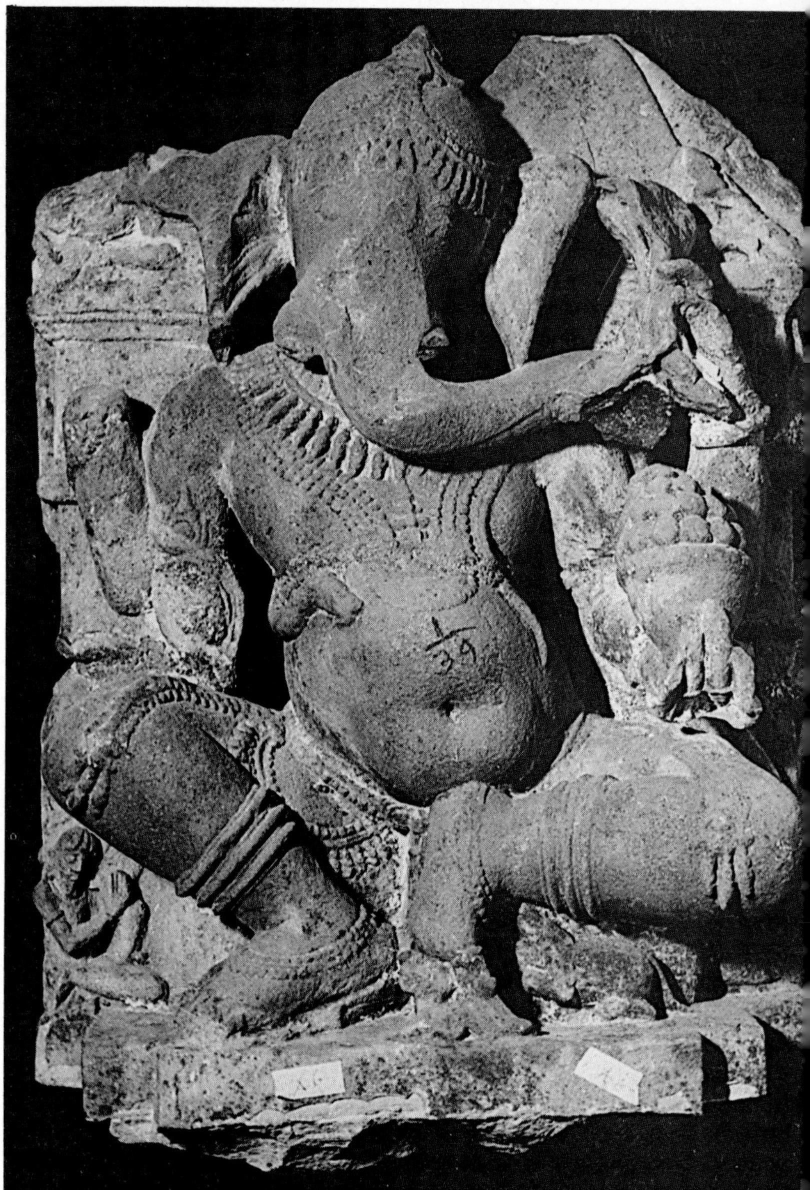

Mutilated Ganesh Figure.

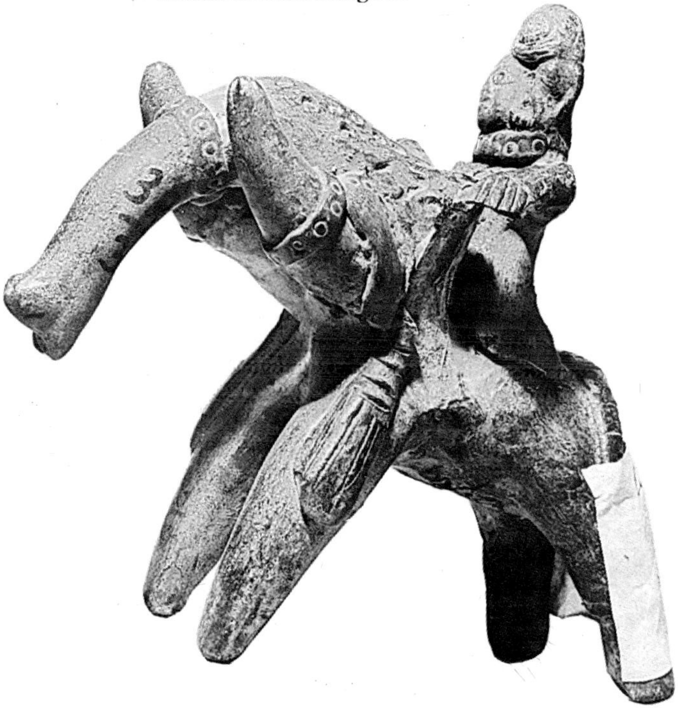

Elephant Terracotta.

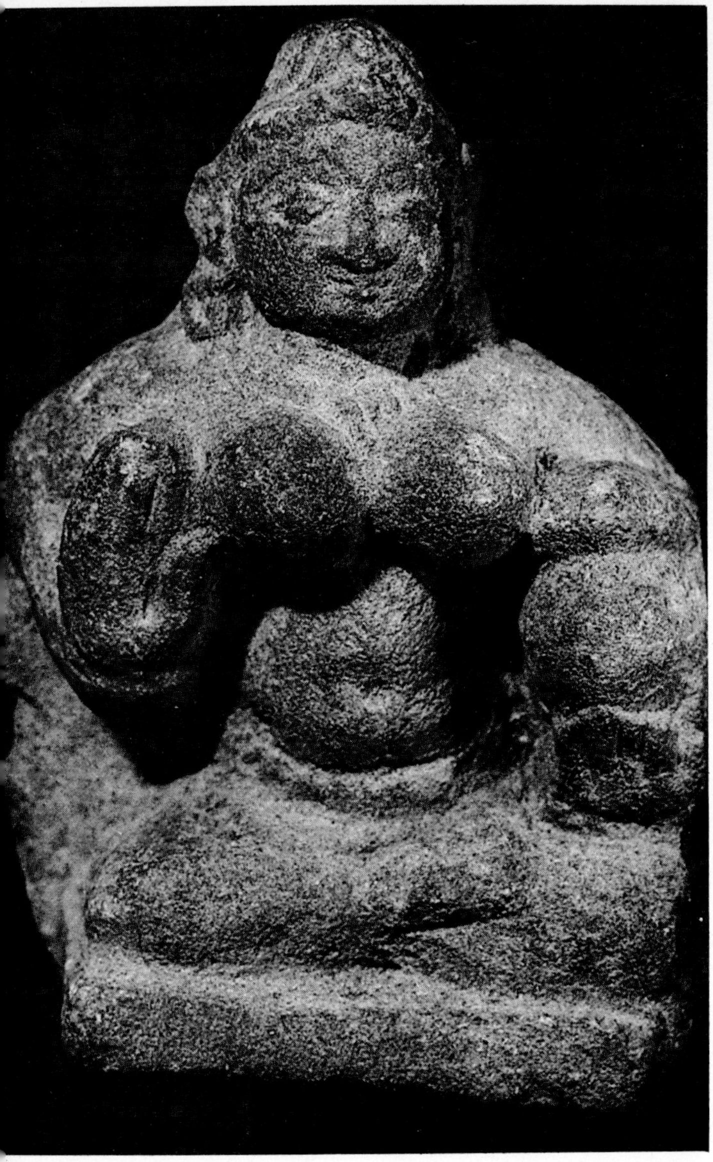

A seated female deity.

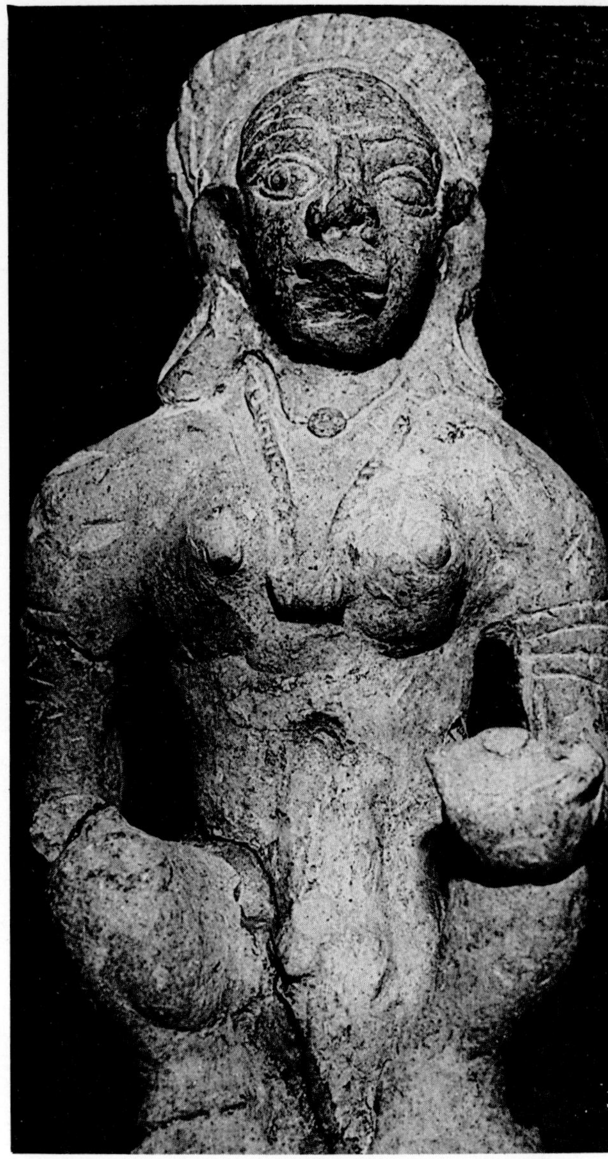

Folk seated female figure holding a bowl.

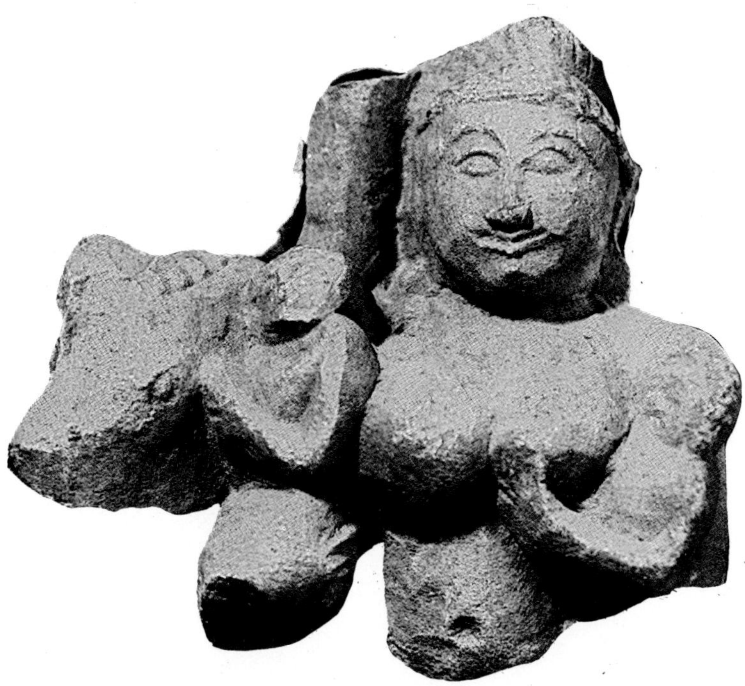

A matrika with child.

Lower portion of a pedestal of standing deity showing two flying whisk attendants.

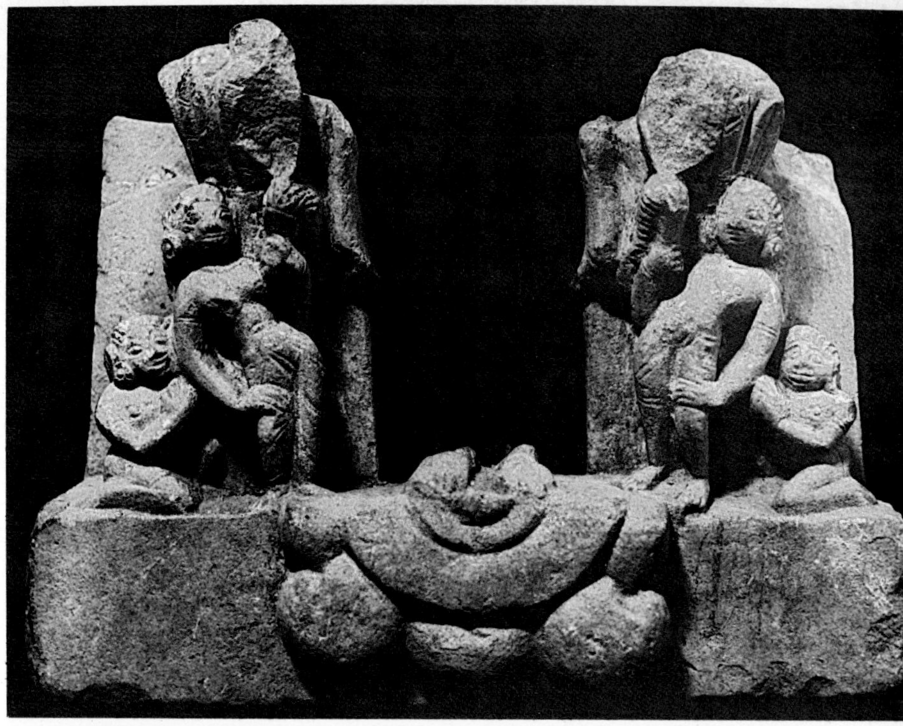

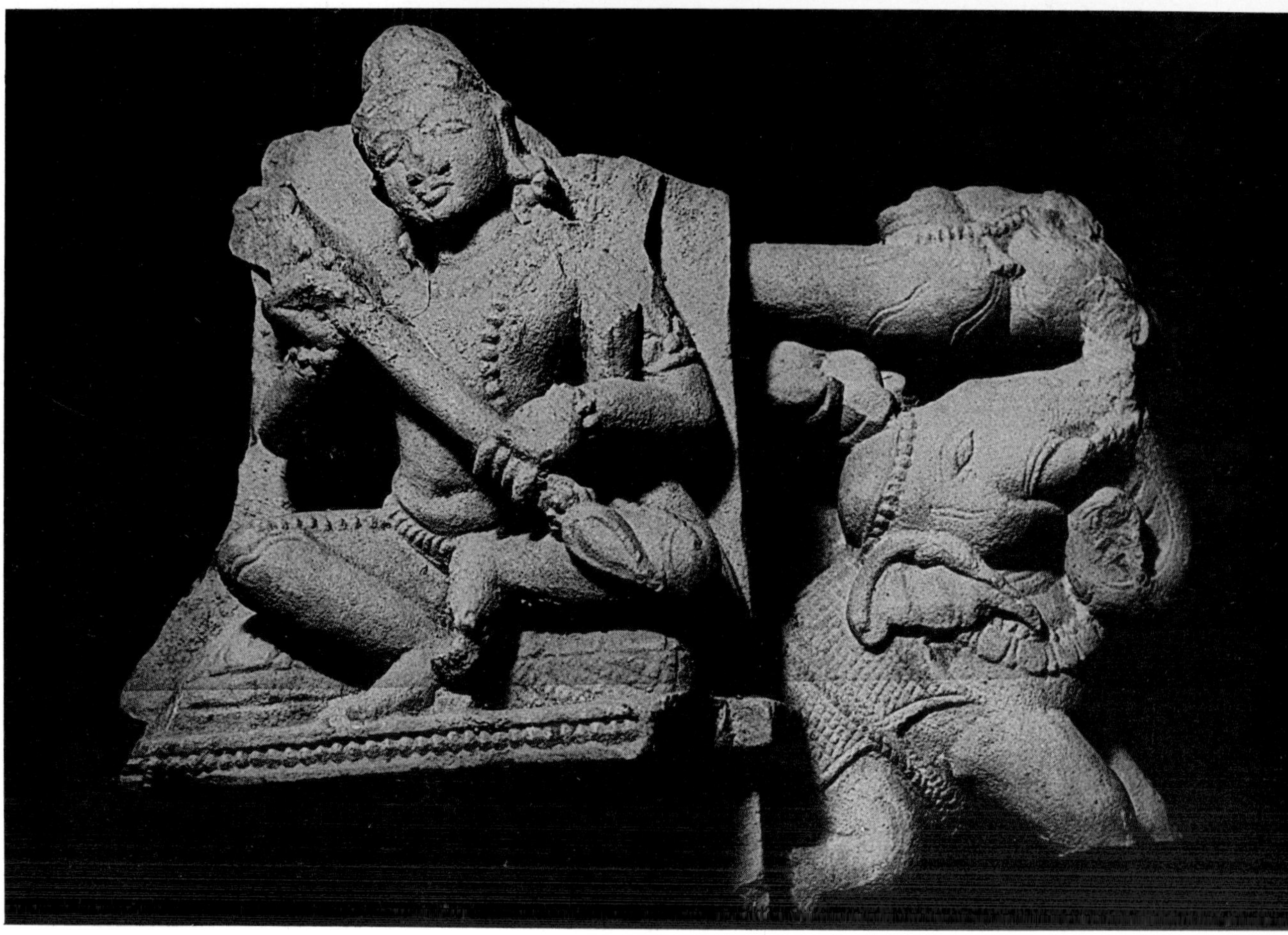

A male figure holding a staff in both hands on the right, left in recass, on charging elephant.

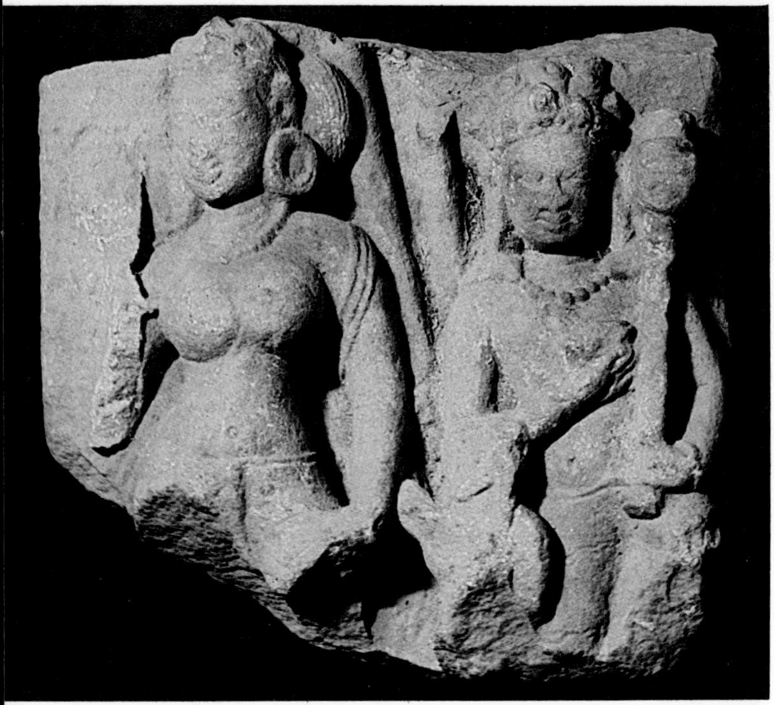

Female flanked by Bhairav.

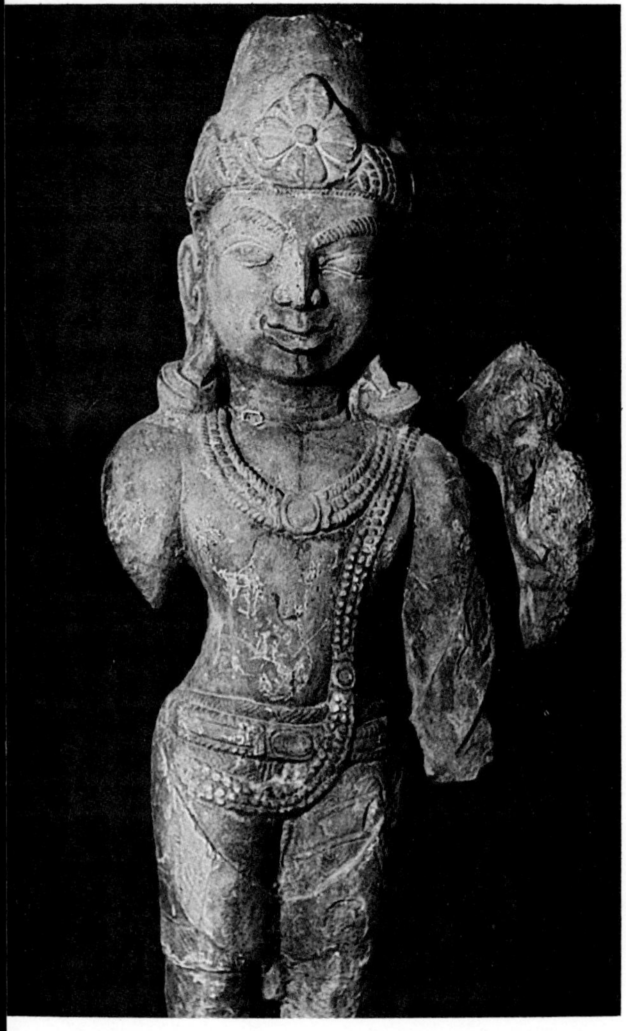

Male standing deity (legless and broken hands).

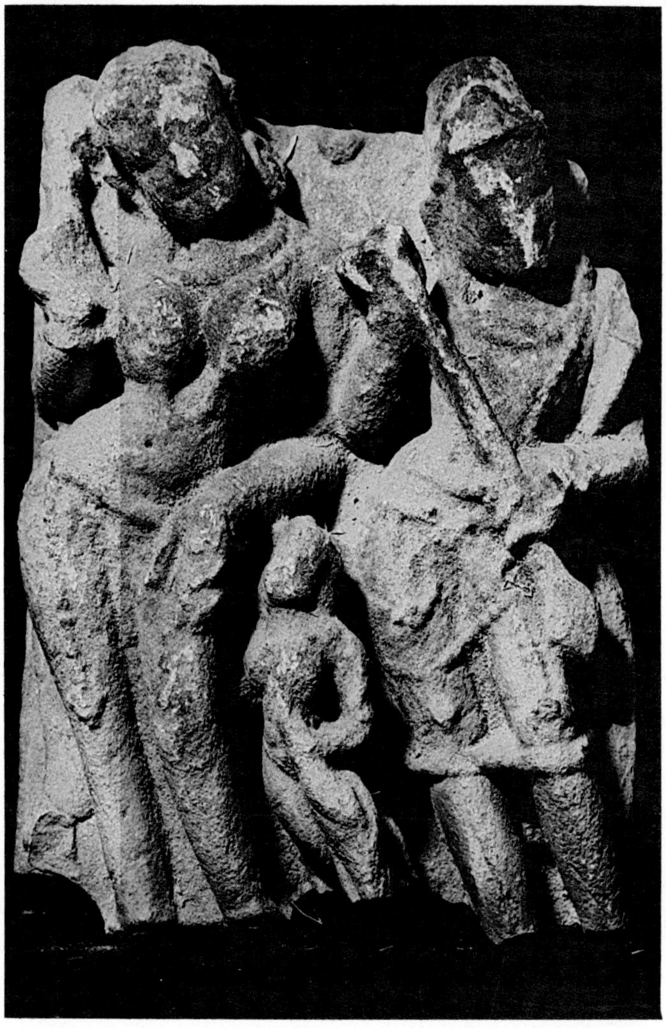

Kamdeva and Rati.

A standing female chauri bearer with four attendants on her right.

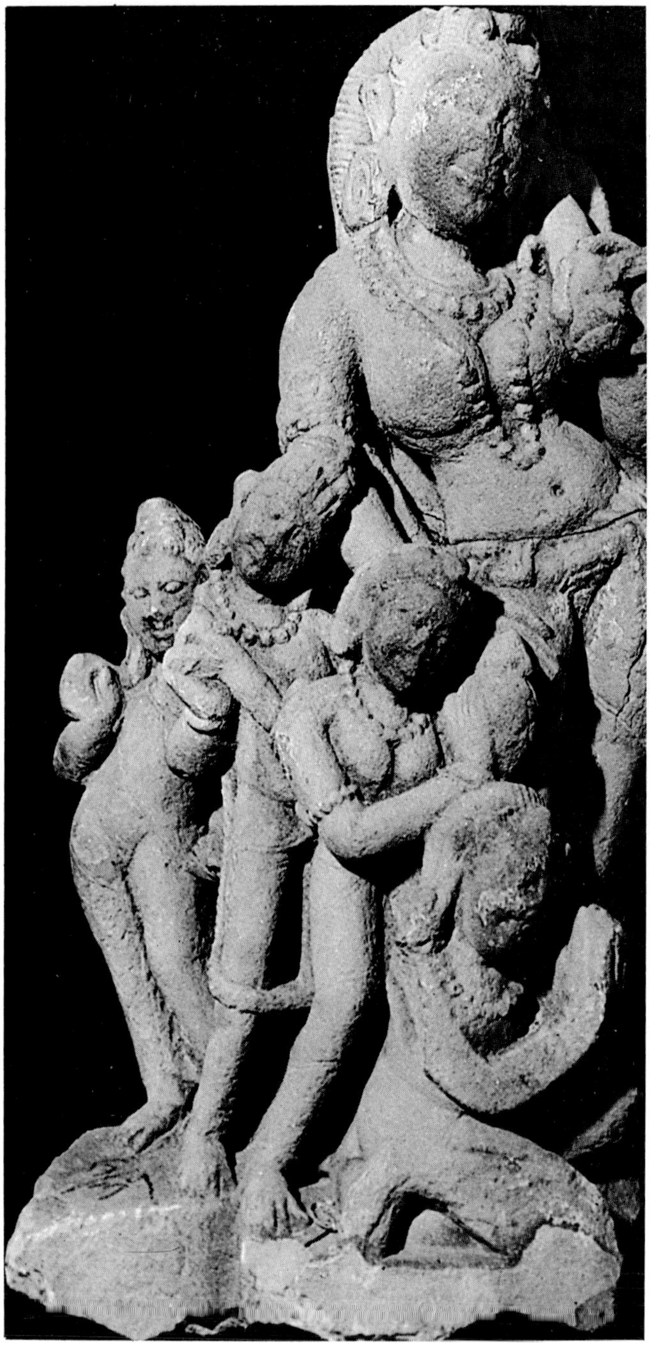

A standing Surya deity.

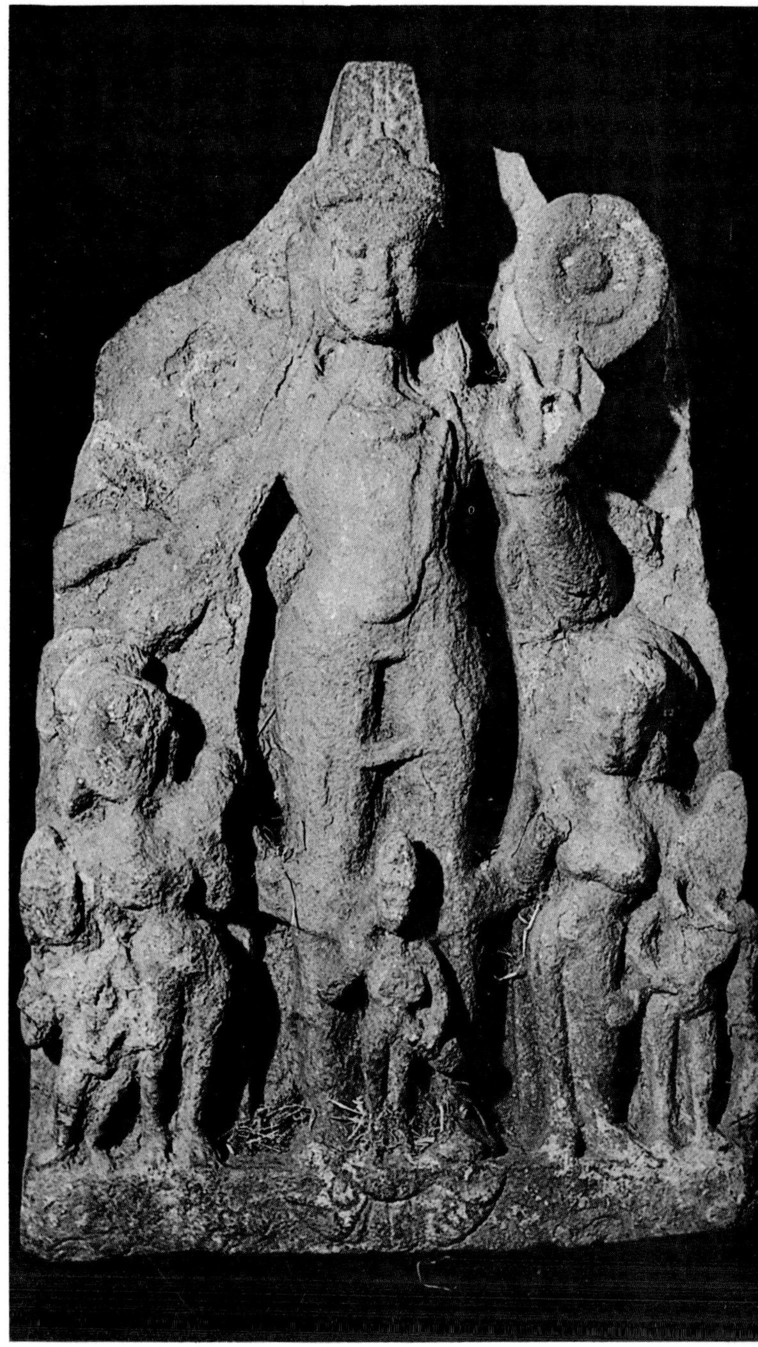

Buddha with a chatra on his head inscribed.

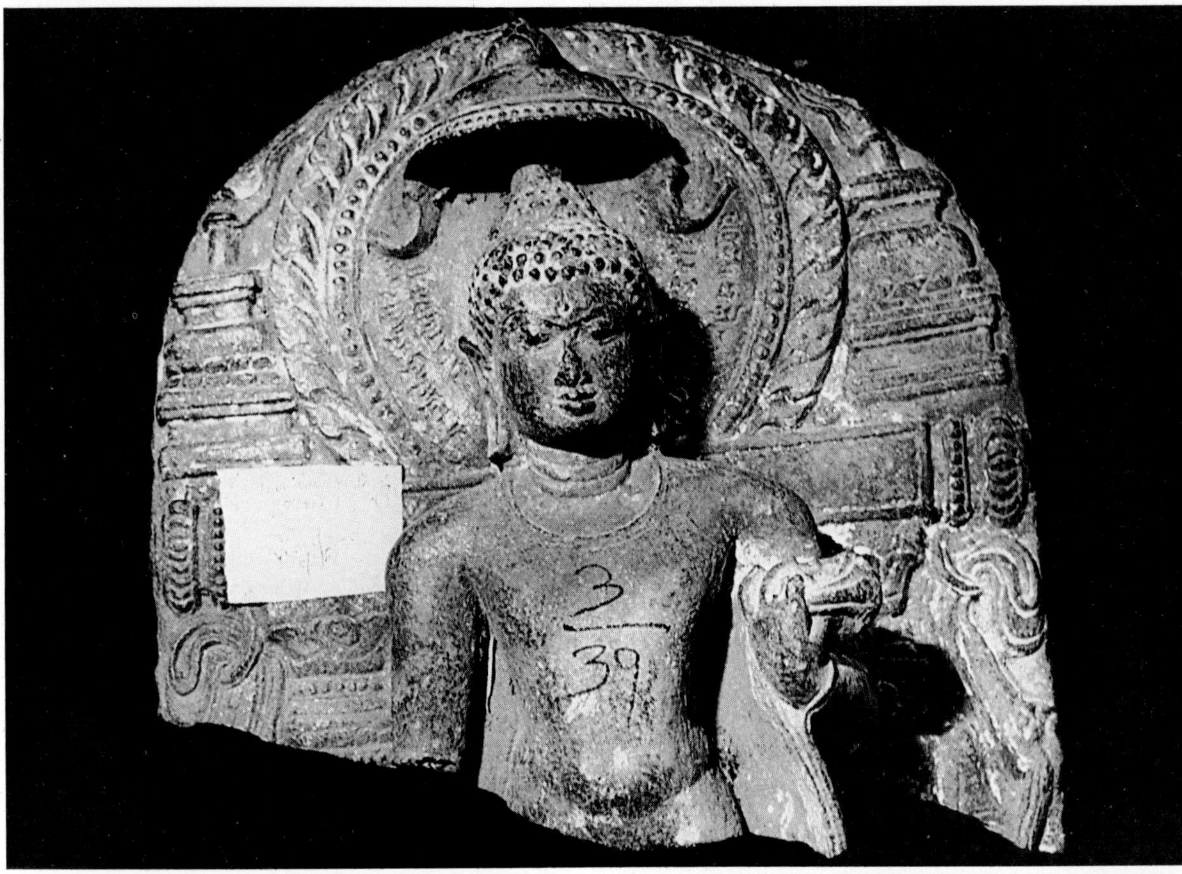


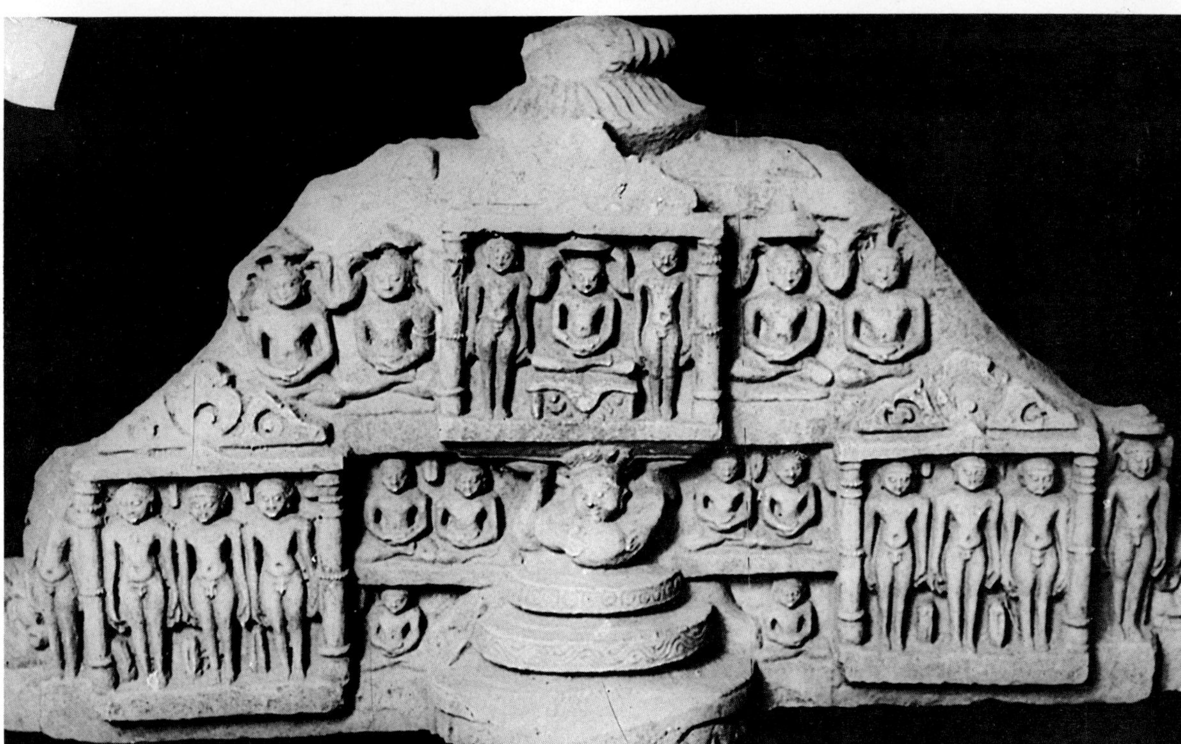

Lintel depicting figures of Jain Tirthankaras.

Burnt brick depicting flying figure.

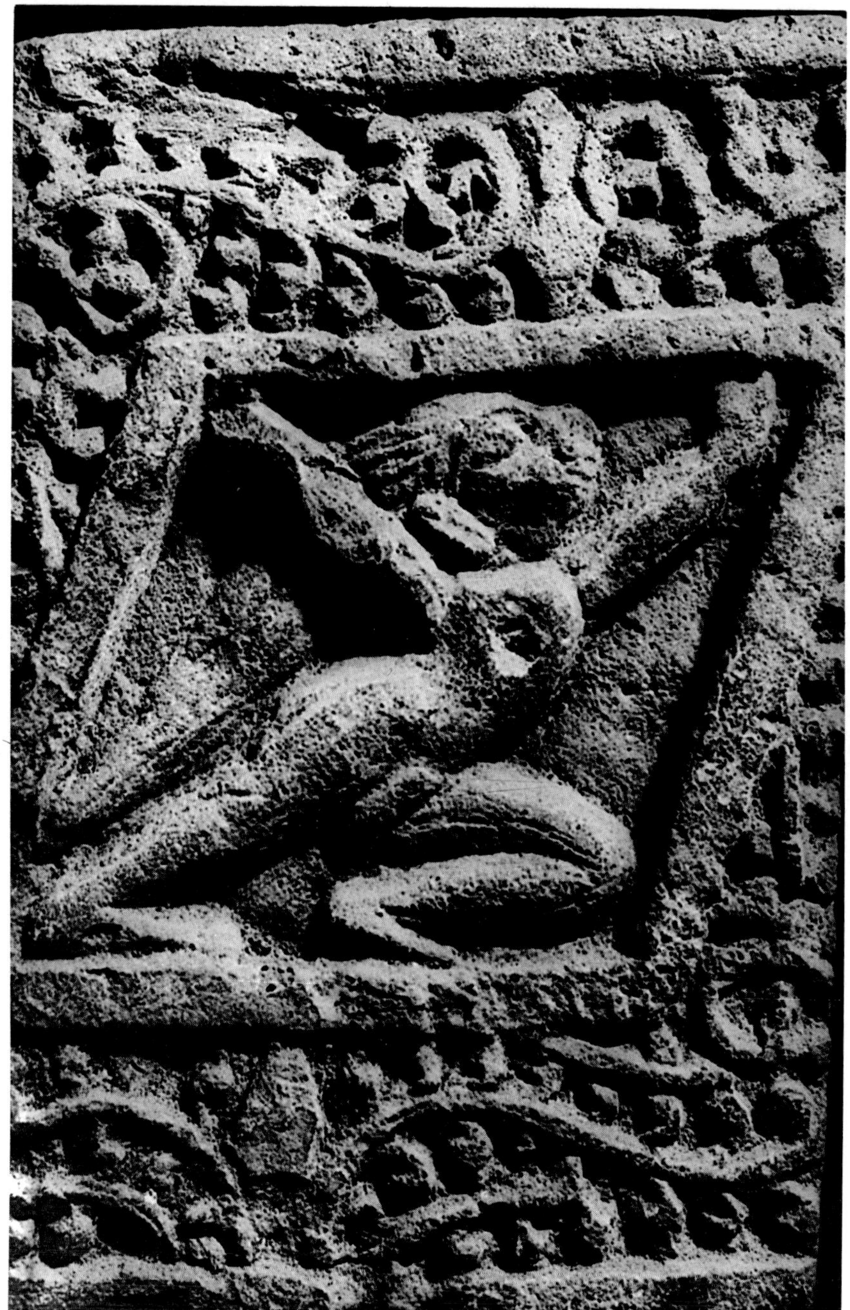

Architectural fragment showing seated Brahma holding sacred waterpot, manuscript, ladle in his three arms, the lower right arm being broken.

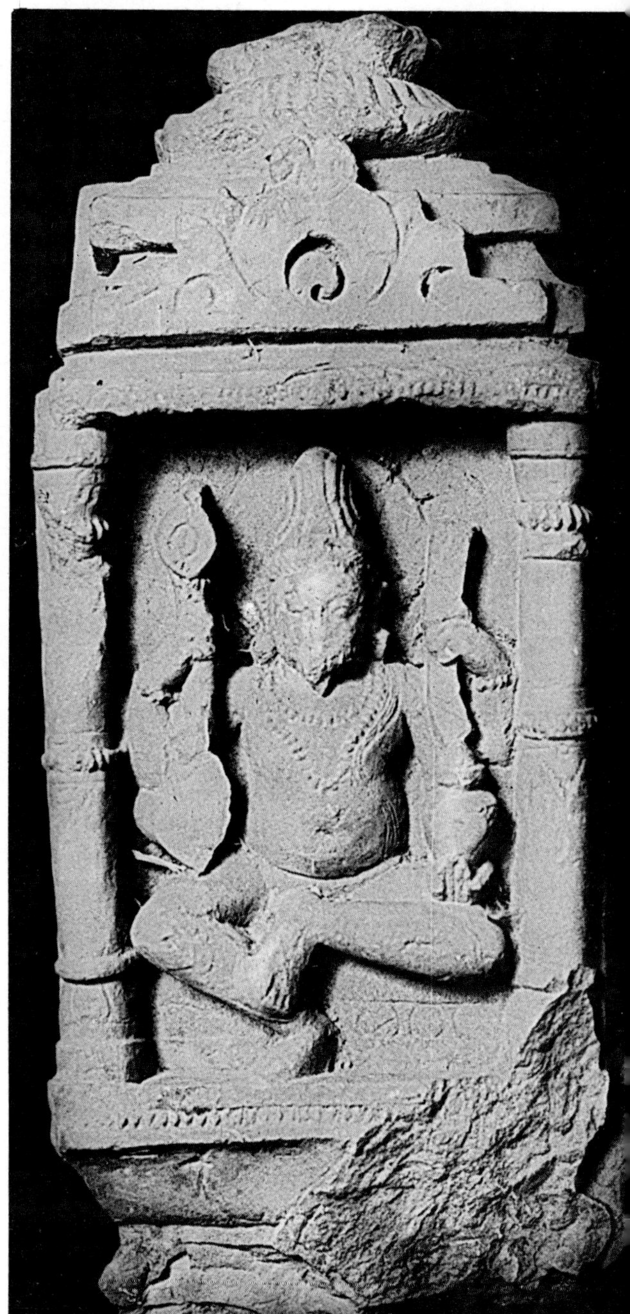

Mithun figures in a door jamb.

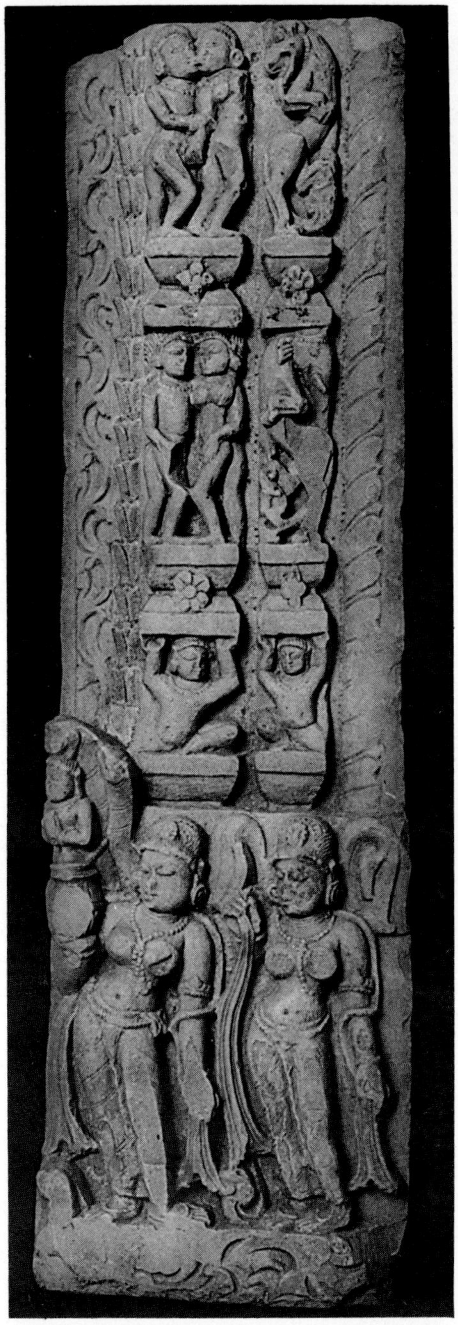

Dancing figures in a door jamb.

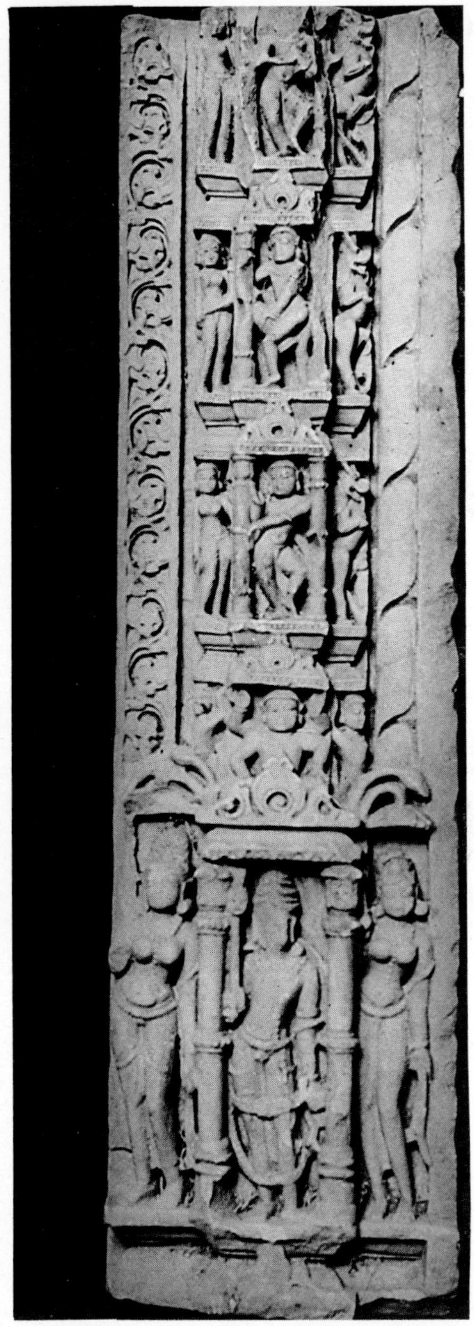

Fragment of a male figure.

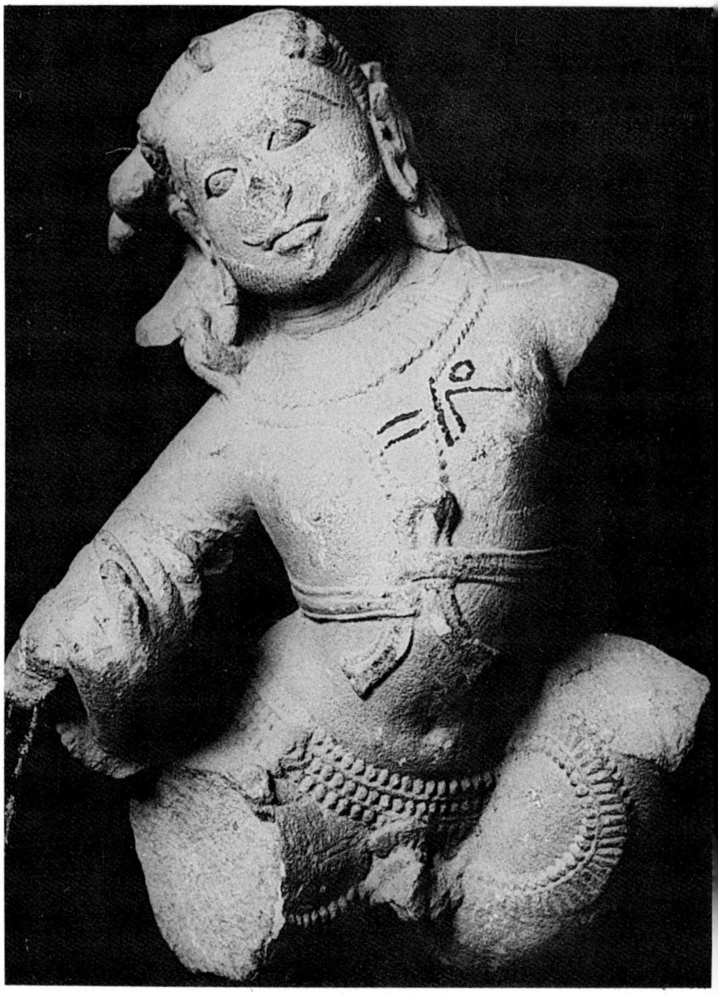

Emaciated human figure.

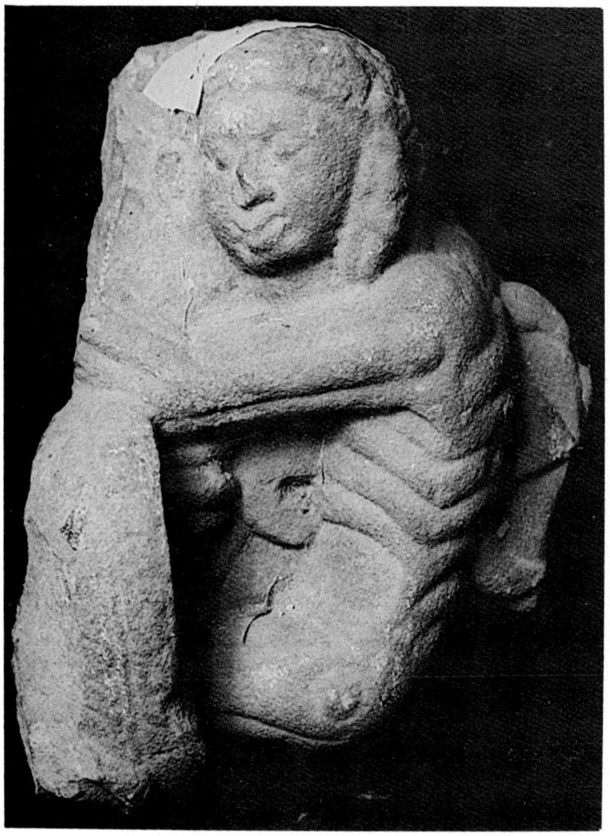

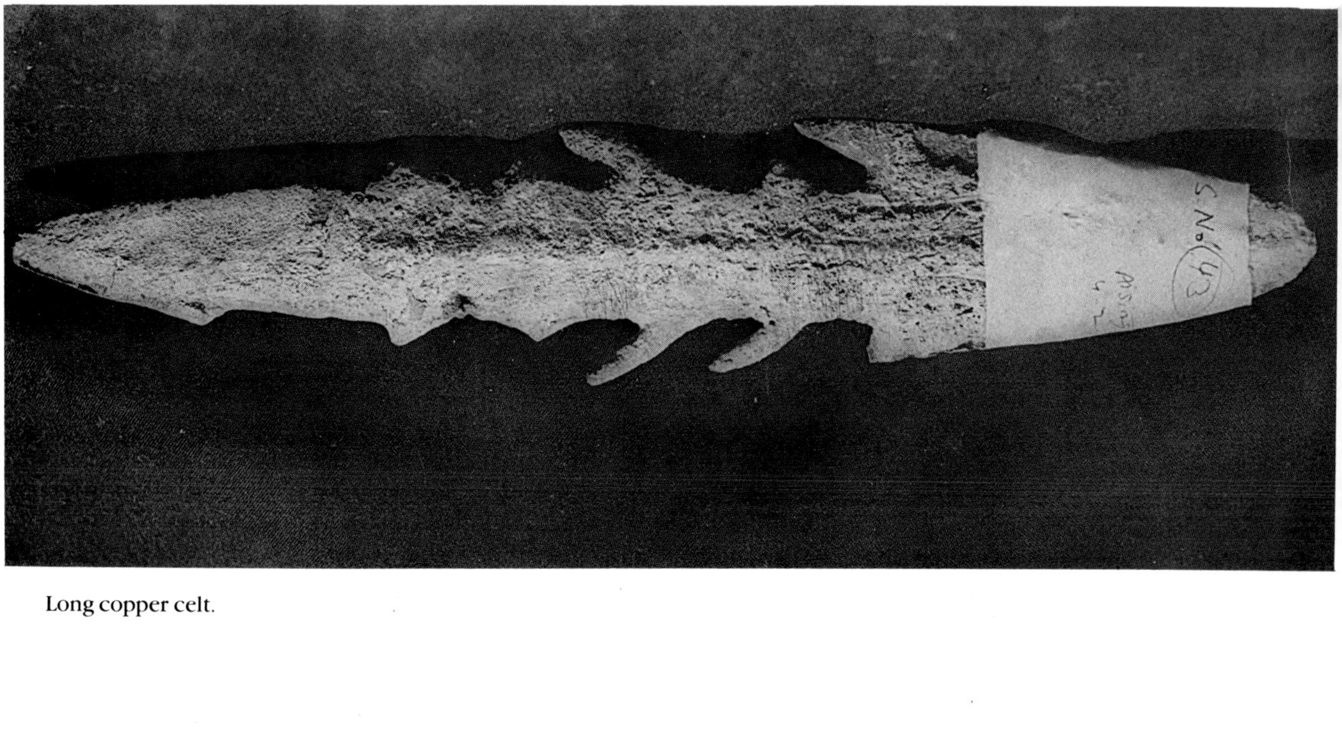

Long copper celt.

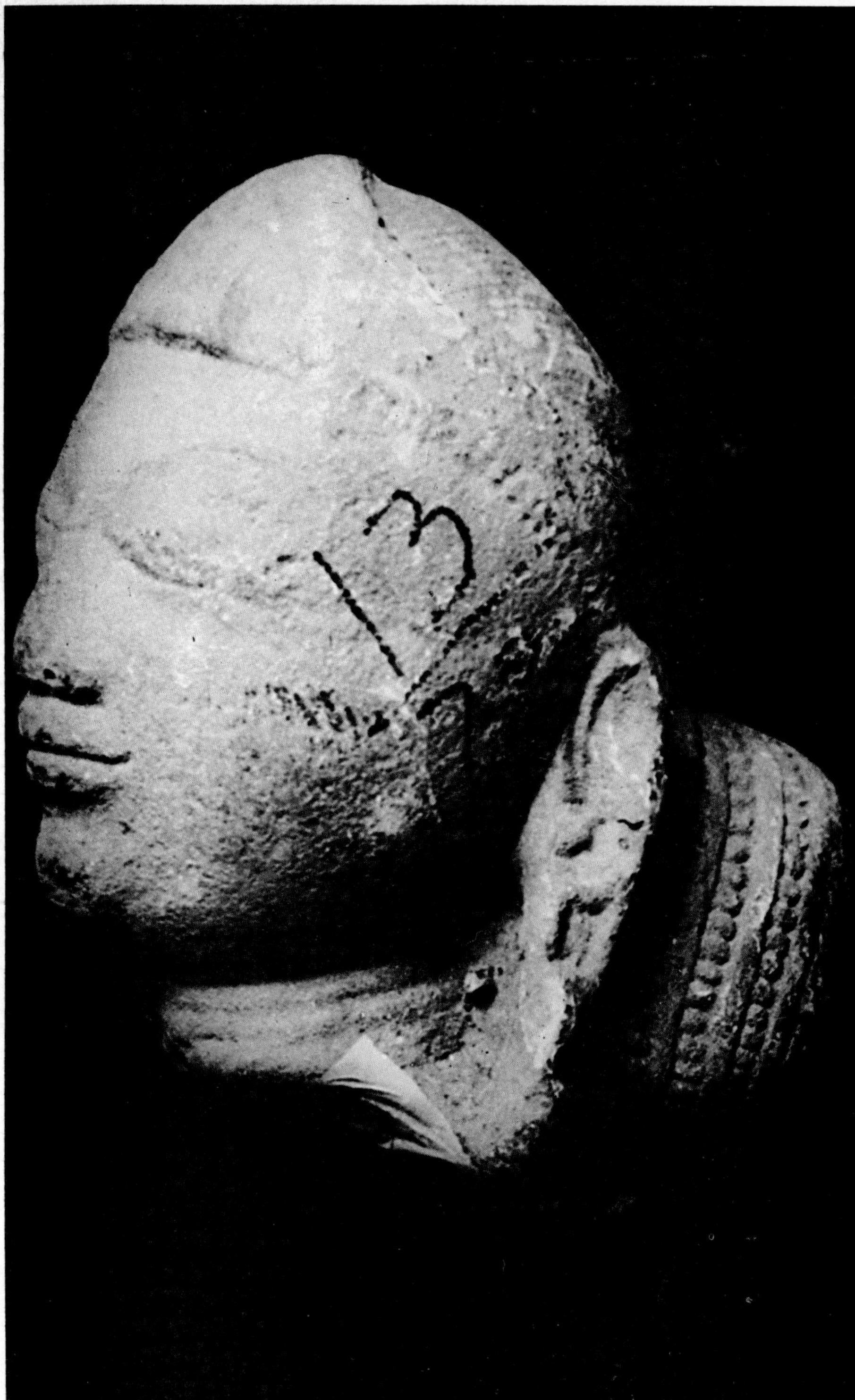

Fragment of a Female Head.

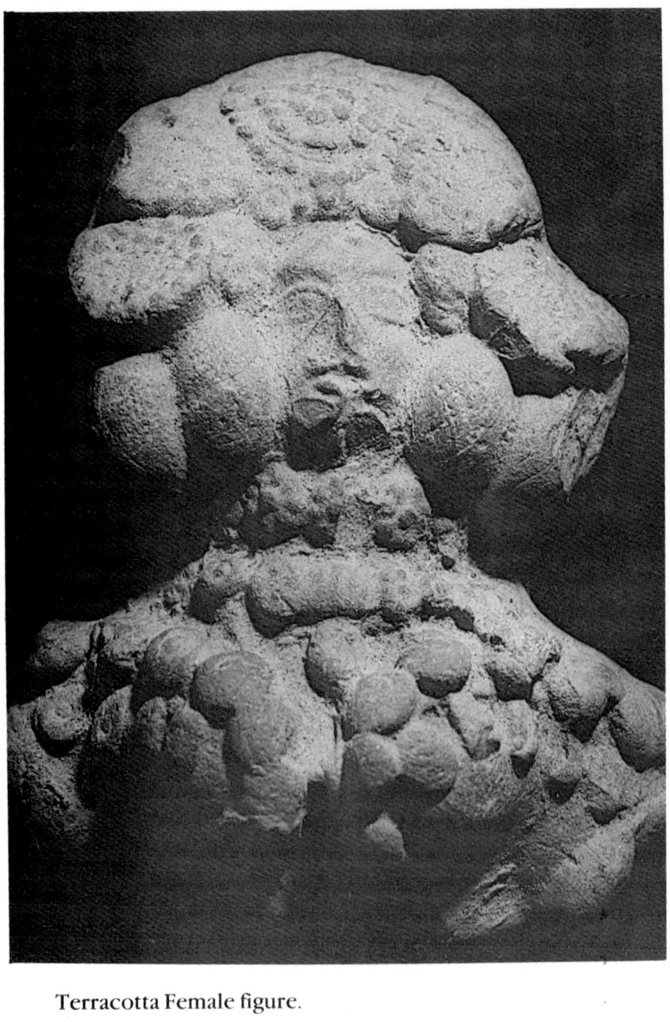

Terracotta Female figure.

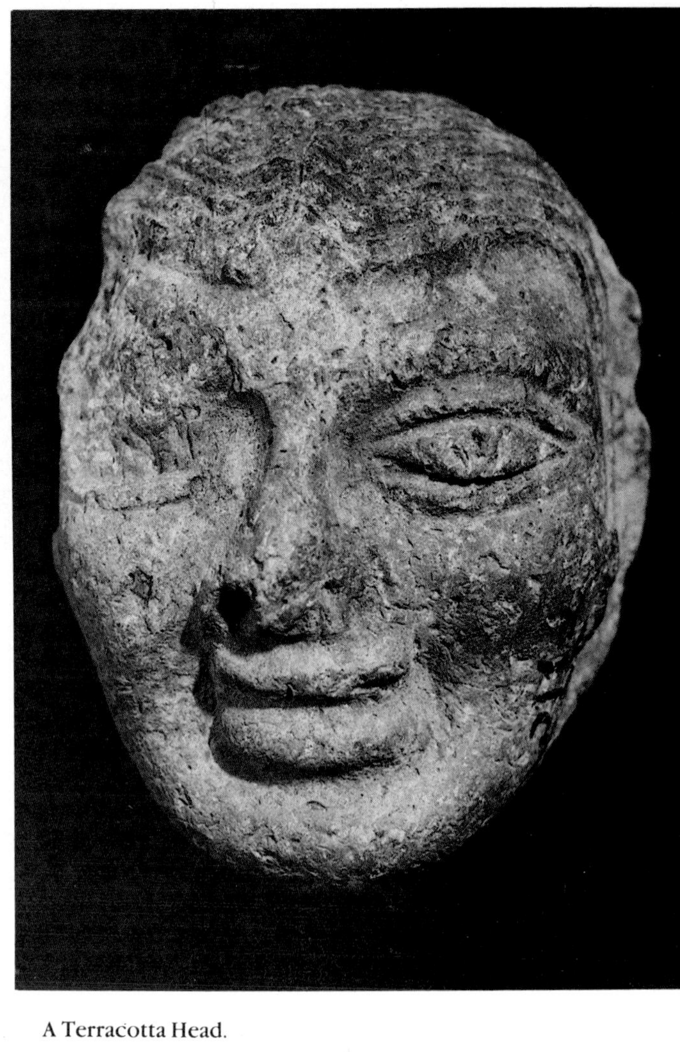

A Terracotta Head.

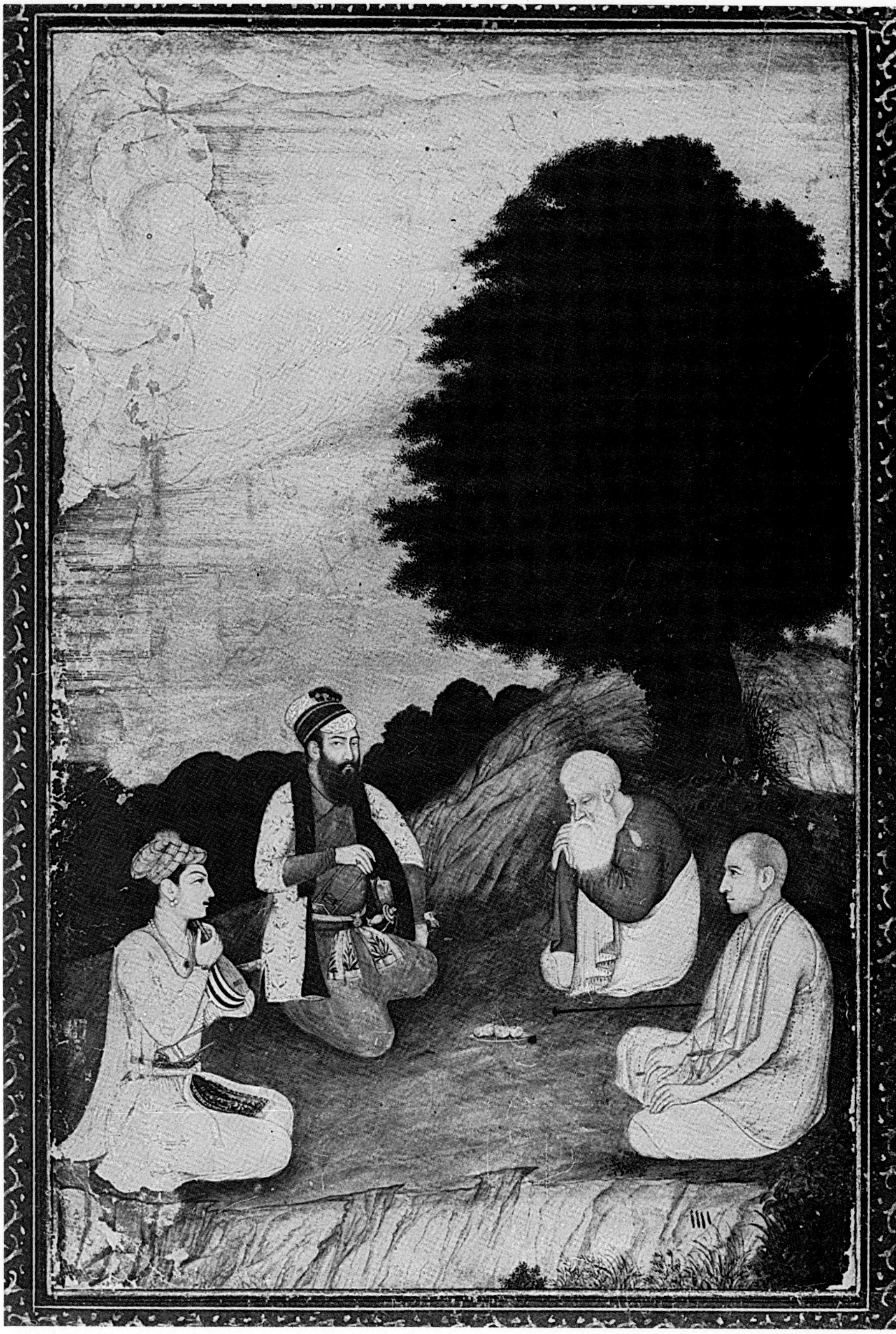

Painting of a Royalty visiting a Saint—early 17th century (Jahangir period).

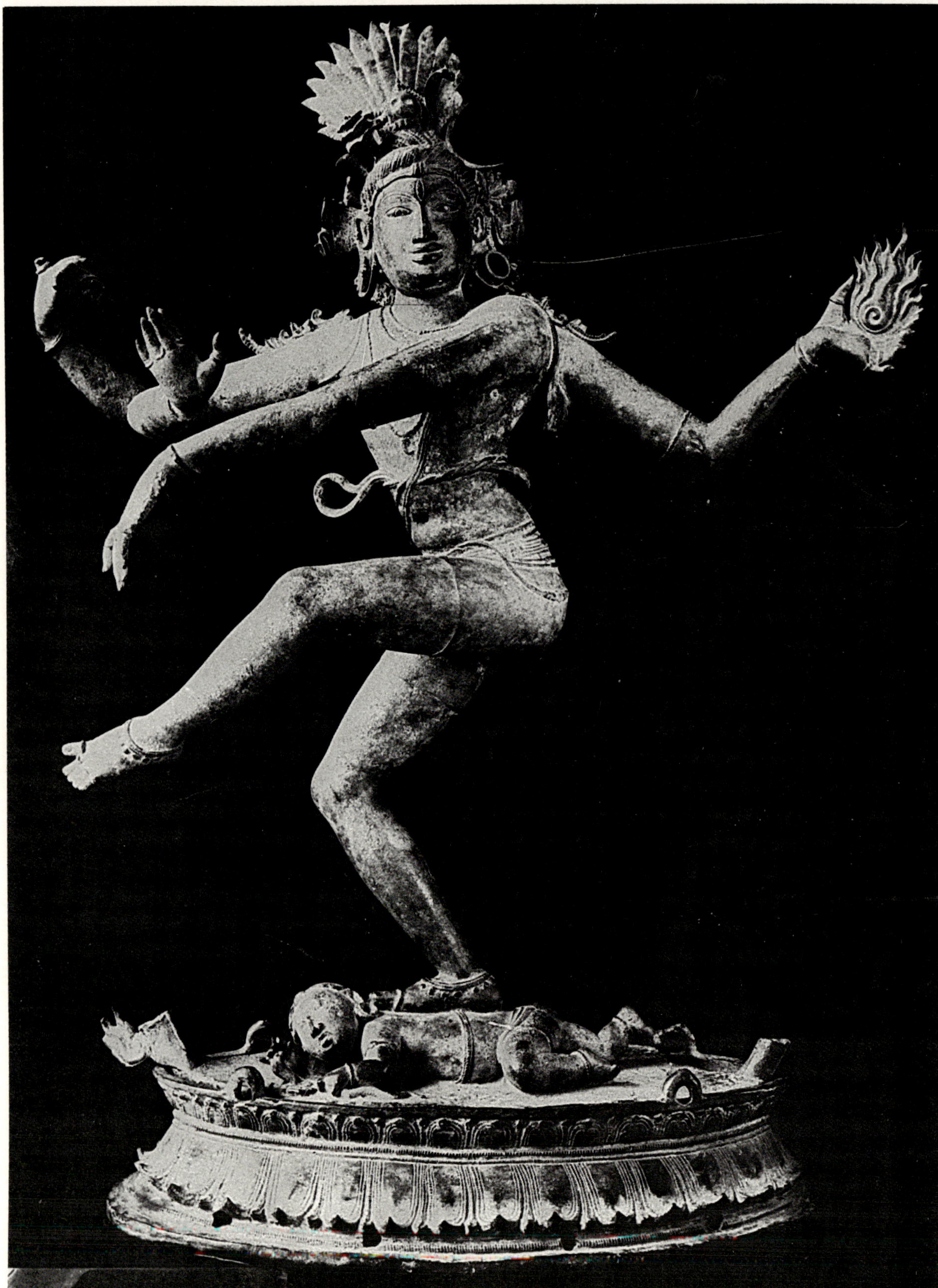

Nataraja. To recover this idol litigation is going on in the American court.

on art and antiquities may prove to be a safe investment. Moreover, there is the additional advantage of tax incentive. Because of these prevailing circumstances, coupled with man's inherent desire to possess things not easily available or procurable, the clandestine traffic in antiquity and works of art has the passive or active patronage of the business magnates and other influential sections of the society. This explains why the concerted efforts of various world bodies fail to stem the tide of illicit trade endangering more and more the safety of the cultural property of these countries which own rich cultural and artistic wealth (H. Sarkar).

Alarmed by the mounting wave of thefts of antiques, the Indian National Committee for International Council of Museums commented as far back as 1970: In some of the Western countries, particularly America, art collecting in all its ramifications has developed into a mania. The Director of National Gallery, London has already warned the British people that dwindling resources of Britain can no longer safeguard her art treasures against depletion by American wealth and that the only remedy is an embargo on exports. The position of India is no better than that of Britain. Indian art objects, both metal and stone, have always evoked world-wide admiration because of their aesthetic appeal. The Americans vie with one another in acquiring precious art pieces. This has made objects in our museums unsafe and vulnerable.

What really created an atmosphere conducive to the growth and proliferation of this crime is the lack of effective legislation. The 1947 Antiquities Export Control Act did not provide effective safeguard, any control on trade, sufficient deterrents for culprits nor for compulsory acquisition. The lack of proper documentation of antique items on a national scale also added to the problem. Even if stolen objects were traced, the police had a difficult time linking the object with the place of its origin due to lack of documentation.

The huge profit involved in the smuggling trade of antiquities has resulted in the growth of innumerable idol lifters. With very little effort he can make a lot of money and the law also takes a long process for the offence, even if he is caught to book him. One survey has commented: "It is not suggested that there is one single pyramid of criminal organisation—there may be several small, big and sequestered groups operating."

The major thefts like life size bronze statue of Vishnu from Chamba and several sandstone Apsaras, Shalabhanjikas and other figures worth several million dollars caused an uproar in the Parliament in 1971 and the Government had to come out with an assurance that a comprehensive legislation would be brought soon.

To streamline the market of antiquities, and prevent its illegal export and of art smuggling and also to plug the loop-holes of previous acts, the Parliament passed the Antiquities and Art Treasures Act, 1972. It was implemented almost four years later in April, 1976. The Ordinance issued on 4th June, 1976 amending the Antiquities and Art Treasures Act, went a long way to remove the genuine grievances about some of the provisions of the original Act. The time given to the dealers to apply for licences was extended by four months. The production of photographs was made obligatory, only, in respect of such antiques or class of antiques as the Government may specify by notification. The Ordinance gave assurance that the Government proposed to exempt from registration many types of articles usually kept by ordinary private collectors, such as coins, medals and jewellery pieces. Fresh items requiring registration would be notified from time to time so that the entire process of registration might be done progressively without causing hardship to any individual or institution.

The purpose of enacting the Antiquities and Art Treasures Act, 1972 was to regulate the export trade in antiquities and art treasures, to provide for the prevention of smuggling of, and fraudulent dealings in antiquities, to provide for compulsory acquisition of antiquities and art treasures for preservation in public places and to provide for certain other matters connected therewith or incidental or ancillary thereto. The provisions of this Act which repeals the Antiquities (Export Control) Act of 1947 institute a comprehensive system of control over the antiquities market.

As specified in the Antiquities and Art Treasures Act, 1972, antiquity includes—

1. (i) any coin, sculpture, painting, epigraph or other work of art or craftsmanship;
   (ii) any article, object or thing detached from a building or cave;
   (iii) any article, object or thing illustrative of science, art, crafts, literature, religion, customs, morals or politics in bygone ages;
   (iv) any article, object or thing declared by the Central Government, by notification in the official Gazette, to be an antiquity for the purposes of this Act, which has been in existence for not less than one hundred years; and

2. (i) any manuscript, record or other document which is of scientific, historical, literary or aesthetic value and which has been in existence for not less than seventy-five years;
   (ii) "Art Treasure" means any human work or art, not being an antiquity, declared by the Central Government by notification in the official Gazette to be an Art Treasure for the purposes of this Act having regard to its artistic or aesthetic value:

Provided that no declaration under this clause shall be made in respect of any such work so long as the author, thereof, is alive.

The 1970 UNESCO Convention on the Illicit Movement of Art Treasures contains a much broader and comprehensive definition of "Cultural Property". This term in fact refers to property "which, on religious or secular grounds, is specifically designated by each State as being important for archaeology, prehistory, history, art or science." It includes not only objects which are traditionally considered as part of the National Heritage, but also objects which as in the case of specimens of flora and fauna, or property related to the social, technological and scientific history—are part of the whole of the natural, cultural, social and historical patrimony of a country.

As regards "Ancient Monument", the Ancient Monuments and Archaeological Sites and Remains Act of 1958 defines it as:

"Any structure, erection or monument or any tumulus or place of internment or any cave, rock-sculpture, inscription or monolith which is of historical, archaeological or artistic interest and which has been in existence for not less than one hundred years and includes:

(i) the remains of an ancient monument;
(ii) the site of an ancient monument;
(iii) such portion of land adjoining the site of an ancient monument as may be required for fencing or covering in or otherwise preserving such monument; and
(iv) the means of access to, and convenient inspection of, an ancient monument."

## PENAL LAW

Among the relevant provisions are Articles 378 and 379 of the Indian Penal Code related to theft, which imposes punishment upto three years and/or a fine. Section 410 provides as follows: "Property, the possession whereof has been criminally misappropriated or in respect of which criminal breach of trust has been committed is designated as 'stolen property', whether the transfer has been made, or the misappropriation or breach of trust has been committed within or out of India. But, if such property subsequently comes into the possession of a person legally entitled to the possession thereof, it then ceases to be stolen property." The expression "Stolen Property" includes things which have been extorted, robbed or obtained by criminal misappropriation or criminal breach of trust. Section 411, which is quite comprehensive, reads as follows: "Whoever dishonestly receives or retains any stolen property, knowing or having reason to believe the same to be stolen property, shall be punished with imprisonment of either description for a term which may extend to three years or with fine or with both." Section 414 extends the same punishment to anyone who "voluntarily assists in concealing or destroying or making away with property which he knows or has reason to believe to be stolen property." To be punishable under the Indian Penal Code the receipt or retention of "Stolen Goods" must take place within India, unless the person "receiving" or "retaining" outside India is an Indian citizen.

The Indian Evidence Act (1872) establishes a permissible and rebuttable presumption that a man found in possession of stolen goods soon after the theft is either the thief or has received the goods knowing them to be stolen. With some exceptions, confessions made before a police officer and not confirmed by subsequent facts (i.e. the recovery of a stolen object as identified in the fonfession) are not admissible in evidence.

Under the Criminal Procedure Code of 1973, importance is given to First Information Report which should give full details of the stolen property. Recovered property is put for identification by witnesses. The house of the suspect can be searched in the presence of two or more independent and respectable habitants of the locality as provided in Section 100(4) of the 1973 Code. In case of an urgency, search can be made without a warrant.

## CIVIL LAW

Except as provided by special legislation, general norms of Indian Civil Law apply to titles and possession of art and archaeological goods, as well as to the position of purchasers in good faith; it should be noted that to establish the bad faith of a purchaser a preponderance of the evidence is sufficient in contrast to the stricter standards of proof in the Criminal Law.) Foreign nationals and residents and foreign governments acting in a proprietary capacity have access to Indian courts of competent jurisdiction (Section 83 Code of Civil Procedure, 1908).

The Antiquities and Art Treasures Act, 1972 provides a deterrent to the smugglers. Besides, the accused are also dealt with penal law of the land for theft of cultural property. Some of the provisions of the Act for punishment are as follows:

**SECTION 25.** 1) If any person, himself or by any other person on his behalf, exports or attempts to export any antiquity or art treasure in contravention of Section 3, he shall, without prejudice to any confiscation or penalty to which he may be liable under the provisions of the Customs Act, 1962 as applied by Section 4, be punishable with imprisonment for a term which shall not be less than six months but which may extend to three years and with fine.

2) If any person contravenes the provisions of Section 5 or Section 12 or sub-section 2 or sub-section 3 of Section 13 or Section 14 or Section 17, he shall be punishable with imprisonment for a term which may extend to six months or with fine or with both and the antiquity in respect of which the offence has been committed shall be liable to confiscation.

3) If any person prevents any licensing officer from inspecting any record, photograph or register maintained under Section 10 or prevents any officer authorised by the Central Government under sub-section 1 of Section 23 from entering into or searching any place under that sub-section, he shall be punishable with imprisonment for a term which may extend to six months, or with fine, or with both.

## COGNIZANCE OF OFFENCES

**SECTION 26.** 1) No prosecution for an offence under sub-section 1 of Section 25 shall be instituted except by or with the sanction of such officer of Government as may be prescribed in this behalf.

2) No court shall take cognizance of an offence punishable under sub-section 2 or sub-section 3 of Section 25 except upon complaint in writing made by an officer generally or specially authorised in this behalf by the Central Government.

3) No court inferior to that of a Presidency Magistrate or a Magistrate of the First Class shall try any offence punishable under this Act.

## MAGISTRATE'S POWER TO IMPOSE ENHANCED PENALTIES

**SECTION 27.** Notwithstanding anything contained in Section 32 of the Code of Criminal Procedure, 1898, it shall be lawful for any Presidency Magistrate or any Magistrate of the First Class to pass any sentence under this Act in excess of his power under Section 32 of the said Code.

## OFFENCES BY COMPANIES

**SECTION 28.** 1) Where an offence under this Act has been committed by a company every person who at the time the offence was commtted was in charge of, or was responsible to the company for the conduct of the business of the company, as well as the company, shall be deemed to be guilty of the offence and shall be liable to be proceeded against and punished accordingly: provided that nothing contained in this sub-section shall render any such person liable to any punishment under this Act if he proves that the offence was committed without his knowledge or that he exercised all due diligence to prevent the commission of such offence.

2) Notwithstanding anything contained in sub-section 1, where an offence under this Act has been committed with the consent or connivance of, or is attributable to,any neglect on the part or any Director, Manager, SEcretary or other officer of the company, such Director, Manager, Secretary or other officer shall also be deemed to be guilty of that offence and shall be liable to be proceeded against and punished accordingly.

**EXPLANATION:** For the purpose of this Section (a) 'Company' means any body corporate and includes a firm or other association of individuals, and (b) 'Director', in relation to a firm, means a partner in the firm.

## PROTECTION OF ACTION TAKEN IN GOOD FAITH

**SECTION 29.** No suit, prosecution or other legal proceeding shall lie against the Government or any officer of the Government for anything which is in good faith done or is intended to be done under this Act.

The Government of India had set June 5, 1976 as the last date for traders in antiques and art objects and July 5, 1976 for individual owners to declare their possessions under the Antiquities and Art Treasures Act of 1972. The Act which came into force on April 1, 1976, aims at checking cladestine trade in antique objects and plugging the leakage of India's cultural heritage through illegal export.

Under the provisions of the Act, individuals, institutions and traders were required to get their possessions registered with photographs with a registering official. The Act covered all antiques, 100 years old or more and manuscripts which were 75 years old or more. As a result of this announcement in Delhi, an individual collector gifted over a hundred rare and ancient pieces to the National Museum. A private art gallery and four dealers requested the Museum authorities to examine their collections and take the genuine antiques to their rightful place, the Museum. The museums in Rajasthan received large quantities of ancient coins, arms and ammunition from the old feudal houses of the state. Many of them surrendered these items as they felt that they were in no position to maintain them according to the procedures of this Act.

About 5000 applications were received for registration from all over the country. One hundred and four registration officials were appointed throughout the country, each of them handling from 1 to 10 districts. Some of the important places from the point of view of antiquities like Jaipur, Madras, Bombay and Calcutta had one registration official each. In Delhi alone, there were three officials.

The original registration requirements included supply of four photographs of each antiquity in at least postcard size. The registration covered (i) sculptures in all media (except wood); (ii) paintings in all media; and (iii) manuscripts containing illustrations, illuminations or paintings. All these items ought to be not less than one hundred years old.

In the initial stages the Act created a stir and resentment among the antique dealers of the capital. They formed a Federation of Association of Collectors and Dealers of Art and Antiquity. They put their viewpoints more vigorously. Their first complaint was the time limit of two months given to them after the enforcement of the Act. It was felt that it was too short a time to complete all documentations because earlier they had not been maintaining any record of source of procurement or antiquity of the object except the commercial record of their daily transactions. They also complained of the procedures of the Act, like compulsory photographic documentation, which were too cumbersome. Sometimes the cost of the photography far exceeded the procurement prices of items like trinkets and coins.

The federation also submitted a memorandum in 1976 to the Union Education Minister and the Director General of Archaeology, in which they sought exemption of antiquities of non-Indian origin. Archaeological Survey sources explained that clandestine trading and pilferage of cultural properties had assumed such alarming proportions that the Government had to bring in this legislations. It could not make any exemptions because a tiny stone inscription could have a valuable bearing on the country's unknown history. These officials wondered why the antique traders, who had been amassing fortunes, could not spend a little more on documentation and include that in the cost of their wares. They also pointed out that the Act was passed in 1972 and its rules were framed in 1973—the dealers had ample time for inquiries. They also asked, why the Delhi dealers should be so agitated when their counterparts in Bombay and other individual collectors all over the country were voluntarily coming for disclosure?

The Government warned the parties concerned that any attempt to destroy the procedures recommended would not be tolerated. "If some people find the formalities of keeping antiques too difficult and expensive, who do not they turn them over to the safe custody of museums? Displaying antiquity in well appointed drawing rooms is a craze of the new rich. If they want to show off, let them accept the legal obligations." It further said, "The illicit traffic would not have been possible without the help and connivance of at least a section of the antique dealers."

The Antiquities Act of 1972 also attracted criticism from various quarters. Mr. N.J. Nanporia in his article in the Statesman dated 13th July, 1976 said, "What has been overlooked by those who drafted the Act and most of those who have criticized it, is the role and position of the modest (financially and otherwise) collector. He is not a hoarder, a black-marketeer, a snob who thinks that antique is the thing, a businessman with an eye on investment, or someone in the grip of an irresistible passion for acquisition. The Act's major failing is in not distinguishing between these intruders in the field of collecting and the genuine collector to whom it is a way of life, sustained by a philosophy and a non-academic expertise that is entirely his own.

Yet it should be conceded that this is a distinction, difficult if not impossible to capture in the legalisation of legislations; and this also applies to the cultivation of aesthetic sense and good taste, something which no law can undertake to do. It is the collector in every country, even more than the usual run of museum curator, who has helped to preserve the spirit and the intuitive faculties associated with genuine collecting. Inevitably he belongs to a minority and perhaps nowhere more so than in a vast country like India; and in most places he is set apart as someone beyond the reach of normal understanding. His interests are too vital and positive to be described by so anaemic a word as "Hobby". It is not a question of something being more than a hundred years old or less. It is rather a matter of integrity which many but not all old things manage to acquire by virtue of the personalised craftsmanship that has produced them."

With the passage of time it was observed that the effective enforcement of the Act was felt more in metropolitan cities and by antique dealers. The rural areas were outside the control of the Act. In fact many antiques were smuggled from the rural areas, and it was here that the real wealth of antiques lay with erstwhile Jagirdars. With the political transition their Jagirs were abolished and for getting quick money and to meet their financial exigencies they clandestinely disposed of their antiques to the smugglers. To avoid registration they made deals with unscrupulous dealers.

Despite the strict measures of security taken by the museums, posting of vigilant staff at all national monuments by the Archaeological Survey of India and vigorous tracking of antique smugglers by local police and the Central Bureau of Investigation sleuths, thefts of antiques have yet not stopped. To make the 1972 Antiques Act more effective, the Archaeological Survey of India is considering to bring several amendements to the said Act. One of the amendments proposed is to make smuggling or theft of antiques a cognizable offence. The other amendments, which are to be recommended to the Government, include making punishment more stringent, compulsory registration within 15 days of acquisition of an antique and shifting the onus of proving innocene on the possessor of an antique.

# PREVENTIVE MEASURES

THE Government of India reiterated its firm commitment for preventing antique smuggling and emphasized that photographic documentation was essential for the detection of theft and smuggling. The theft of the 9th century Ponaraja image from Jogeshwar in Uttar Pradesh and the public agitation that followed it, prompted the Government to launch a countrywide operation and as a result, the idol was recovered. The Government could take action on this scale because the Ponaraja and other images at Jogeshwar had been photographed in detail. The Boston Museum of Fine Arts in the U.S.A. returned a rare Vishnu idol to the Bangiya Sahitya Parishad Museum in Calcutta because the identity of the image could be established with the help of photographs. The other example in support of photographic documentation was the recovery of priceless original of the Quran Sharif and a few other original paintings, stolen from Aligarh Muslim University at Palam when an attempt was being made to take them out of the country.

Enforcement officials have underlined the gravity of the problem posed by the theft of art objects and their sale on an international scale. There has been steady stream of thefts from museums, ancient monuments and even churches and temples.

In the seventies, in Italy antique thefts had become such a national scandal that the Government had given the problem urgent attention and instituted new and more stringent regulations to prevent such thefts. These art objects are a major tourist attraction in many countries. A Titian, stolen from Italy, was estimated to be priced at one million pound at least. In England too several thefts of valuable antiques were reported.

Big museums and even well-organised exhibitions have so far found themselves unable to keep the crafty thieves at bay. In India too, effective protection of ancient monuments has not been possible. Neither the agents nor the collectors are bothered as to how these objects of art would bring value and pride to a nation. To the agent these purchases represent a very good investment and to the collector ownership of invaluable rarities brings special personal joy. Hence, fabulous prices are being offered for paintings, sculptures and other art objects of guaranteed old and quality.

UNESCO has time and again brought these issues in its conventions. Under its terms any country would be able to recover such stolen objects from the country to which they have been sent with the whole-hearted cooperation of the Government concerned.

One shudders to think of travails the owners would have had to undergo to recover them if the idols and the paintings had been smuggled out of India. The sad truth is that while the Antique and Art Treasure Act, 1972 provides, though inadequate, some protection domestically, internationally the Law provides no protection at all. International art markets do not bother about legal restraints or moral inhibitions. Not only Asia, Africa and South America, but even parts of Europe, like Italy, still suffer from smuggling and illegal traffic of art treasures. According to the Italian Government's estimate, art treasures worth more than $ 50 million are stolen every year. While some countries like Mexico have imposed a total ban on export of art property, others like India have made legislation and established a system of licensing.

Whatever measures the countries have taken in enacting the legislations, their efficacy has so far been very limited. It may work as some sort of deterrent but not wipe out completely the menace of art thefts. There are hardly any avenues of redress if the laws are successfully flouted. What would be far more effective than to put a ban on the import of works of art which are either illegally acquired or exported? Government should take effective steps to check the imports undertaken through treaties as this will help the interests of developing countries to safeguard their art possessions.

At the General Conference of UNESCO held in 1970, an international convention on the means of prohibiting and preventing illicit import-export and transfer of ownership of cultural property was adopted. Much of the convention comprised admirable formulations, such as that cultural property found within the national territory "forms part of the cultural heritage of each State." It was the operative part which mattered most but it was in this vital respect that the convention found itself inadequate. Under article 7, the States will "take the necessary measures, consistent with national legislation to prevent museums and similar institutions within their territories from acquiring cultural property originating in another State party which has been illegally exported after entry into force of this convention, in the States concerned."

The States also undertook "to prohibit the imports of cultural property stolen from a museum or a religious or secular public monument or similar institution" in another State party to this convention after the entry into force of this convention for the State concerned, provided that such property is documented as per the inventory of that institution." There is also an obligation to take steps to recover and return stolen cultural property at the request of the country of its origin, provided it has been imported after the convention has come into force and the requesting State pays "just compensation to the person who has valid title to that property." These obligations could be implemented only by enacting suitable legislation after adherence to the convention.

Commenting on the convention, Professor Leonard D. Du Bott recorded that the original draft of the convention would have enacted regulations which, in essence, would have prohibited importation of works, removed from another country in violation of its export laws.

Drafting the domestic legislation was not an easy task, as it posed many problems. Such has been the fate all through a decade of convention which by no means was unfair to the importing countries and was far from satisfactory to countries which have suffered the plunder of their cultural property. Discussions regarding demands of restitution of cultural property took place in the General Conference of UNESCO in 1978. A resolution was passed for the creation of an Advisory Inter-governmental Committee for promoting the return of cultural property to its countries of origin.

In India, a coordinated scheme for completion of photographic documents of monuments and art objects in museums was recommended by the Conference held in 1971 under the chairmanship of the then Union Education Minister, Mr. Siddhartha Shanker Ray. The conference was attended by representatives of Education and Home Ministries, the Archeological Survey of India and the State Governments. It recommended that a scheme should be prepared by the Director General of the Archaeological Survey of India in consultation with the State Governments. It also suggested that the States shall establish separate cells under the charge of responsible police officers for investigating expeditiously cases of theft of art objects. The State Governments were also urged to request the Judiciary to try the cases expeditiously on priority basis.

The posting of police guards at important monuments and recruitment, preferably, of ex-servicemen, to posts of monument attendants created recently for the Archaeological Survey, was also recommended at the Conference. It was also suggested that senior police officers should occasionally inspect important tourist places.

On 4th August, 1971, Mr. S.S. Batliwala, President of the Society for the Preservation of Art Heritage, demanded the setting up of an 'Ombudsman' to prevent large-scale antique smuggling from India. According to him a knowledgeable and upright Ombudsman would be quite effective in preserving the art heritage of India. The police, the customs and other authorities should be under the direction of the Ombudsman and forced to act quickly. He also stressed the need for setting up of scientific laboratories where the genuineness of antique could be tested. Since sophisticated antique smugglers were using scientific methods, the only way to fight them would be with the help of experts in the field. The age of any metal or alloy would easily be determined in a well-equipped laboratory with a trained staff. He also recommended that a National Commission be established and instructed to submit a list of national treasures within a specified time. It should register all such treasures and be empowered to buy them. The tax structure could be utilised for preserving the art heritage.

Enforcement agencies like the customs and the police are ill-equipped to prevent the continuous drain of idols and antiques. The only agency is CBI, on which the Indian authorities can depend. After a valuable antique has left the country, it takes interest in chasing the antique smugglers by contacting their counterparts in other countries.

A UNESCO resolution drafted in 1964 calling for a strict control on sale and purchase of stolen antiques by various nationals has remained unimplemented so far. As a result, the antique smuggling trade has acquired huge dimensions the world over. Asian countries like India, Nepal and Sri Lanka, West Asian countries like Egypt and Latin American countries like Mexico have continued to suffer colossal losses of their cultural wealth while the affluent countries have been dillydallying to accept the UNESCO resolution. The most shocking aspect is that even well-known American museums display no scruples in acquiring precious art objects knowing fully well that these were stolen from other countries.

According to a research conducted on behalf of the United Nations Social Defence Research Institute, a report from Madras concludes as: "Actually it is very difficult, if not impossible, to get permits for the export of antiquities and so the only way open to anti-social elements is to resort to smuggling. Curio shops have sprung up in practically all the big cities where such works of art are exhibited for sale. Many of them are known to be repositories of stolen articles and some of them indulge in clandestine export. Practically every district in the State has its own idol thieves and receivers."

The Orissa report suggests a correlation between the phenomenon of idol and temple thefts and the increasing materialistic attitude towards life, implying a gradual erosion of spiritual values. It further concluded that the antique thieves generally belonged to the lower strata of society addicted to heavy smoking and liquor. The copper idols were often stolen for the sale of metal in return for quick money. The report from Madhya Pradesh noted that art thefts were no longer confined to abandoned idols; they occurred even in temples where regular worships are being held. It concluded that generally vigilance in most of the important sites was insufficient despite the supervision by the Department of Archaeology. In response to this, some positive steps has been taken by the State Inspector General of Police, who gave explicit instructions to his force to increase their vigilance, and to treat thefts of cultural property as Special Report Cases.

Law enforcement agencies do not have any special cells of antique experts who can quickly distinguish the fake from the genuine. Whenever, there is a request for the export of non-antique curios or after seizure to verify the genuineness of antiques, they are referred to the experts in the Archaeological Survey of India. But the process is very tedious and time consuming and therefore large-scale identification of objects is well-nigh impossible.

Another factor contributing to the unchecked loot of country's sculptural treasures is that there is nothing like a strong museum movement here. Finding no guaranteed buyers, the legitimate owners of private collections of famous antiques often sell them on the sly to unscrupulous foreign buyers. It is also true that smugglers and thieves have better knowledge about the location of priceless art treasures. The authorities often discover the value of a piece only after it has been stolen.

To prevent thefts from the museums experts have suggested certain measures to be adopted by the authorities concerned. Some of the measures suggested are as follows:

1) All weak points in the building should be fully illuminated.
2) The doors, windows, ventilators, skylights, staircases and all unusual openings should be made secure. The windows and ventilators should invariably be provided with thick grills.

3) A museum should have single point of entry and exit.
4) The dark and inconspicuous corners of the museum must be provided with adequate light.
5) Special strong rooms should be provided for keeping the valuable objects.
6) General construction of walls and fixtures should make it impossible for thieves to enter the building, to pierce holes in walls or break the outside doors, windows etc.
7) Vigilant watch and ward staff should be posted in the museums. They should be recruited after proper verification of their antecedents.
8) Employees of the museum should be oriented from security angle. Regular courses should be conducted of the staff members in order to create security environment in the museum.
9) Surprise checks by security officers and other senior officers should take place frequently.
10) Guards and other employees concerned should ensure that no person remains inside at the time of closing of the museum. After the museum is closed all rooms should be checked and counter-checked.
11) Electronic and mechanical devices like burglary alarm, cameras at concealed positions and circuit television be provided.

## POLICE INVESTIGATION

Many thefts from private collections are not even reported and as such the police cannot do anything about them. Another factor that hinders police investigation is that even when thefts are reported it is too late and in the meantime the antique pieces have left for their destinations. For example, the theft of the famous Nataraja idol came to notice only when it reached a foreign country. Another problem faced by the police is that rarely do they get a complete and apt description of the stolen piece. With the result, identification becomes very difficult in the absence of a photograph or a document. Accurate description of the stolen piece is the most important factor. There have been cases when police were able to arrest a smuggler with a stolen piece but failed to detect its place of origin, with the result, courts have sometimes ordered the return of the piece to the smuggler.

Despite these handicaps, most police forces in the States are doing their best to curb such thefts or smuggling. Thefts of antique pieces are given a special rating and special officers have been posted in the sensitive districts. Cases with inter-state or international connections are handed over to the Central Intelligence Department (CID). The CID seeks the help of the Interpol to apprehend the international smugglers. Watch is also kept on suspected antique dealers. Scrutiny of vehicles belonging to suspected foreign nationals is also done and surveillance kept on them.

## NEW POLICIES

The Archaeological Survey of India in collaboration with the law enforcement authorities has taken the following steps to protect the cultural heritage:

1) Sculptures in centrally protected monuments which cannot be adequately safeguarded in site are collected and stored in central sculpture sheds where they can be better looked after.
2) Watch and ward staff at centrally protected monuments has been increased and stricter measures of supervision have been enforced.
3) Cases of theft from centrally protected monuments are being promptly reported. (Formerly there was no arrangement for reporting thefts to the Headquarters of the Archaeological Survey of India; at present, however, telegraphic reports are made to the Director General of Archaeological Survey in all such cases. Reports are also required to be lodged promptly with the police.)
4) As soon as cases of theft from centrally protected monuments are detected, intimation is also given to the Export Advisory Committee and Customs authorities at major ports to watch out for the stolen antiques being smuggled out of the country. Ten Superintendents are charged with this task.
5) For improved vigilance, police guards have been posted at selected museums and monuments.
6) A collection of complete documentation on centrally protected monuments and sculptures to facilitate identification has been initiated by the Director General of Archaeological Survey.
7) The Archaeological Survey of India has started an inservice training course for the Customs staff to enable them to identify antiques.
8) Since the CBI as the Central Coordination Agency for international crime in the country has started maintenance of records relating to cases of idols and antiquities commencing from 1969, State Police Agencies all over the country have been reporting losses and recoveries. The details of stolen antiquities and art objects are also being maintained.
9) The information received is tabulated and disseminated among the law enforcement agencies in the country by the CBI through alert notices and reviews in the CBI Bulletin.
10) The Customs officers are alert in cases where there is suspicion or information that a work of art or antiquity is likely to be smuggled out of India.
11) The CBI has been persistently drawing the attention of the State Police through circulars, during conferences etc., towards the problem of art theft, and making suggestions to counteract this form of crime.
12) Adequate cooperation is now being secured in the efforts made by the CBI, Customs authorities, the Archaeological Survey and State Police authorities to prevent the loss of such cultural property.
13) The CBI has been assisting the State Police in working out a number of difficult and important cases. In some cases investigations were carried out by the CBI itself while in others it provided expert guidance and advice. In view of the high incidence of thefts of antiquities and art objects in the country, some State Governments have set up separate cells for detection of such cases, the strength of the cell varying with the seriousness of the problem.

At a conference of Deputy Inspectors General of Police (CID) held in Delhi in 1972, the following resolution was passed:

(i) Every case of theft and recovery of cultural property should be made a special report case.
(ii) Copies of the special report should be sent to the Central Bureau of Investigation by the CID or its special cells.
(iii) In every State, affected by the problem of art theft, special cells should be set up to investigate.
(iv) Adequate measures should be taken to ensure identification of cultural property in the event of its loss.
(v) The Central Bureau of Investigation should act as a data bank and keep information about cases, persons and property involved. It should also coordinate with the States on the one hand and with the Customs and the the Interpol authorities on the other.

## ANTIQUITIES WING OF THE CBI

To combat the growing incidence of thefts and smuggling of the cultural property of the nation which had assumed alarming proportions and was viewed with grave concern at the DIGs (CID) Conference and also by the press and the public at large, a small investigating unit was set up in the CBI in 1973. Ever since, it has been undertaking investigation of all important inter-state and international offences relating to cultural property.

The cell has been taking up cases mainly on reference from the State Police Forces as well as from the Archaeological Survey of India, especially those cases not solved at the State Police level. Of late, as a result of the information obtained and developed on its own suo motu investigation of cases has also been taken up. Even though the jurisdiction of the branch is all-India, due to the inadequacy of the investigating staff, the cases have been restricted more to Northern India. This is apart from the cases taken from some States like Orissa, on the State Government's reference.

As an investigating unit at the Central level, this wing has tried within its limited resources to assist the other police forces to recover stolen antiquities and also provide information about the possible inter-state gangs and the big time dealers and smugglers operating from Delhi. The provisions of the Antiquities and Art Treasures Act, 1972 are also enforced in the case of bigger operators. The Archaeological Survey of India is also provided assistance in matters of verification and in the discharge of the powers vested in ASI officers as and when called for. The Central Unit located in Delhi also makes efforts to coordinate with Customs authorities at the Delhi International Airport in order to check smuggling to Western countries.

Some of the more important cases successfully conducted by the Antiques Branch may be recapitulated briefly here:

1) A gang of professional thieves in U.P. committed a dacoity in the godown of the Archaeological Survey of India, situated at the Jogeshwar Temple, Almora. The stolen piece was a very valuable life-size idol of 'Pawan Raja' made of 'Asht Dhatu' estimated at Rs. 100 crores. This case came to CBI Antiques Wing as a reference from the U.P. Government. The case was worked out by the CBI and the idol was recovered from some Delhi dealers who had purchased the same from the dacoits. All the accused were traced, arrested and charge-sheeted. They were recently convicted to imprisonments ranging from 3 to 5 years in addition to fine.

2) In a case involving a notorious gang, it came to the notice of the CBI that two invaluable antique pillars of Sunga period of second century B.C. were stolen from the Suraj Temple in village Amin, District Karnal in Haryana. Later when they were recovered some accused had the pillars taken from the court's custody on the fraudulent plea that they were required for a temporary period in the interest of archaeological research and study. However, three sets of fake replicas of the originals were prepared by the accused and one such set returned to the court. The originals were smuggled to the U.K. where the accused tried to dispose them of to some parties from U.S.A. through a London broker. With the help of the Scotland Yard Police, they were brought back to India and the accused charge-sheeted by the CBI. He was convicted to undergo imprisonment for 2 years and 9 months.

3) A complaint that 64 rare Mughal miniature paintings were stolen from the house of a person in Varanasi in 1971, was after investigation by the U.P. Police closed without the culprits and the property being found. On the request from the State Police, the CBI Antiques Wing took up the case of investigation in February, 1977. Although six years had elapsed and it was difficult to get evidence either enough clues were not available or had disappeared, the case however was successfully worked out and some of the paintings recovered by the CBI. Seven accused persons have been prosecuted by the CBI in UP and the case is pending trial. The accused have been filing miscellaneous petitions on matters of jurisdiction, bail etc. in the High Courts, hence the case is at present under stay orders from the Allahabad High Court.

4) On receipt of information from Director General, ASI, about the detention of 18 antiques, stone sculptures and terracottas by the Delhi Customs at Palam Airport, the CBI took up the investigation of the case. The investigations revealed that a notorious antique dealer and smuggler of Delhi had booked these antiquities as personal luggage to be taken with him to New York in May-June, 1981 but was caught by the Customs on suspicion. He, however, managed to give the slip to the Customs authorities and later left for New York via Nepal and was absconding. The five VIP suitcases in which the 18 objects were found were seized and they all were certified as antiques by the Director General of Archaeological Survey of India.

One of these antiquities was later traced to a theft committed in an old temple of Taksheshwar Mahadev in Allahabad in April, 1981 for which there was a registered case with the local police who had, however, closed that case. The six accused arrested and charge-sheeted in this case included the above-mentioned dealer. The case is under trial in Delhi.

5) On information obtained by the CBI, searches were conducted at various places including those of a big antique dealer of Delhi in 1983. Some of the antiques seized were invaluable terracottas stolen from a famous temple of Gupta period located at Bhitargaon in Kanpur District in U.P. A case of receiving stolen property and offences under the Antiquities and Art Treasures Act, 1972 was registered and charge-sheeted against the accused. The case is pending in the court on the petition of the accused as well as the prosecutor.
6) On a reference from the Orissa Government, a case of theft at Narsingh Nath Temple in Sambalpur District, Orissa was taken up for investigation by the CBI Antiques Wing. The idol could be recovered and was later installed in the temple. The accused were also identified. While some of the accused were arrested others are absconding. The case of burglary has been registered and pending trial in an Orissa court.
7) Orissa Police requested the CBI Antiques Wing for assistance in tracing a very important and valuable Garuda idol made of black stone stolen from a temple in the Puri Temple Complex in November, 1985. Accordingly an alert signal was given and an all-out effort was made to find the possible hideout of the gang responsible for the theft in U.P. and M.P. and on receiving some information the Garuda idol was recovered from Delhi in January, 1987 and a few gang members were also arrested. The case is under investigation and efforts are on to apprehend the other gang members.

Among the priceless art and historical objects that the Central Bureau of Investigation seized in Mysore in December, 1985 during raids carried out in the offices of some antique dealers and some private residences, there was the famous golden sword belonging to Tippu Sultan. It was seized along with its wooden casket which bore the indication that it was from the collection of the Duke of Richmond. The Duke of Wellington had presented it to him. This sword had been used by Tippu in his last fatal battle on May 4, 1799 before the British stormed his fort at Srirangapatnam and found him dead.

Among the jewels looted by the British was a pair of Tippu's armlets, set in diamonds. One Dr. Nair who bought them for Rs. 1500 two years later sold them for a sum which brought him an annual income of £ 2000.

The other articles included Panchaloha idols and a big Rudraksha garland strung together on a golden chain with a pendant the size of a soap-box in solid gold, a glittering gold neckless with rubies, emeralds and diamonds worth lakhs of rupees and a large ornamental chair inlaid with ivory and with the inscription OM in Tamil on the arm-rest suggesting that it could have been a gift to the Mysore Royal family from some Tamil king.

Perhaps the biggest raid conducted so far in the country in February 1987 on the business premises of two well-known antique dealers of Old Delhi yielded more than 180 antique pieces of very old antiquity and high value in the international market. Investigation revealed that most of the antiquities had been stolen from ancient temples and archaeological sites mostly in northern and central India. Some of the documents seized from the dealers pointed to the possibility of their trying to sell them to foreigners in U.K., U.S.A. etc.

## PREVENTIVE MEASURES UNDERTAKEN BY THE GOVERNMENT

There is no precise information available regarding smuggling of antiquities out of the country. However, 15,556 cases have been registered as a result of concerted efforts of the agencies of the Government. The yearwise break-up is as follows:

1985—637
1986—435
1987—484

The Government of India has taken various measures for proper security and to prevent thefts and smuggling of antiquities. Some of the measures taken by the Government are as follows:

1) Enforcement of Antiquities and Art Treasures Act, 1972, which *inter alia* provides for the following:
   (i) Compulsory registration of certain categories of antiquities (sculptures in all media, paintings and illustrated and illuminated manuscripts) with the Registering Officer;
   (ii) Registering Officers to be informed regarding movement of such registered antiquities;
   (iii) Dealing in antiquities to be restricted to licensed dealers;
   (iv) Restriction on export of antiquities.

2) In addition, armed guards have been posted in some of the important centrally protected monuments and museums under the control of Archaeological Survey of India, besides tightening of watch and ward arrangements and appointment of security officers in some Circle Headquarters. Sculpture sheds to house the loose sculptures for safety and new site museums to display the antiquities at the site itself have been constructed.

3) In 1977, India has ratified the UNESCO Convention on the Means of Prohibiting Illicit Import, Export and Transfer of Cultural Properties. The convention *inter alia* provides that the contracting parties would take steps for preventing illicit import into their territories of stolen cultural property prospective to the signing of the convention and not retrospective.

4) An Antique Cell has been opened in the Central Bureau of Investigation for investigation into cases of thefts and loss of antiquities.

5) Steps are being taken for documentation of loose sculptures, paintings, illustrated manuscripts, etc.

6) Archaeological Survey of India has posted its officers at important international seaports and airports in India to help the Customs authorities in preventing illegal export of antiquities by identifying objects which are antiquities. Further, Expert Advisory Committees have been set up in important towns in India to examine the objects meant for export in order to find out if any of the objects is an antiquity in terms of the Antiquities and Art Treasures Act, 1972.

The Archaeological Survey of India has registered over three lakh antiquities in its antiquities data bank. Still many priceless antiquities, unrecognised and uncatalogued, are lying at temple ruins and excavation sites. The ASI has been trying its best to catalogue and document every antique to put a check on the smuggling activities and help the researchers to pursue their research on pantheon of Indian gods, miniature paintings or temple art. But in a surprise move in May 1987, the Central Advisory Board for Museums had passed a resolution against compulsory registration for State and Central Government museums.

The Archaeological Survey of India proposes to build a National Catalogue of antiquities so that at any given time information supported by photographs would be available on India's heritage in sculptures, paintings and manuscripts. With this Catalogue the ASI could keep an eye on the important antiques in the country and it may also be of immense help to police in their search for stolen antiques. Transfer of antiques is permitted but each transfer or sale is to be recorded at the ASI.

Though a complete documentation of all types of antiques would be of immense value to collectors and other officials concerned but there is also a fear that it may be misused by art thieves and smugglers as a ready compendium.

Mere seizures and raids are not enough to protect the traditional wealth of this vast country from being looted. A strong and effective measure has to be taken is the belief of the police and CBI. Initially, when the Antiquities and Art Treasures Act of 1972 was enforced, some dealers got their items registered and obtained licences for running their trade but most of the stock went underground thus pushing up their prices. The Act they realised was toothless. Thus, the trade flourished and is not handled by well organised groups.

It is for the law makers to take substantive action to prevent these businessmen from depleting the heritage of the country. Perhaps an amendment to the Antiquities and Art Treasures Act, 1972 to which serious thought is being given, may ensure a safer future for the remaining art treasures of the country.

# INTERPOL AND ART THEFT

THE various measures undertaken by the enforcement agencies to curb the smuggling of antiques from the country have not been very successful. According to some conservative estimate by experts more than 1000 art objects valued at nearly Rs. 100 crores are being smuggled every year. These are taken mainly from the ancient temples which fetch them fabulous price from the art collectors of the West. In India, legislative measures like the Antiquities and Art Treasures Act, 1972 regulate the export of antiquities and art treasures and prevention of smuggling of and fraudulent dealings in antiquities. The Act also envisages the licensing of antique dealers for regulating the trade and control of illicit export. The object has been to eliminate the acquisition of these antiquities by dubious means.

The international ramifications in the nefarious activity of art smuggling posed a major problem and this could be solved only at international level. It is here that the Interpol can play an effective role in busting international rackets of art smuggling. In dealing with art thefts, the Interpol—the International Criminal Police Organisation—with its headquarters in Paris has to bank upon the cooperation of its member-states. There are 146 countries as members and each has its Interpol wing. Interpol spreads its tentacles far and wide, across continents with the help of effective monitoring and operation of different police systems among the member-countries.

Many a time the clever smugglers keep the national police and the Interpol on tenterhooks; the stolen goods might be neatly concealed after the theft, and once the vigil is relaxed, they would smuggle the goods out. Once it is confirmed or even suspected that the objects have passed across international borders, Interpol swings into action at the instance of the national government. A message is flashed by radio or telex to the countries linked to the Interpol communication network.

## NATIONAL CENTRAL BUREAU—INDIA (INTERPOL)

India joined the International Police Commission in 1938 to actively share the facilities pooled by the organisation. India is presently contributing Rs. 15 lakhs annually as its share for the services, for which Central Bureau of Investigation has been chosen as National Central Bureau for India and the Interpol Wing of the CBI has been entrusted with the coveted task. The Director, CBI, is the head of the Indian National Central Bureau, i.e., Interpol—New Delhi which functions under the immediate control of an officer of the rank of an Assistant Director.

In addition to normal communication channels, Interpol, New Delhi has its own radio station for rapid and discrete contacts with ICPO — Interpol General Secretariat and other National Central Bureaus connected on the Interpol radio network. About 65 National Central Bureaus have set up Interpol radio stations and this totally independent network allows them to contact each other and the General Secretariat. Besides, a photo-telegraphy equipment has also been acquired by Interpol radio station for quick exchange of photographs and fingerprints.

While communicating with other police forces of the country some photographs of the stolen antiques are required for identification which are generally not easily available. Generally a smuggler thinks that his antique may not be detected during its transhipment since he applies a foolproof method to conceal the art items. As such he never bothers to photograph them but for police this is a handicap in locating the stolen antiques and also in apprehending culprits.

In a case of theft of a painting committed in a Belgium Museum, the police of another country asked the curator of the Museum to visit them to identify what they thought might be the missing picture. The curator was visibly surprised that the police, who had come across the painting during a search carried out as part of quite another investigation, had been able to connect the painting with the photograph and the description he had provided at the time of the theft. A cross-reference file of stolen works, with descriptions and photos, date of notification of theft and when investigations were stopped, as well as details about the works and the schools and periods to which they belong, helps the Interpol to galvanise into action against the sophisticated criminals.

Interpol is also concerned about the security measures in museums. Even as early as in 1959, at the request of ICOM—the International Council of Museums—the Interpol asked member-states to tell them about the measures they were taking or planned to take to protect their museums. The purpose of the enquiry was that both the personnel and equipment at the museums need periodic updating.

In 1971, the General Council of the Interpol had asked its affiliated member-nations to facilitate the return to the country of origin any work of art found in fraudulent circumstances in another country. Interpol adopted a resolution urging all national departments and institutions responsible for conserving cultural property not to buy any property without first verifying its origin.

The Indian delegation presented to the Interpol a report on theft of cultural property. Taking note of this report, the Interpol voiced concern at the alarming rate of thefts in certain countries. The Interpol urged upon member-countries to step up international police co-operation in tracing any missing work of art and in this respect exchange of information should be as complete and detailed as possible. It also recommended that member-countries should try to make available the (stolen) property to judicial authorities of the requesting country of origin so as to facilitate its identification and prosecution of the concerned persons.

The General Council directed the Interpol General Secretariat to draw up a list of the most important stolen works of art for purposes of investigation and circulation among National Central Bureaus. Description of such valuables should also be grouped together to underline Interpol's activities and to alert world public opinion. It has also suggested to the heads of National Central Bureaus to persuade their Governments to adopt more suitable legislation on art crimes.

At the Interpol meet in 1983 conflicting views regarding ownership rights of stolen antiques between developing and developed nations were aired. Interpol issued a circular to seek their views again. Continuous flow of antiques from India and some other countries rich in cultural heritage to Europe and the USA was at an alarming stage. In India alone about 1000 cases of theft of antiques and other cultural property are reported every year.

In the affluent countries of Europe and the USA, the craze to possess antiques is responsible for their outflow from the countries of their origin. These smuggled items are bought by the rich people or institutions at fabulous prices. It is stated that even if the Central Bureau of Investigation and other agencies manage to locate the stolen items in foreign countries, legal difficulties crop up in retrieving them. Most of the affluent countries take the stand that in accordance with their laws, a bonafide buyer of stolen property cannot be deprived of it without adequate compensation. This position is different from the one prevailing in India where stolen property does not belong to its buyer.

**The Case of Nataraja Idol:** On 17th February 1988, India won a long-drawn legal battle in the London High Court, getting back a 12th century bronze statue of Lord Shiva in the Nataraja posture belonging to the Pathur temple in Thanjavur district of Tamil Nadu from where it was stolen in 1976. The priceless bronze statue considered a rare piece of antique belongs to the Chola period in the 11th century and was stolen by one Ramamoorthy from the Arul Thiru Vishwanatham temple at Pathur. This Nataraja—the panchaloha idol—is 100 cm tall and weighs 65 kg.

The Indian Government professed that the Nataraja had been stolen in the autumn of 1976 from a temple at Pathur village. Investigations revealed that the idol had been buried along with others close to the temple, to protect them from Muslim invaders. This had been dug out by thieves and sold to a Madras dealer. The latter sold it to a dealer in Bombay. It was subsequently smuggled out of Bombay in contravention of the Indian laws and sold to the Bumber Development Corporation (a Canadian Oil Company). The idol was then sent to the British Museum by the Corporation for restoration. Company Chairman Robert Borden, a noted art collector, had bought the Nataraja idol for £ 2,50,000 from a London antique dealer, Julian Sherrier who claimed the idol had been in his family's possession for some years. Michael Dollard, the art adviser to Bumber Development Corporation, said the Company had checked out the idol's provenance from the dealer who gave them a clean record.

The verdict rung down the curtain on a controversial court battle which began in August 1982 after the Scotland Yard seized the dancing Shiva following a tip-off from the

British Museum. The Union of India, the State of Tamil Nadu and the temple authorities filed a plaint seeking restoration of the statue to its rightful owner, Vishwanathaswamy temple. The Government proceeded to sue both Bumber Development Corporation and the Metropolitan police as co-defendants. Mr. Bhaskar Ghorpade, barrister-at-law, represented the Union of India and the State of Tamil Nadu in the case which went on for 44 working days; over 40 decisions of the Supreme Court, several high courts of India and the Privy Council were cited in support of India's contention that the statue must be returned to the temple.

The case before the High Court was unique as for the first time articles of the Constitution of India, Indian laws and in particular Hindu Law were referred before Mr. Justice Kennedy. It was argued by Mr. Ardian Hamilton Q.C. that the well established legal conventions of Hindu temples were entitled to protection in English Courts. Hamilton and Ghorpade's arguments evoked much legal curiosity. They maintained that "once a deity, always a deity. An idol remains a juristic person however long buried or damaged, since the deity and its juristic entity survive the total destruction of its earthly form." They argued that the temples' rights were not affected by the mere fact of the idols' clandestine removal and export. Several witnesses were flown from India to give evidence in the court who included experts from India and Britain. The identification of the statue was first established by Ramamoorthy who had stolen it. Meveil, Maqbool Hussain and Balraj Nadar, receivers of the stolen property, also appeared in the court.

Justice Kennedy in his far-reaching and fascinating judgement said: "I am entirely persuaded that the London Nataraja is Pathur Nataraja." Referring to the defendant's case, he said: "The defendent has pointed out, and pointed out correctly that there are many idols in the museums and private collections of India, some of which can be identified to particular temples. Logic would dictate that they too should return to their own restored temples. Yet there is no suggestion that they will."

Mr. Justice Kennedy further observed: "It may be that claims akin to that in this case could be made which could be pursued outside the jurisdiction of the Union of India. Many will fail, but some will succeed, particularly if the criminal character of their taking could be proved. I am sure that the real energy behind the present claim is that of the Government of the Union which wants to stop, and if possible reverse the outward flow of a precious part of the nation's cultural heritage."

This judgement has opened new frontiers for India, though fighting a case abroad is very costly. The case has set an example for future, a country to challenge and plead for restoration of arts and antiques smuggled out of its territory clandestinely. Even in this case, the court appreciated the role of the Canadian art collector and conceded that his motive was genuine. But, it held that his ignorance of the channel through which it was secured could not entitle him for its possession.

Kennedy's verdict has created a sensation in the British institutions that hold millions of pounds worth of Indian antiquities. The Victoria and Albert Museum possesses a collection of about 33,000 Indian paintings, sculptures, textiles and almost countless Indian religious objects. There is no doubt that many of these objects were clandestinely imported from India. Interpol thus can play an important role in tracing stolen objects and retrieve them to the rightful owners. This can be achieved by active cooperation of the public, state police forces and the Central Government's law-enforcement agencies.

A Nataraja idol stolen from Tamil Nadu is now in the Kambell Art Museum in the United States. The Museum had purchased it for Rs. 6 lakhs. Even though the CBI located the idol it could not be retrieved and ultimately a compromise was arrived at in accordance with which the idol would be retained in the USA for 10 years and thereafter it would be returned to India. In another case, an idol stolen from India was traced to a multi-millionaire in the U.S.A. who had purchased it for $ 1 million. Civil suits for its recovery were filed and ultimately an agreement was arrived at whereby though the ownership rights of the idol would remain with the owner in India, the idol would remain in USA for 10 years.

The Indian delegation had taken up these issues at the Interpol meetings and pleaded that the rights of the owner must be given priority over the rights of the bonafide buyer.

## COMPUTERIZATION OF DATA

Participants at the 2nd International Symposium on 'Theft of Works of Art and Cultural Property' held from 14th to 16th September 1983 and the 12th European Regional Conference (1983) recommended that computerization of data on stolen cultural property should be standardized so as to facilitate international cooperation. The ICPO-Interpol General Assembly meeting in Cannes from 18th to 25th October, 1983, at its 52nd session decided to set up a Standards and Documentation Committee to study existing applications of electronic data processing to stolen cultural property, and those under development, and to recommend specific criteria common to all applications.

The work of this Committee was completed in February, 1987 and a revised CRIGEN/ART form and a manual of guidance was produced. At the 56th session of the General Assembly (Nice, 1987) by Resolution No. AGN/56/RES/6, these documents were adopted for use within the organization. This form is to be solely used for reporting either the thefts or discovery of an item of cultural property or work of art.

In order to facilitate computer processing of data, NCBs should use these documents. In cases where a telegram is sent out before the form or even instead of it, NCBs are requested to ensure that the information supplied in the telegram is drafted in such a way as to follow the headings on the CRIGEN/ART form and the order of those headings. The manual of guidance had also been produced to enable officers at NCBs to describe the items of cultural property.

## THE CODE OF ETHICS

According to Mr. Hughes de Varine Bohan, Director of the International Council of

Museums, the root of the problem of art pillage lies in the false conception of museum. "An object of scientific interest should not be considered primarily as an art work. Yet, museums, which are supposed to educate the public, often contribute to spread the idea that such and such a culture is represented only by uniquely beautiful objects." The picture that the public builds of ancient cultures can be permanently distorted when the past is consistently presented as a kaleidoscope of masterpieces. Tourists and collectors, art dealers and museum curators become obsessed by this quest for unique works. And this "Monalisa Complex" can give rise to an illegal market, leading in turn to excavations, looting and the destruction of monuments.

International Council of Museums (ICOM) has laid a clear code of ethics. Any object offered for sale or as a gift to a museum should have a clean bill of health—that is, it should be accompanied by a certificate showing its origin and also carry scientific documentation.

If every country adheres to these principles and its enforcement agencies actively cooperate with each other the illegal smuggling of art objects can be effectively checked. Illicit trade in works of art will disappear, especially in many affluent countries where donors to museums benefit from tax exemption.

According tó UNESCO guide to the world decade for cultural development 1988-97, on preserving the cultural heritage—urban development, industrialization, pollution, armed conflicts or the unplanned development of mass tourism present an ever increasing threat to our cultural heritage whether in the form of works of art and architecture or cultural and natural sites.

Measures to defend mankind's cultural heritage, like those designed to combat the illicit traffic in works of art and archaeological treasures, are rooted in a widespread awareness of present-day problems. This is why training and information have a decisive role to play in mobilizing public opinion. Moreover all possible traditional technical resources, and new technologies, must be put to use in order not only to preserve, but also to revitalize this heritage which is in danger.

# THE ROLE OF UNESCO

MANY nations have passed laws to protect their works of art, antiques and archaeological objects. But lack of adequate protection and the growing demands for these objects result in continuous thefts and the archaeological sites being regularly plundered. The countries like Egypt, Italy, Greece, Turkey and the Arab world are suffering from extensive tomb robbing. Organised smuggling gangs unhesitatingly plunder the castles and churches of Europe, and so is the case of temples in Asia. It not only results in losing the cultural heritage, but in defacing the archaeological sites and thus berefting the scholars to study the history of human race.

The UNESCO has taken steps to check such cases of thefts, to regulate the export and import of cultural objects so that countries are not deprived of those items which are of fundamental significance to their national heritage.

In 1970 the UNESCO adopted an international convention, i.e., "Convention on the means of prohibiting and preventing the illicit import, export and transfer of ownership of cultural property", with the object of building cooperation among all countries in the field. One of its key provisions concerns the return by a State Party of cultural property stolen from a museum or similar public institution in another State Party (see Appendix I).

Till 15th June 1983, 65 states have become signatories to the Convention, most of whom have been victims of illicit traffic. Most of these states have passed laws in their countries protecting certain cultural objects or categories of objects and laying down rules regulating export. The rules, however, vary widely in scope. In some countries there is a total ban on the export of cultural property; in others export is subject (in all cases) to authorization; and in some, authorization to export has to be obtained in the case of certain categories of objects.

As regards legal provisions governing import, different approaches have been adopted. For instance, the Canadian Cultural Property Export and Import Act provides that "it is illegal to import into Canada any foreign cultural property that has been illegally exported from a reciprocating State." The legislation adopted in the USA in application of the Convention focuses on the steps to be taken in response to a request from a State party whose cultural heritage is in danger because of extensive looting of archaeological sites; these steps include strict import controls on items coming from the State Party concerned.

The main impact of the Convention is undoubtedly the change in attitudes. By adopting this agreement, the international community exerts moral pressure not only on those concerned with protection of the cultural heritage, but also on those dealing in cultural objects even in States which are not parties to the Convention. On the one hand, States are encouraged to take adequate measures to ensure proper protection in collaboration with the concerned public services (museums, police, customs, etc.); on the other, those acquiring cultural property (museums, collectors and dealers) are now more aware and cautious of what is considered by the international community to be right and wrong. The impact can be seen in the codes of ethics adopted by many museums in the industrialized countries on the acquisition of cultural property, based on the Code of Professional Ethics of the International Council of Museums (ICOM) which states: "A museum should not acquire, whether by purchase, gift, bequest or exchange, any object unless the governing body and responsible officer are satisfied that the museum can acquire a valid title to the specimen or object in question and that in particular it has not been acquired in, or exported from, its country of origin...in violation of that country's laws." Other examples are the codes of practice of antique dealers' associations, such as the Code of Practice for the Control of International Trading in Works of Art adopted by members of the U.K. Fine Art and Antiques Trade.

Few cases have so far been brought before the courts under legislation adopted in implementation of the 1970 Convention. In fact, the only case known to the UNESCO Secretariat is a case brought to a court in Canada which concerned the importation into Canada of an ancient Noh sculpture illegally exported from Nigeria. However, the principles embodied in the convention have been evoked in several other cases. One case concerned 12,000 pre-Columbian objects illicitly exported from Ecuador to Italy that were eventually returned by court order to Ecuador. Another case was brought before the courts of the Federal Republic of Germany concerning a contract entered into by a Nigerian company with a German Insurance Company covering the transport of cultural objects from Nigeria to Hamburg. The objects had been exported in contravention of Nigerian law. The plaintiff (the Nigerian company) was seeking damages for the loss of some of the objects. The court considered that the UNESCO Convention expressed the internationally accepted fundamental convictions on the right of each country to the protection of its cultural heritage and on the fact that practices which prejudice this right are condemnable and must be combated. The Court held that the contract was unenforceable in the Federal Republic since the export of cultural property was contrary to a prohibition in the country of origin. In the interest of maintaining proper standards for the international trade in cultural objects, no protection from the civil law was provided.

UNESCO's role is essentially to encourage States to ratify the Convention; to collect information on measures taken to implement it and circulate this information widely; to study questions raised by States concerning the application of the Convention and to make proposals to States on these matters; to circulate information concerning thefts of cultural property from museums or similar institutions in States parties to the Convention; and to help develop cooperation among the different services concerned (museums, customs administrations, police services, etc.).

Given below is one such case. Following the theft in December 1985 of 140 archaeological objects, many of them in gold, from the National Museum of Anthropology of Mexico, the Organization circulated to all States Parties an illustrated booklet on the items in question, asking them to provide all possible assistance for the recovery and return of the stolen objects (Interpol and the International Council of Museums also circulated details of the theft through their own channels).

UNESCO has published two volumes in English and French of a compendium of national laws and regulations in force in 45 States concerning the protection of movable cultural property as well as booklets, in English and French, containing the full texts of national laws and regulations on the same question in some 20 other States; a commentary on the Convention has been prepared in French. A study was conducted on problems of implementation of the Convention raised by States and the results were reviewed by a group of experts in March 1983, which proposed possible solutions to some of the problems; a report prepared for UNESCO on measures that can be taken at the national and international levels to stem illicit trafficking has been published under the title "National legal control of illicit traffic in cultural property".

# APPENDIX I

## CONVENTION ON THE MEANS OF PROHIBITING AND PREVENTING THE ILLICIT IMPORT, EXPORT AND TRANSFER OF OWNERSHIP OF CULTURAL PROPERTY

(Adopted by the General Conference at its 16th session in Paris, 14 November, 1970)

The General Conference of the United Nations Educational, Scientific and Cultural Organisation, meeting in Paris from 12 October to 14 November 1970 at its sixteenth session,

Recalling the importance of the provisions contained in the Declaration of the Principles of International Cultural Cooperation, adopted by the General Conference at its fourteenth session,

Considering that the interchange of cultural property among nations for scientific, cultural and educational purposes increases the knowledge of the civilization of man, enriches the cultural life of all peoples and inspires mutual respect and appreciation among nations,

Considering that cultural property constitutes one of the basic elements of civilization and national culture, and that its true value can be appreciated only in relation to the fullest possible information regarding its origin, history and traditional setting,

Considering that it is incumbent upon every State to protect the cultural property existing within its territory against the dangers of theft, clandestine excavation, and illicit export,

Considering that, to avert these dangers, it is essential for every State to become increasingly alive to the moral obligations to respect its own cultural heritage and that of all nations,

Considering that, as cultural institutions, museums, libraries and archives should ensure that their collections are built up in accordance with universally recognized moral principles,

Considering that the illicit import, export and transfer of ownership of cultural property is an obstacle to that understanding between nations which it is part of Unesco's mission to promote by recommending to interested States international conventions to this end,

Considering that the protection of cultural heritage can be effective only if organized both nationally and internationally among States working in close cooperation,

Considering that the Unesco General Conference adopted a Recommendation to this effect in 1964,

Having before it further proposals on the means of prohibiting and preventing the illicit import, export and transfer of ownership of cultural property, a question which is on the agenda for the session as item 19,

Adopts this Convention on the fourteenth day of November 1970.

**Article 1**

For the purposes of this Convention, the term "cultural property" means property which, on religious or secular grounds, is specifically designated by each State as being of importance for archaeology, prehistory, history, literature, art or science and which belongs to the following categories:

(a) rare collections and specimens of fauna, flora, minerals and objects of palaeontological interest;

(b) property relating to history, including the history of science and technology and military and social history, to the life of national leaders, thinkers, scientists and to events of national importance;

(c) products of archaeological excavations (including regular and clandestine) or of archaeological discoveries;

(d) elements of artistic or historical monuments or archaeological sites which have been dismembered;

(e) antiquities more than one hundred years old, such as inscriptions, coins and engraved seals;

(f) objects of ethnological interest;

(g) property of artistic interest, such as:

  (i) pictures, paintings and drawings produced entirely by hand on any support and in any material (excluding industrial designs and manufactured articles decorated by hand);
  (ii) original works of statuary art and sculpture in any material;
  (iii) original engravings, prints and lithographs;
  (iv) original artistic assmblages and montages in any material;

(h) rare manuscripts and incunabula, old books, documents and publications of special interest (historical, artistic, scientific, literary, etc.) singly or in collections;

(i) postage, revenue and similar stamps, singly or in collections;

(j) archives, including sound, photographic and cinematographic archives;

(k) articles of furniture more than one hundred years old and old musical instruments.

**Article 2**

1. The States Parties to this Convention recognize that the illicit import, export and transfer of ownership of cultural property is one of the main causes of the impoverishment of the cultural heritage of the countries of origin of such property and that international cooperation constitutes one of the most efficient means of protecting each country's cultural property against all the dangers resulting therefrom.

2. To this end, the States Parties undertake to oppose such practices with the means at their disposal, and particularly by removing their causes, putting a stop to current practices, and by helping to make the necessary reparations.

**Article 3**

The import, export or transfer or ownership of cultural property effected contrary to the provisions adopted under the Convention by the States Parties thereto, shall be illicit.

**Article 4**

The States Parties to this Convention recognize that for the purpose of the Convention property which belongs to the following categories forms part of the cultural heritage of each State:

(a) cultural property created by the individual or collective genius of nationals of the State concerned, and cultural property of importance to the State concerned created within the territory of that State by foreign nationals or stateless persons resident within such territory;

(b) cultural property found within the national territory;

(c) cultural property acquired by archaeological, ethnological or natural science missions, with the consent of the competent authorities of the country of origin of such property;

(d) cultural property which has been the subject of a freely agreed exchange;

(e) cultural property received as a gift or purchased legally with the consent of the competent authorities of the country of origin of such property.

**Article 5**

To ensure the protection of their cultural property against illicit import, export and transfer of ownership, the States Parties to this Convention undertake, as appropriate for each country, to set up within their territories one or more national services, where such services do not already exist, for the protection of the cultural heritage, with a qualified staff sufficient in number for the effective carrying out of the following functions:

(a) contributing to the formation of draft laws and regulations designed to secure the protection of the cultural heritage and particularly prevention of the illicit import, export and transfer of ownership of important cultural property;

(b) establishing and keeping up to date, on the basis of a national inventory of protected property, a list of important public and private cultural property whose export would constitute an appreciable impoverishment of the national cultural heritage;

(c) promoting the development or the establishment of scientific and technical institutions (museums, libraries, archives, laboratories, workshops...) required to ensure the preservation and presentation of cultural property;

(d) organizing the supervision of archaeological excavations, ensuring the preservation *in situ* of certain cultural property, and protecting certain areas reserved for future archaeological research;

(e) establishing, for the benefit of those concerned (curators, collectors, antique dealers, etc.), rules in conformity with the ethical principles set forth in this convention; and taking steps to ensure the observance of those rules;

(f) taking educational measures to stimulate and develop respect for the cultural heritage of all States, and spreading knowledge of the provisions of the Convention;

(g) seeing that appropriate publicity is given to the disappearance of any items of cultural property.

**Article 6**

The States Parties to this Convention undertake:

(a) to introduce an appropriate certificate in which the exporting State would specify that the export of the cultural property in question is authorized. The certificate should accompany all items of cultural property exported in accordance with the regulations;

(b) to prohibit the exportation of cultural property from their territory unless accompanied by the above-mentioned export certificate;

(c) to publicize this prohibition by appropriate means, particularly among persons likely to export or import cultural property.

**Article 7**

The States Parties to this Convention undertake:

(a) to take necessary measures, consistent with national legislation, to prevent museums and similar institutions within their territories from acquiring cultural property originating in another State Party which has been illegally exported after entry into force of this Convention, in the States concerned. Whenever possible, to inform a State of origin Party to this Convention of an offer of such cultural property illegally removed from that State after the entry into force of this Convention in both States;

(b) (i) to prohibit the import of cultural property stolen from a museum or a religious or secular public monument or similar institution in another State Party to this Convention after the entry into force of this Convention for the States concerned, provided that such property is documented as appertaining to the inventory of that institution;

(ii) at the request of the State Party of origin, to take appropriate steps to recover and return any such cultural property imported after the entry into force of this Convention in both States concerned, provided, however, that the requesting State shall pay just compensation to an innocent purchaser or to a person who has valid title to that property. Requests for recovery and return shall be made through diplomatic offices. The requesting Party shall furnish, at its expense, the documentation and other evidence necessary to establish its claim for recovery and return. The Parties shall impose no customs duties or other charges upon cultural property returned pursuant to this Article. All expenses incident to the return and delivery of the cultural property shall be borne by the requesting Party.

**Article 8**

The States Parties to this Convention undertake to impose penalties or administrative sanctions on any person responsible for infringing the prohibitions referred to under Articles 6(b) and 7(b) above.

**Article 9**

Any State Party to this Convention whose cultural patrimony is in jeopardy from pillage of archaeological or ethnological materials may call upon other States Parties who are affected. The States Parties to this Convention undertake, in these circumstances, to participate in a concerted international effort to determine and to carry out the necessary concrete measures, including the control of exports and imports and international commerce in the specific materials concerned. Pending agreement each State concerned shall take provisional measures to the extent feasible to prevent irremediable injury to the cultural heritage of the requesting State.

**Article 10**

The States Parties to this Convention undertake:

(a) to restrict, by education, information and vigilance, movement of cultural property illegally removed from any State Party to this Convention and, as appropriate for each country, oblige antique dealers, subject to penal or administrative sanctions, to maintain a register recording the origin of each item of cultural property, names and addresses of the suppliers, description and price of each item sold and to inform the purchaser of the cultural property of the export prohibition to which such property may be subject.

(b) to endeavour by educational means to create and develop in the public mind a realization of the value of cultural property and the threat to the cultural heritage created by theft, clandestine excavations and illicit exports.

**Article 11**

The export and transfer of ownership of cultural property under compulsion arising directly or indirectly from the occupation of a country by a foreign power shall be regarded as illicit.

**Article 12**

The State Parties to this Convention shall respect the cultural heritage within the territories for the international relations of which they are responsible, and shall take all appropriate measures to prohibit and prevent the illicit import, export and transfer of ownership of cultural property in such territories.

**Article 13**

The States Parties to this Convention also undertake, consistent with the laws of each State:

(a) to prevent by all appropriate means transfers of ownership of cultural property likely to promote the illicit import or export of such property;

(b) to ensure that their competent services cooperate in facilitating the earliest possible restitution of illicitly exported cultural property to its rightful owner;

(c) to admit actions for recovery of lost or stolen items of cultural property brought by or on behalf of the rightful owners;

(d) to recognize the indefeasible right of each State Party to this Convention to classify and declare certain cultural property as inalienable which should therefore ipso facto not be exported, and to facilitate recovery of such property by the State concerned in cases where it has been exported.

**Article 14**

In order to prevent illicit export and to meet the obligations arising from the implementation of this Convention, each State Party to the Convention should, as far as it is able, provide the national services responsible for the protection of its cultural heritage with an adequate budget and, if necessary, should set up a fund for this purpose.

**Article 15**

Nothing in this Convention shall prevent States Parties thereto from concluding special agreements among themselves or from continuing to implement agreements already concluded regarding the restitution of cultural property removed, whatever the reason, from its territory of origin, before the entry into force of this Convention for the States concerned.

**Article 16**

The States Parties to this Convention shall in their periodic reports submitted to the General Conference of the United Nations Educational, Scientific and Cultural Organization, on dates and in a manner to be determined by it, give information on the legislative and administrative provisions which they have adopted and other action which they have taken for the application of this Convention, together with details of the experience acquired in this field.

**Article 17**

1. The States Parties to this Convention may call on the technical assistance of the United Nations Educational, Scientific and Cultural Organization, particularly as regards:

(a) information and education;
(b) consultation and expert advice; and
(c) coordination and good offices.

2. The United Nations Educational, Scientific and Cultural Organization may, on its own initiative, conduct research and publish studies on matters relevant to the illicit movement of cultural property.

3. To this end, the United Nations Educational, Scientific and Cultural Organization may also call on the cooperation of any competent non-governmental organization.

4. The United Nations Educational, Scientific and Cultural Organization may, on its own initiative, make proposals to States Parties to this Convention for its implementation.

5. At the request of at least two States Parties to this Convention which are engaged in a dispute over its implementation, Unesco may extend its good offices to reach a settlement between them.

**Article 18**

This Convention is drawn up in English, French, Russian and Spanish, the four texts being equally authoritative.

**Article 19**

1. This Convention shall be subject to ratification or acceptance by States members

of the United Nations Educational, Scientific and Cultural Organization in accordance with their respective constitutional procedures.

2. The instruments of ratification or acceptance shall be deposited with the Director-General of the United Nations Educational, Scientific and Cultural Organization.

**Article 20**

1. This Convention shall be open to accession by all States not members of the United Nations Educational, Scientific and Cultural Organization.

2. Accession shall be effected by the deposit of an instrument of accession with the Director-General of the United Nations Educational, Scientific and Cultural Organization.

**Article 21**

This Convention shall enter into force three months after the date of the deposit of the third instrument of ratification, acceptance or accession, but only with respect to those States which have deposited their respective instruments on or before that date. It shall enter into force with respect to any other State three months after the deposit of its instrument of ratification, acceptance or accession.

**Article 22**

The States Parties to this Convention recognize that the Convention is applicable not only to their metropolitan territories but also to all territories for the international relations of which they are responsible, they undertake to consult, if necessary, the governments or other competent authorities of these territories on or before ratification, acceptance or accession with a view to securing the application of the Convention to those territories, and to notify the Director-General of the United Nations Educational, Scientific and Cultural Organization of the territories to which it is applied, the notification to take effect three months after the date of its receipt.

**Article 23**

1. Each State Party to this Convention may denounce the Convention on its own behalf or on behalf of any territory for whose international relations it is responsible.

2. The denunciation shall be notified by an instrument in writing, deposited with the Director-General of the United Nations Educational, Scientific and Cultural Organization.

3. The denunciation shall take effect twelve months after the receipt of the instrument of denunciation.

**Article 24**

The Director-General of the United Nations Educational, Scientific and Cultural

Organization shall inform the States members of the Organization, the States not members of the Organization which are referred to in Article 20, as well as the United Nations, of the deposit of all the instruments of ratification, acceptance and accession provided for in Articles 19 and 20, and of the notifications and denunciations provided for in Articles 22 and 23 respectively.

**Article 25**

1. This Convention may be revised by the General Conference of the United Nations Educational, Scientific and Cultural Organization. Any such revision shall, however, bind only the States which shall become Parties to the revising convention.

2. If the General Conference should adopt a new convention revising this Convention in whole or in part, then, unless the new convention otherwise provides, this Convention shall cease to be open to ratification, acceptance or accession, as from the date on which the new revising convention enters into force.

**Article 26**

In conformity with Article 102 of the Charter of the United Nations, this Convention shall be registered with the Secretariat of the United Nations at the request of the Director-General of the United Nations Educational, Scientific and Cultural Organization.

Done in Paris this seventeenth day of November 1970, in two authentic copies bearing the signature of the President of the Sixteenth Session of the General Conference and of the Director General of the United Nations Educational, Scientific and Cultural Organization, which shall be deposited in the archives of the United Nations Educational, Scientific and Cultural Organization, and certified true copies of which shall be delivered to all the States referred to in Articles 19 & 20 as well as to the United Nations.

The foregoing is the authentic text of the Convention duly adopted by the General Conference of the United Nations Educational, Scientific and Cultural Organization during its sixteenth session, which was held in Paris and declared closed the Fourteenth day of November 1970.

IN FAITH WHEREOF we have appended our signatures this seventeenth day of November, 1970.

The President of the General Conference
Atilio Dell'Oro Maini
The Director-General
Rene Maheu
Director, Office of International
Standards and Legal Affairs,
United Nations Educational,
Scientific and Cultural Organization.
Certified copy.
Paris.

# RECOMMENDATION FOR THE PROTECTION OF MOVABLE CULTURAL PROPERTY
## (Paris, 1978)

The General Conference of the United Nations Educational, Scientific and Cultural Organization meeting in Paris from 24 October to 28 November 1978, at its twentieth session.

Noting the great interest in cultural property now finding expression throughout the world in the creation of numerous museums and similar institutions, the growing number of exhibitions, the constantly increasing flow of visitors to collections, monuments and archaeological sites, and the intensification of cultural exchanges,

Considering that this is a very positive development which should be encouraged, in particular by applying the measures advocated in the Recommendation concerning the International Exchange of Cultural Property adopted by the General Conference at its nineteenth session in 1976,

Considering that the growing desire of the public to know and appreciate the wealth of the cultural heritage, of whatever origin, has nevertheless led to an increase in all the dangers to which cultural property is exposed as a result of particularly easy access or inadequate protection, the risks inherent in transport, and the recrudescence, in some countries, of clandestine excavations, thefts, illicit traffic and acts of vandalism,

Noting that because of this aggravation of the risks, but also as a consequence of the increase in the market value of cultural items, the cost of comprehensive insurance in countries where there is no adequate system of governmental guarantees is beyond the means of most museums and is a definite impediment to the organization of international exhibitions and other exchanges between different countries,

Considering that movable cultural property respresenting the different cultures forms part of the common heritage of mankind and that every State is therefore morally responsible to the international community as a whole for its safeguarding,

Considering that States should accordingly intensify and give general effect to such measures for the prevention and management of risks as will ensure the effective protection of movable cultural property and, at the same time, reduce the cost of covering the risks incurred,

Wishing to supplement and extend the scope of the norms and principles laid down in this respect by the General Conference, in particular in the Convention for the Protection of Cultural Property in the Event of Armed Conflict (1954), the Recommendation on International Principles Applicable to Archaeological Excavations (1956), the

Recommendation on the Most Effective Means of Rendering Museums Accessible to Everyone (1950(, the Recommendation on the Means of Prohibiting and Preventing the Illicit Export, Import and Transfer of Ownership of Cultural Property (1964), the Convention on the Means of Prohibiting and Preventing the Illicit Import, Export and Transfer of Ownership of Cultural Property (1970), the Recommendation concerning the Protection, at National Level, of the Cultural and Natural Heritage (1972), the Convention concerning the Protection of the World Cultural and Natural Heritage (1972) and the Recommendation concerning the International Exchange of Cultural Property (1975). Having before it proposals concerning the protection of movable cultural property,

Having decided, at its nineteenth session, that this question should take form of a recommendation to Member States,

Adopts, this twenty-eighth day of November 1978, the present Recommendation.

The General Conference recommends that Member States apply the following provisions by taking whatever legislative or other steps may be required, in conformity with the constitutional system or practice of each State, to give effect within their respective territories to the principles and norms formulated in this Recommendation.

The General Conference recommends that Member States bring this Recommendation to the attention of the appropriate authorities and bodies.

The General Conference recommends that Member States submit to it, by dates and in the form to be decided upon by the Conference, reports concerning the action taken by them in pursuant of this Recommendation.

**I. DEFINITIONS**

1. For the purposes of this Recommendation:

   (a) "movable cultural property" shall be taken to mean all movable objects which are the expression and testimony of human creation or of the evolution of nature and which are of archaeological, historical, artistic, scientific or technical value and interest, including items in the following categories:

      (i) products of archaeological exploration and excavations conducted on land and under water;
      (ii) antiquities such as tools, pottery, inscriptions, coins, seals, jewellery, weapons and funerary remains, including mummies;
      (iii) items resulting from the dismemberment of historical monuments;
      (iv) items relating to history, including the history of science and technological interest;

(v) items relating to history, including the history of science and technology and military and social history, to the life of peoples and national leaders, thinkers, scientists and artists and to events of national importance;

(vi) items of artistic interest, such as:

(a) paintings and drawings, produced entirely by hand on any support and in any material (excluding industrial designs and manufactured articles decorated by hand);

(b) original prints, and posters and photographs, as the media for original creativity;

(c) original artistic assemblages and montages in any material;

(d) works of statuary art and sculpture in any material;

(e) works of applied art in such materials as glass, ceramics, metal, wood, etc.

(vii) manuscripts and incunabula, codices, books, documents or publications of special interest;

(viii) items of numismatic (medals and coins) and philatelic interest;

(ix) archives, including textual records, maps and other cartographic materials, photographs, cinematographic films, sound recordings and machine-readable records;

(x) items of furniture, tapestries, carpets, dress and musical instruments;

(xi) zoological, botanical and geological specimens;

(b) "protection" shall be taken to mean the prevention and coverage of risks as defined below:

(i) "prevention of risks" means all the measures required, within a comprehensive protection system, to safeguard movable cultural property from every risk to which such property may be exposed, including those resulting from armed conflict, riots or other public disorders;

(ii) "risk coverage" means the guarantee of idemnification in the case of damage to, deterioration, alteration or loss of movable cultural property resulting from any risk whatsoever, including risks incurred as a result of armed conflict, riots or other public disorders whether such coverage is effected through a system of governmental guarantees and indemnities, through the partial assumption of the risks by the State under a deductible or excess loss arrangement, through commercial or national insurance or through mutual insurance arrangements.

2. Each Member State should adopt whatever criteria it deems most suitable for defining the items of movable cultural property within its territory which should be given the protection envisaged in this Recommendation by reason of their archaeological, historical, artistic, scientific or technical value.

## II. GENERAL PRINCIPLES

3. The movable cultural property thus defined includes objects belonging either to the

State or public bodies or to private bodies or individuals. Since all this property constitutes an important element of the cultural heritage of the nations concerned, the prevention and coverage of the various risks, such as damage, deterioration and loss, should be considered as a whole, even though the solutions adopted may vary from case to case.

4. The growing perils which threaten the movable cultural heritage, should indicate all those responsible for protecting it, in whatever capacity, to play their part: staff of national and local administrations in charge of safeguarding cultural property, administrators and curators of museums and similar institutions, private owners and those responsible for religious buildings, art and antique dealers, security experts, services responsible for the suppression of crime, customs officials and the other public authorities involved.

5. The cooperation of the public is essential for truly effective protection. The public and private bodies responsible for information and teaching should strive to instil general awareness of the importance of cultural property, the dangers to which it is exposed, and the need to safeguard it.

6. Cultural property is liable to deterioration as a result of poor conditions of storage, exhibition, transport and environment (unfavourable lighting, temperature or humidity, atmospheric pollution), which in the long run may have more serious effects than accidental damage or occasional vandalism. Suitable environmental conditions should consequently be maintained in order to ensure the material security of cultural property. The responsible specialists should include in the inventories data on the physical state of the objects and recommendations concerning the requisite environmental conditions.

7. The prevention of risks also calls for the development of conservation techniques and restoration workshops and the installation of effective protection systems in museums and other institutions possessing collections of movable cultural property. Each Member State should endeavour to ensure that the most suitable measures are taken in accordance with local circumstances.

8. Offences concerning works of art and other cultural property are increasing in some countries, most frequently being linked to fraudulent transfers across frontiers. Thefts and plunder are organized systematically and on a large scale. Acts of vandalism are also increasing. To combat these forms of criminal activity, be they of an organized nature or the action of individuals, strict control measures are necessary. Since fakes can be used for theft or the fraudulent transformation of authentic objects, measures must also be taken to prevent their circulation.

9. Protection and the prevention of risks are much more important than compensation in the event of damage or loss, since the essential purpose is to preserve the cultural heritage, not to replace by sums of money objects which are irreplaceable.

10. Because of the considerable increase in the risks resulting during transport and temporary exhibition, from environmental changes, inept handling, faulty packaging or

other unfavourable conditions, adequate coverage against damage or loss is essential. The cost of risk coverage should be reduced through the rational management by museums and similar institutions of insurance contracts or by means of full or partial governmental guarantees.

## III. MEASURES RECOMMENDED

11. In accordance with the principles and norms set out above Member States should take all necessary steps, in conformity with their legislation and constitutional system, to protect movable cultural property effectively and, in the case of transport in particular, should ensure the application of the necessary measures of care and conservation and the coverage of the risks incurred.

### Measures for the Prevention of Risks in Museums and Other Similar Institutions

12. Member States should take all necessary steps to ensure adequate protection for cultural property in museums and similar institutions. In particular, they should:

(a) encourage the systematic inventorying and cataloguing of cultural property, with the fullest possible details and in accordance with methods specially developed for the purpose (standardized niches, photographs—and also, if possible, colour photographs—and, as appropriate, microfilms). Such an inventory is useful when it is desired to determine damage or deterioration to cultural property. With such documentation the necessary information can be given, with all due precautions, to the national and international authorities responsible for combating thefts, illicit trading and the circulation of fakes;

(b) encourage, as appropriate, the standardized identifications of movable cultural property using unobtrusive means offered by contemporary technology;

(c) urge the museums and similar institutions to reinforce the prevention of risks by a comprehensive system of practical security measures and technical installations and to ensure that all cultural property is kept, exhibited and transported in such a way as to protect it from all elements likely to damage or destroy it, including in particular heat, light, humidity, pollution, the various chemical and biological agents, vibration and shock;

(d) provide the museums and similar institutions for which they are responsible with the necessary funds for implementing the measures set out in subparagraph (c) above.

(e) take the necessary steps to ensure that all the tasks associated with the conservation of movable cultural property are carried out in accordance with the traditional techniques best suited to the particular cultural property and the most advanced scientific methods and technology; for the purpose, a suitable system for training and the vetting of professional qualifications should be established, in order to ensure that all those involved possess the required level of competence. The facilities for this should be strengthened or, if necessary, established. If appropriate, for the sake of economy, the establishment of regional conservation and restoration centres is recommended;

(f) provide suitable training for supporting staff (including security staff) and draw up guidelines for such staff, laying down standards for the performance of their duties;

(g) encourage regular training for protection, conservation and security staff;

(h) ensure that the staff of museums and similar institutions also receive the necessary training to enable them, in the event of disasters, to cooperate effectively in the rescue operations carried out by the competent public services;

(i) encourage the publication and dissemination to those responsible, if necessary in confidential form, of the latest technical and scientific information on all aspects of the protection, conservation and security of movable cultural property;

(j) issue performance standards for all security equipment for museums and public and private collections and encourage their application.

13. No effort should be spared to avoid giving in to ransom demands, so as to discourage the theft or illegal appropriation of movable cultural property carried out for that purpose. The persons or institutions concerned should consider ways and means of making this policy known.

**Private Collections**

14. Member States should also, in conformity with their legislation and constitutional system, facilitate the protection of collections belonging to private bodies or individuals by:

(a) inviting the owners to make inventories of their collections, to communicate the inventories to the official services responsible for the protection of the cultural heritage and, if the situation requires, to grant access to the competent official curators and technicians in order to study and advise on safeguarding measures;

(b) if appropriate, providing for incentives to the owners, such as assistance for the conservation of items listed in the inventories or appropriate fiscal measures;

(c) studying the possibility of granting fiscal benefits to those who donate or bequeath cultural property to museums or similar institutions;

(d) entrusting an official body (the department responsible for museums or the police) with the organization of an advisory service for private owners on security installations and other protective measures, including fire protection.

**Movable Cultural Property Situated in Religious Buildings and Archaeological Sites**

15. To ensure that movable cultural property situated in religious buildings and archaeological sites is suitably preserved and protected against theft and plunder, Member States should encourage the construction of installations for storing it and the application of special security measures. Such measures should be in proportion to the value of the property and the extent of the risks to which it is exposed. If appropriate, governments should provide technical and financial assistance for this purpose. In view of the special

significance of movable cultural property situated in religious buildings, Member States and the competent authorities should endeavour to provide for the proper protection and presentation of such property where it is located.

**International Exchanges**

16. Since movable cultural property is particularly exposed, during transport and temporary exhibition, to risks of damage which can arise from inept handling, faulty packaging, poor conditions during temporary storage or climatic changes, as well as inadequate reception arrangements, special measures of protection are required. In the case of international exchanges Member States should:

(a) take the necessary measures to ensure that appropriate conditions of protection and care during transport and exhibition as well as adequate coverage of risks are specified and agreed on between the parties concerned. Governments through whose territory the cultural property will transit should provide assistance, if so requested;

(b) encourage the institutions concerned to:

  (i) ensure that cultural property is transported, packed and handled in accordance with the highest standards. The measures to be taken to this effect could include the determination of experts of the most appropriate form of packaging, as well as the type and timing of transport, it is recommended that, where appropriate, the responsible curator of the leading museum accompany the property during transport and certify its conditions; the institutions responsible for the shipping and packing of the objects should attach a list describing their physical appearance, and the receiving institutions should check the objects against those lists;

  (ii) take appropriate measures to prevent any direct or indirect damage which might arise from the temporary or permanent overcrowding of the exhibition premises;

  (iii) agree, where necessary, on the methods to be used for measuring, recording and regulating the degree of humidity in order to maintain the relative humidity within definite limits, and on the measures to be taken to protect light-sensitive objects (exposure to daylight, type of lamp to be used, maximum level of illumination in lux, methods used to measure and control this level);

(c) simplify the administrative formalities relating to the lawful movement of cultural property and arrange for appropriate identification of crates and other forms of packaging containing cultural property;

(d) take steps to protect cultural property in transit or temporarily imported for the purpose of cultural exchanges, and in particular facilitate rapid customs clearance in suitable premises, which should be situated close to, and if possible, on the premises of the institution concerned, and ensure that clearance is effected with all the desirable precautions; and

(e) whenever necessary, give instructions to their diplomatic and consular representatives to enable them to take effective action to accelerate customs procedures and ensure the protection of cultural property during transport.

**Education and Information**

17. To ensure that the population as a whole becomes aware of the value of cultural property and of the need to protect it, particularly with a view to the preservation of their cultural identity, Member States should encourage the competent authorities at national, regional or local level to:

(a) provide children, young people and adults with the means of acquiring knowledge and respect for movable cultural property, using all available educational and information resources for that purpose;
(b) draw the attention of the public at large by every possible means to:
   (i) the significance and importance of cultural property, but without stressing the purely commercial value of that property;
   (ii) the opportunities available to them for participating in the activities undertaken by the competent authorities in order to protect such property.

**Control Measures**

18. To combat thefts, illegal excavations, vandalism and the use of fakes, Member States should, where the situation demands, establish or strengthen services specifically responsible for the prevention and suppression of these offences.

19. Member States should, where the situation calls for it, take the necessary measures to:

(a) provide for sanctions or any appropriate measures, whether under the penal or civil code or administrative or other measures, in the case of the theft, pillage, receiving or illegal appropriation of movable cultural property, and of damage intentionally caused to such property; these sanctions or measures should take into account the gravity of the offence;
(b) ensure better coordination between all services and sectors working for the prevention of offences concerning movable cultural property and organize a system of rapid dissemination of information on such offences, including information on fakes, among official bodies and the various sectors concerned, such as museum curators and art and antique dealers;
(c) ensure proper conditions for the safeguarding of movable cultural property by taking steps to counter the neglect and abandon to which it is very often exposed and which is conducive to its deterioration.

20. Member States should also encourage private collectors and art and antique dealers to transmit all information concerning fakes to the official bodies mentioned in paragraph 19(b).

**Measures to Improve the Financing of Risk Coverage**

**Governmental Guarantees**

21. Member States should:

(a) give special attention to the problem of covering adequately the risks to which movable cultural property is exposed during transport and temporary exhibitions;

(b) in particular, consider instituting in any legislative, statutory or other form, a system of governmental guarantees such as those which exist in certain countries, or a system of partial assumption of the risks by the State or any community concerned with a view to covering an insurance franchise deductible or an excess of loss;
(c) within the framework of such systems and in the forms mentioned above, provide for compensation to lenders in the event of damage to, or the deterioration, alteration or loss of cultural objects loaned for the purpose of exhibition in museums or similar institutions. The provisions instituting these systems should specify the conditions and procedures governing the payment of such compensation.

22. The provisions concerning governmental guarantees should not apply to cultural property which is the object of transactions for commercial purposes.

### Measures at the Level of Museums and Similar Institutions

23. Member States should also urge museums and other similar institutions to apply the principles of risks management, comprising the determination, classification, assessment, control and financing of risks of all kinds.

24. The risk management programme of all institutions which have taken out insurance should include the internal drafting of a procedures manual, periodic surveys on types of risks and the probable maximum loss, analysis of contracts and rates, market studies and a competitive bidding procedure. A person or body should be specifically entrusted with risk management.

## IV. INTERNATIONAL COOPERATION

25. Member States should:

(a) collaborate with inter-governmental and non-governmental organizations competent in regard to the prevention and coverage of risks;
(b) strengthen at international level cooperation between official bodies responsible for the suppression of thefts and illicit trading in cultural property and for the discovery of fakes, and, in particular, urge these bodies to circulate rapidly among themselves, through machinery provided for this purpose, all useful information on illegal activities;
(c) if necessary conclude international agreements for cooperation in regard to legal aid and the prevention of offences;
(d) take part in the organization of international training courses in the conservation and restoration of movable cultural property, and in risk management, and ensure that they are regularly attended by their specialized staff;
(e) establish, in collaboration with the specialized international organizations, ethical and technical standards in the fields covered by the present Recommendation and encourage the exchange of scientific and technical information, particularly on innovations relating to the protection and conservation of movable cultural property.

# APPENDIX II

## SOME REPORTS FROM NEWSPAPERS AND PERIODICALS

### 1) 100 PAINTINGS STOLEN FROM MUSEUM
**(The Statesman:** 25-7-1970)

A Central Bureau of Investigation team from Delhi had been summoned to investigate the theft of rare art pieces costing several lakhs of rupees from the Chandigarh Museum on Wednesday night.

The museum had lost over 100 rare and priceless miniature paintings of Mughal, Persian, Kangra, Rajkot and Basohli schools. The museum has a collection of about 3,000 such paintings according to its Director, Mr. Sushil Sarkar.

Mr. S.N. Bhanot, Home Secretary of the Chandigarh Union Territory, told reporters this evening that the CBI team was expected here by tomorrow. "It is however not yet known whether the CBI team will handle the investigation or just guide the local police in the matter", he added.

The administration has sent messages throughout the country to alert the authorities.

Mr. Bhanot who visited the museum with the Chief Commissioner Mr. B.P. Bagchi, said the theft was noticed on July 23 morning, when a senior staff member of the museum opened the galleries.

According to Mr. Sarkar, the galleries are locked at 6 p.m., in the presence of the guard on duty, when the museum is closed for the day. There is a nine-man police guard which keeps round-the-clock vigil of the museum.

The Home Secretary said preliminary investigations showed that the thief could escape through a door on the eastern side of the museum building. The door could be opened by unscrewing a latch of the door. This was confirmed when a screw-driver and some screws were found near the door.

The galleries, where the paintings were hung, are on the first floor of the building.

According to Mr. Bhanot, the thieves must have taken three to four hours to do their job. The paintings had been removed from the frames "very neatly", he said.

After removing the paintings the frmes were put in a drk corner on the eastern side of the building.

**Safety Steps:** Mr. Bhanot swaid, for the present the administration has reinforced the gurds. But, it was thinking of introducing other modern devices, like electronic bells to ensure greater sfety of the museum.

The book vlue of the stolen pintings was below Rs. 20,000, he sid. He sid it wasdifficult to scertin the present market vlue of the paintings. However, Mr.Sarkar said the internationl market vlue could be easily between Rs. 3 and Rs. 4 lakhs.

The museum, before it was transferred to the present building, was housed in an adjoining building of School of Arts.

Some of the rare and priceless pieces of art in the museum were collected through Dr. M.S. Randhawa, former Chief Commissioner of Chandigarh.

The museum has been closed until primary investigations are completed.

**IDOL THEFT IS BIG BUSINESS IN M.P.**
**The Times of India:** 22-7-1971)

By all accounts idol theft is big business in Madhya Pradesh which abounds in antiques dating form the Buddhist and Ashoka period to the Moghul days. That some antique dealers have grown affluent from this illicit trade is evident from the fact that some of them have been kidnapped by bandits for ransom. In a recent case in the Gwalior region, a ransom of Rs. 8 lakyhs was demanded. Nobody knows for certain how mucyh money changed hands, but knowlegeable sources put the figure at Rs. 5 lakhs.

**Influential Men Involved:** The banits themselves are not known to be directly ihnvolved in the lifting of iddols. But some influentil people andd politicians are suspected to have a hand in this nefarious business which has a wide network of agents and subagents, operating through petty criminals who lift idols and other curious for comparatively small payments. some low-paid Government employees are also involved in this racket. Only recently a vaccinator in Vidisha district was prosecuted.

The Buddhist Stupa at Sanchi, the temples of Khajuraho and the forts of Gwalior and Mandu have attracted worldwide tourist interest. Besides, there are exquisite antiques in Mandsaur, Shivpuri, Ujjain, Dhar, Shahdol, Guna, Damoh, Tikamgarh, Satna, RAtlam, Rajgarh, Durg, Mandla and Rewa districts But the arrangements made for their preservation and protection are woefully inadequate.

Officials concerned with the prevention of thefts claim that the incidence of idol lifting has come down considerably over the past two years. But they avoid giving any statistics. On the other hand, archaeological officials have made a fetish of secrecy, notwithstanding the fact that the clandestine trade in curios has admittedly a turnover of lakhs of rupees.

Going by the available data, in 1969 and 1970 the number of reported cases of idol theft was 51 and 38 against 89 and 105 in the preceding two years. But it is a moot point whether all thefts have been reported.

Among the important thefts in 1969 was the lifting of the idol of Radha Nath in January from the court premises at Rajnagar in Chhatarpur district. Prompt police investigation resulted in the prosecution of four culprits.

Hardly six months later five idols of Deviji were removed from a temple at Sidhi. Here too the culprits were apprehended. An idol of Mahavir Swami was stolen from a temple at Rafatpura village in Morena district. Four persons were arrested and their car was impounded. The case is pending in a court.

Seven culprits were taken into custody by the delhi Police in Guna district after they had stolen two stone idols from Chanderi. In Gwalior district one person was caught while removing two Ganesh idols from Singhpur forest in March 1970.

Curiously, authentic information on the number of cases which have resulted in convictions is lacking. The archaeological outfit, such as it is in Bhopal, apparently does not possess relevant information or is unwilling to disclose it for reasons best known to itself. The only piece of corroborative evidence about the decline in such crimes has come from the police.

On the basis of random sampling, it is claimed that only two thefts have been reported in the February-May period this year against 12 during the corresponding period last year. This by itself, it can be argued, does not mean except perhaps as a pointer to greater awareness on the part of the authorities of their responsibility to protect the country's cultural heritage. Even archaeological authorities point out that till recently the police, especially the lower ranks, paid scant attention to this aspect in their preoccupation with the maintenance of law and order.

**Police Circular:** To overcome this apathy, the police headquarters had issued a circular two years ago to the police stations in Madhya Pradesh, drawing their attention to the need for preventing theft of antiques and protecting monuments.

It is not the police alone who have of late been evincing interest in this field. Early last year the Shukla Ministry issued an ordinance amending the Ancient Monuments and Archaeological Sites and Remains Act. This ordinance, later replaced by an Act, provides for stringent punishment. The term of imprisonment has been raised from one year to three years and the fine from Rs. 1,000 to Rs. 10,000. Further, a minimum prison term of six months has been stipulated, unless the trial court specifies the reason for not awarding it.

The amended Act makes it obligatory for people to declare the curios in their possession and to intimate to the authorities sale, purchase and gifting away of antiques. The Government has also assumed powers to acquire antiques from private individuals if they are considered to be of national importance. What is more important, one of the amendments makes theft of idols and curios a cognisable offence, enabling the authorities to take prompt action on their own without formal complaints.

A list of monuments in the State has been obtained from the Archaeological Department and sent to the districts to enable the police to keep an effective watch on them. Circle inspectors supervise the investigation of theft of idols. Important cases of theft are investigated by a gazetted police officer. Cases involving inter-State criminals are taken up by CID inspectors. Over the past few years eight cases were investigated by the CID.

Though it is too early to say how far the amended Act has helped curb idol thefts, the authorities certainly can no longer complain of lack of powers. How the powers are being actually exercised is, at least at the moment, a debatable point. All the same, it is patent that such thefts cannot be controlled by the authorities alone. Public cooperation is necessary on a much wider scale for keeping the pirates away from the monuments.

As the archaeological monuments are mostly located in deserted and secluded places, the police find the protection chore tough. Besides, the supervision arrangements made by the Archaeological Department are not up to the mark. Caretakers of the Archaeological Department are supposed to look after a very wide area. This explains why thefts are either not detected in time or are reported to the police after considerable delay.

Another factor which hampers efficient supervision of the monuments is the lack of correlation between the Archaeological Department's zones and the State boundaries. For instance, the two important sites in Madhya Pradesh—Khajuraho and Barhut—come under the Agra circle. Likewise the Chattisgarh area is looked after by the Hyderabad circle of the Archaeological Department. The central zone, with its headquarters at Bhopal, is responsible for the monuments in the Madhya Bharat region and in parts of Maharashtra and Rajasthan.

These zones are no doubt based on archaeological classification. But they do not make coordination easy. Even within the the same zone, the archaeological authorities have to depend on the police of different States.

**Half-Hearted Replies:** The central zone has 320 listed monuments and sites spread over three States, most of them being in M.P. Of these the more important are Sanchi, Badhopathari, Gavaspur, Udaigiri, Chanderi, extensive areas around Gwalior, Bagh caves and Mandu. At Mandu part of the site is looked after by the State Government authorities. The dependence of the archaeological authorities on the police and the people becomes evident from the fact that for the 320 monuments and sites in the central zone there are only 150 attendants. A substantial number of sites have no attendants at all. Plans are under way to raise the number of attendants to 350.

Have all possible protective steps been taken with the available resources? Half-hearted and laconic replies by the archaeological authorities to queries hardly inspire confidence that all that is possible is being done. It is claimed, for instance, that the Department has carried out a number of successful raids in cooperation with the police. How many, where and with what results? No details are provided.

Such reticence is hard to understand in the wake of the nationwide interest aroused by the recent theft of the Vishnu idol from Chamba in Himachal Pradesh and the inter-State hunt that led to its recovery from a godown in Bombay. It was with considerable difficulty that this reporter could elicit the otherwise heartening piece of information that one of the raids led to the recovery of a truckload of exquisite stone-heads and idols in Gwalior last year. Again no information is available on the action taken against the culprits.

Meanwhile, the Archaeological Department plans repairs to monuments this year at an estimated cost of Rs. 1 lakh. The total annual budget of the central zone is Rs. 6 lakhs, admittedly too low for the work it has to handle. As more funds become available, documentation with iconographic details and photographic records of the monuments in the zone are proposed to be undertaken.

Provision of enclosed shelters for safe custody and display of sculptures at selected sites is urgently needed. At Chanderi, for instance, it is stated that 2,500 exquisite idols were collected by the Departmental authorities in the course of a few months last year. A shelter is being built there as also at two other sites in Vidisha district. About 25 such shelters are needed in the central zone itself. Though such shelters are not classified as museums, they meet the requirements of display and study by scholars.

### 3) LAWYER, 4 OTHERS HELD ON IDOL-LIFTING CHARGE
**(The Times of India:** 4-9-1971)

A lawyer and a grandson of a former MLA from Mathura are among the five persons who have been arrested in connection with the recent theft of ancient Durga idol from a temple in Itora village on the outskirts of the city.

According to the police, the arrested men belong to an inter-State gang of idol lifters. Besides the Durga idol, a small statue of Vishnu stolen from Janger village, 75 km from here, has been recovered from them.

The Durga idol, which apparently belongs to the Gupta period, is 1.20 metres high and 0.75 metre wide. Carved in black sandstone, the exquisite statue has been attracting devotees for centuries.

**Idol Replaced:** It is stated that a villager, Karuna Shankar, who was held earlier on smuggling charges, was among those engaged by the gang to steal the idol after a Delhi firm offered Rs. 60,000 for it. Ten per cent of the amount is said to have been given as advance to the gang.

Members of the gang entered the temple one night after breaking open steel door of the temple and stole the idol. It was first hidden in a pond and then buried in a field.

For a few days, only the temple authorities knew about the theft. The priest, perhaps fearing that the importance of the shrine might be reduced, put up another idol and wrapped it in pieces of cloth in such a way that no one could notice the difference. A report was, however, lodged with the police.

The police got their first clue when they traced two residents of Delhi, alleged to be members of the gang, to a small hotel in the Daresi area. Their movements were closely watched. A few days later, the two men held a secret meeting with three others in a hut near Akola village. The police raided the hut and arrested all the five men. The idol was recovered subsequently.

The lawyer is stated to have admitted that he was responsible for the theft of numerous idols. Some months ago, he is reported to have sold a truckload of statues to art dealers in Delhi.

The MLA's grandson is said to have told the police about the 'modus operandi' of the gang and disclosed the names of several members of the gang in Delhi, Mathura and Hathras.

**4) IDOL STOLEN AT GUN-POINT**
**(National Herald: 30-6-1971)**

A stone image of Lord Mahavira, dated eleventh century A.D., is reported to be the latest victim of the antique thieves. The Jain image, installed in the Nasia Jain Mandir, about one-and-half kms from Etawah city (Uttar Pradesh), was stolen in the early hours of June 25 at gun-point by a group of eight men. While they were taking the image from the temple to a car a furlong away they dropped the idol breaking it into two.

According to the superintendent of police, Etawah, the thieves left the lower part of the image and escaped with the torso with the head intact. The image was about three-and-half feet in height.

The SP told the Herald over the telephone that police parties had been sent to Agra and Delhi. In addition wireless messages had been sent to other cities. A spokesman of Delhi police, however, said that they had so far not been contacted by any officer of the UP police. "Maybe, they are making independent inquiries in some part of the city", he added. But he admitted that a letter from the Etawah police was received by them in the late afternoon today.

The Mahavira image bears an inscription which specifically mentions the date 1111 Samvat. The current Samvat year is 2028. The temple, in which the image was installed, according to the local Jain tradition, was constructed in 1095 Samvat (1070 A.D.).

According to the report lodged by the temple authorities, the antique vandals were armed—at least two of them with guns. The chowkidar of the temple was threatened by the gunmen who kept him pinned down to the ground while the other six took out the five-maund image.

So far there is no trace of the image or the culprits.

**Vandalism in Jammu:** According to a PTI message from Jammu, four idols have been stolen from the Lakshmi Narayan and Gupt-Ganga temples situated in the picturesque valley of Bhaderwah, known as 'Little Kashmir', adjacent to the Chamba district of Himachal Pradesh. Bhaderwah is about 225 kilometres from Jammu.

Among the stolen idols is a blackstone image of a Naga ruler which bears a Sanskrit inscription in the Brahmi script resembling Gupta characters. The sculpture, according to the inscription, belonged to the third century A.D.

The other three idols are of Goddess Lakshmi (sculpted in white marble), Satya Narayan (in black stone) and Nandi (in bronze). Police investigations have drawn a blank.

**5) MAHAVIRA STATUE 900-YEAR-OLD**
**(National Herald:** 1-7-1971)

The image of Lord Mahavira stolen from Etawah was today identified as belonging to the Gahadavala school which flourished during the tenth and eleventh centuries in the area between Allahabad in the east and Delhi in the west.

An expert said today that this school was contemporaneous with the Chandela, Chauhan and Parmar schools which flowered briefly around Khajuraho, Ajmer and Indore, respectively.

The Mahavira image is in Kayotsarga attitude—a rigid standing pose with hands dangling. The image, as far as public memory goes, had been armless but when the vandals dropped it on the road the upper body was separated from the lower part.

The expert, when shown a file picture of the image, as it stood in the temple, explained that the austere looking image was adorned all-round to make the whole aesthetically more acceptable. This is the general characteristic of Jain images.

A lotus halo forms the background to the head with an elephant on each side—a sign of auspiciousness. On the chest the image bears the Srivatsa sign, the mark of a Mahapurusha. Over the head, the usual tri-umbrella and the tree—which are associated with Jain images—are missing like the arms.

Running parallel to the torso, on each side, are miniature images of tirthankaras—those "who are as holy as the holy spots (tirthas)"—12 on each side. At the feet of the Lord are four attendants—two holding chauris or murchhal.

The expert explained that in case of Mahavira images, in addition to the two attendants, as in this case, an image of the donor and his or her spouse was also provided. This lower part, with the two attendants and the donors' images, has been left behind by the thieves.

Another expert expressed the opinion that originally the image could have belonged to Bateshwar or Chandwar—the two centres where the best of the Gahadavala idols were sculpted.

**Idol in Delhi?:** The Etawah police believe that the 11th century sculpture of Lord Mahavira, lifted from the Nasia Jain Temple last Friday, must have found its way to the Delhi antique market.

The crime branch of the Delhi Police has been filled in with all details of the theft, according to a police official in Etawah. A police party from there is already here.

The temple was robbed around 2.30 a.m. last Friday. But the temple authorities did not inform the police till 7.30 a.m., according to the Etawah police.

A police official told the Herald tonight that but for the five-hour delay in reporting the robbery, the police would have nabbed the culprits within hours by blocking the exit points. The police had all details of the vehicles involved in the crime, including their number-plates.

The Etawah police have registered a case of dacoity, as the idol was lifted at gun-point by a gang of eight men who came in a jeep and a car.

Reports of recent dacoities in the temples in Agra and Etawah areas have been received here. It is believed that the Jain temple job was handled by a gang operating in Etah and Agra, with links in Delhi.

Etawah police parties, sent out to Etah and Agra, have collected information on various idol cases in the areas and on the gangs active there. This information is now being passed on to the Delhi police (crime branch) to pursue the investigation.

### 6) STOLEN IDOL SOLD IN U.S. FOR Rs. 75 LAKHS
**(The Hindu: 1-11-1971)**

The Tamil Nadu Police tonight claimed to have unearthed a gang of racketeers who had managed to smuggle out a 1200 year-old famous Nataraja idol from an ancient temple in Sivapuram (ten km from Kumbakonam) to New York.

The 1.4 metre idol of the early Chola period has been sold to an art lover in New York for a sum of $ one million (Rs. 75 lakhs), police said.

Facts came to light when police arrested on Thursday Thilagar of Kuttalam (Thanjavur district) who narrated the startling story of how the idol made its way from Kumbakonam to Madras, then to Bombay and finally to New York, passing innumerable hands.

The Nataraja idol, police said, was among the six other idols recovered when some local people unearthed them in a place, six miles from Kumbakonam in 1952 (other idols were Sivakamasundari, Somaskanda, Vinayagar Tirugnana Sambandar and another Amman). The temple trustees at Sivapuram to whom the idols were handed over, finding them mutilated and tarnished, got them back after being polished by some famous Sthapathis.

Police said that moulds of Nataraja and Somaskanda idols were taken subsequently by some men who had links with Bombay racketeers in idols smuggling and fakes were cast from the idols. The fakes along with the other four idols were returned to the trustees who installed them later in the temple. The original idols of Nataraja and Somaskanda, police said, must have been smuggled out to Bombay and then to New York.

The Sivapuram idols attracted the attention of many people and the State Information and Publicity Department published pictures of the idols at the time of the First World Tamil Conference in Madras. Police began to suspect the genuineness of the two idols (Nataraja and Somaskanda) when the Curator of the Madras Museum and an expert British archaeologist Mr. Douglas Barrett who visited the Sivapuram temple in 1961, traced some differences between the idols installed and photographs of the originals they had seen.

Police assert that the Somaskanda idol must be somewhere abroad and hope to bring it to light soon.

The Tamil Nadu Government was considering a proposal to set up a special cell to prevent idol thefts and trace stolen ones, police said.

The investigation leading to the unearthing of the smuggled Nataraja idol was conducted by Mr. Chandramouli, Deputy Superintendent of Police under instructions from Mr. Krishnaraj, D.I.G. (C.I.D.) and Mr. K.V. Gnanasambandam, Superintendent of Police (C.I.D.).

**7) BIG HAUL OF STOLEN IDOLS**
**(National Herald:** 26-9-1975)

The police today reported a haul of over 50 stolen idols from godowns of antique dealers in Sunder Nagar, Karol Bagh and South Extension areas and in Chatterpur, near Mehrauli.

It is learnt that about eight of these idols were found buried under earth in Chatterpur area. The police got some clues during raids of the city godowns of local antique dealers.

The haul included a bronze statue of Edward VII, larger than life-size, recovered from a godown in Christian Colony on Original Road, Karol Bagh, and a former maharaja figures in the police investigations.

A Sunder Nagar antique dealer and one of his employees have been arrested. The police would not disclose their names or details of the case on the plea that it would hamper their investigation. They are looking for another local antique dealer.

Among the pieces recovered from Sunder Nagar godown was a statue of Ganesh in a dance pose, which was stolen from Ghazipur, UP, in 1969. It was found slightly damaged. Thirty other idols were recovered from two godowns in Sunder Nagar area. A house-cum-godown in South Extension area accounted for 12 stolen antique pieces in the haul.

Among other notable pieces are a Ganesh statue in bronze and a stone idol of Shiva and Uma, dating back to the 11th century.

A crime branch official said that organised gangs were operating throughout the country for lifting the idols from ancient temples and places of historical importance.

**8) IDOL-LIFTER FOUND UNCONSCIOUS IN MYSORE TEMPLE**
**(The Times of India:** 30-12-1975)

A thief who intended to steal the "mangalsutra" of the deity in Katte Parameswari temple was found unconscious in the sanctum sanctorum by the temple priest the next morning in Madagere village, Mysore district, recently.

Ramgowada, 35, managed to open the temple door one night when no one was in sight. But, he told the police, the moment he touched the mangalsutra he "received a powerful electric shock" and fell unconscious.

Giving details of the incident, the Inspector General of Police, Mr. C.V.S. Rao, said today that temple thefts had taken place in Karnataka at the rate of one a day in the past two years. Some thefts had also taken place in mosques and churches.

**Idols Stolen:** Three hundred and two cases of thefts and burglaries from places of worship were reported in the first 10 months of this year as against 302 cases in 1974. Jewels, cash and idols were stolen.

A priest and a servant at the Lakshmi Narsimhaswamy temple at Nuggehalli, Hassan district, had been found killed. Police action led to the conviction of four culprits.

The priest of the Gadarebetta temple was found murdered in March. One person, caught by villagers and handed over to the police, is facing trial.

The incidence of temple thefts has been the highest in South Kanara, Shimoga and Bangalore districts, accounting for nearly a third of the total number of offences of this nature. Of the 32 cases of idol thefts reported in 1974, 20 ended in conviction.

## 9) STEPS TO CHECK ANTIQUE SMUGGLING

**(Patriot: 16-4-1976)**

All international airports and seaports in the country are to have an archaeologist stationed there for identifying art objects attempted to be smuggled.

This is one of the several steps being taken by the Government to check smuggling of antiques.

Besides, all sculptures and pieces of antique value at the Centrally-protected monuments and sites are being documented. The ultimate aim of the combined efforts of documentation and registration of antiques is to prepare a national register of India's antique wealth.

For the convenience of tourists and exporters the Archaeological Survey of India has been issuing non-antique certificates for objects like handicrafts and replicas which are less than hundred years old.

The Government is taking various steps to implement the Antiques and Art Treasures Act 1972, which came into force from 5 April, and which is meant to regulate trade in antiques and art treasures and also to prevent smuggling and fraudulent dealings in antiques.

**Suitable Machinery:** The Archaeological Survey of India is setting up a suitable machinery with the help of all State Governments and Union Territories, for the enforcement of the law.

A training scheme for registering officers was also conducted by the Survey simultaneously at four centres—Bombay, Calcutta, Madras and New Delhi—to achieve this objective.

The task of issuing licences to dealers who are doing business in antiques and of regulating the trade in antiques devolves directly on the Archaeological Survey of India which has appointed Licensing Officers in Bombay, Calcutta, Madras, New Delhi, Patna, Agra, Srinagar, Vadodara, Bhopal, Hyderabad and Bangalore. Their jurisdiction covers the entire country except Sikkim. The dealers who will be given licences for carrying out business in antiques have to maintain stock registers and photo albums for their collections.

**Registration:** Under the Act persons including foreigners holding antiques have to register them with the registering officers of their area.

In most of the States the registering officers have been appointed with the Director of Archaeology as overall incharge of the scheme of registering the antiques. In certain cases some other State officials have been appointed for the purpose.

In Delhi an additional magistrate in the office of the Deputy Commissioner will coordinate the work of registering the antiques.

The Act does not contemplate any export of antiques or art objects by any person other than the Central Government or an authority or agency authorised by the Union Government.

### 10) INDIA SECURES CUSTODY OF NATARAJA IDOL
**(The Times of India:** 15-5-1976)

India has secured the custody of the 10th century bronze Nataraja idol stolen from the Shivapuram temple in Tamil Nadu. But for the next 10 years the idol has been loaned to the Norton Simon Foundation for purposes of exhibition in the United States.

Meanwhile a former Indian citizen, Mr. Manulal Narang, has been arrested in London for receiving sculptures valued at £ 150,000 stolen from an Indian temple. The sculptures—two tall sandstone pillars—were recovered from a London warehouse.

Mr. Narang changed his nationality sometime ago and is described as a consular official at the Liberian Embassy in Paris. But his plea for diplomatic immunity was rejected and he was set free on bail to appear in court on May 28.

The Nataraja was one of the five idols discovered in 1956 during excavations at the Shivapuram temple site. It was sent to a restorer who switched it with a replica.

The idol changed hands several times and was smuggled out of India in 1969. It was eventually bought by the Norton Simon Foundation for $ 1 million.

In November 1974 the idol was traced to a London artist to whom it had been sent for restoration. The Government of India immediately sought an injunction against its removal and the idol has since been in the vault of a London bank.

**New Agreement:** Under the new agreement reached between the Government of India and the Norton Simon Foundation, the idol was flown to the United States yesterday.

Superstition has it that the idol brings ill-luck to whoever owns it. The cleaner in south India who replaced it with a fake lost both his legs. One owner got into serious financial difficulties and another lost his wife.

The flight of the idol to America was also accompanied by drama. The security firm engaged to carry it to London's Heathrow Airport declined the job on the plea that the risk was too high. Scotland Yard obliged by escorting it to the airport. There one international airline demanded full idemnity before it undertook to fly it to America. Finally, an American airline came to the rescue.

## 11) ANTIQUE BUSINESS
**(The Indian Express: 14-6-1976)**

The Ordinance issued on June 4 amending the Antiquities and Art Treasures Act, 1972, goes a long way to remove the genuine grievances about some of the provisions of the original Act. The time given to the dealers to apply for licences has been extended by four months. The production of photographs is made obligatory only in respect of such antiques or class of antiques as the Government may specify by notification. The press note on the Ordinance has also given an assurance that the Government proposes to exempt from registration many types of articles usually kept by ordinary private collectors, such as coins, medals and jewellery pieces. Fresh items requiring registration would be notified from time to time so that the entire process of registration may be done progressively without causing hardship to any individual or institution.

In spite of these significant concessions, the dealers have kept up a hue and cry against the Act. Other vested interests also have been lobbying to water down the salutary provisions of the measure which was long overdue. They have even started a scare that, rather than submit to the new rules, possessors of precious art objects may destroy them. The Government has done well to warn the parties concerned that any attempt to destroy such things will not be tolerated. If some people find the formalities of keeping antiques too difficult and expensive, why don't they turn them over to the safe keeping of museums? Displaying antiquary in well-appointed drawing rooms is a craze of the new rich. If they want to show off, let them accept the legal obligations.

Those who are crying hoarse against the Act were the least concerned when priceless images and other cultural heirlooms were being smuggled out of the country. As the Government press note points out, the illicit traffic would not have been possible "without the help and connivance of at least a section of the antique dealers". While taking care to avoid unnecessary hardship or harassment to law-abiding private collectors and traders, the Government must stand firm against pressures to make things easier for the black sheep in the antique business. Vigilance is also necessary to ensure that antiques in the possession of certain public institutions, exempted from registration under the Ordinance, are not misused or spirited away by fake substitution as has happened in some cases.

## 12) FROM GODOWN TO MUSEUM
**(The Times of India: 10-9-1976)**

Priceless bronze, antique sculptures, rare ivories and wood works are among the 60 antiquities handed over by the Bombay customs to the Prince of Wales Museum on Tuesday.

Among these is a 12th century 22.4-cm tall rare Nepalese bronze of Vaikuntha-Kamalja, one of the finest and rarest pieces in the world.

An eighth-century Siamese bronze Buddha, 28-cm high, and the personal seal of Duke of Wellington, exquisitely shaped and beautifully carved, are among the other valuable objects that the museum has got in the treasure trove.

The museum has acquired these objects after three years of negotiations with the Bombay customs. The customs had seized these pieces over the last 15 years and they were lying in its Ballard Pier godown, almost uncared-for.

The Vaikuntha-Kamalja bronze, a form of Vishnu, half-man and half-woman representing Vishnu and Laxmi, will be displayed immediately in the museum galleries for the public, the museum authorities said.

This form of Vishnu, similar to the concept of Ardhanari-Nateshwara, a form of Shiva, was never worshipped in India, though the literature on it is Indian in origin. The worship began in Nepal during the 12th century.

According to the collectors of art objects, the eight-armed piece is the finest bronze of the deity in antiquity, rarity and beauty.

Mr. B.V. Shetty, curator of archaeology of the museum, took four days to sift through and list the antiquities lying in the customs godown. They were stacked and some of the pieces were seized by the customs as long as 1961.

The objects handed over to the museum include 16 stone sculptures, 13 ivories, 11 wood works, four bronzes, five guns, two swords, an old scent bottle made of crystal, a seal and five ancient carved bricks whose period has not yet been determined. All these objects were seized by the customs while they were being smuggled out of the country.

In addition to these, the museum has also got 830 coins, mostly of copper, and a Nepalese tanka. Most of these objects will have to be cleaned and fumigated before being displayed in the galleries.

The earliest stone sculptures thus acquired by the museum belong to the eighth century, which include a beautiful piece of a Kashmiri Mahadeo.

The museum authorities said the antiques were given to them with the understanding that they would retain them and take care of them pending a final decision of the Government of India.

The museum had begun making efforts to acquire these confiscated antiques in 1973. The customs authorities in Calcutta and Delhi had been handing over such confiscated antiquities to the national museums, but the Bombay customs had not.

The museum authorities had pleaded that since they had helped the customs in assessing the confiscated objects, these should rightfully be given to the museum, which could take proper care of them.

However, the customs were not sure of the policy of the Central Revenue Board and were hesitating to hand over the antiques to the museum pending a clarification from the

Board. Meanwhile the Director-General of the Archaeological Survey of India directed the customs to hand over all confiscated antiquities to museums of national importance.

The customs had intended to sell these pieces. But after the recent passing of the antiquities Act, they could not do so. Hence they decided to hand over the objects to the museum.

The museum authorities appreciated the gesture of the customs and anticipate some more consignments of antiquities seized by the customs in which the museum experts had helped the customs in assessment and evidence.

These consignments include 16 cases containing valuable Hoysala sculptures seized by the customs in 1965, consignments of a Swiss national comprising Kashmiri bronzes, Nepalese tankas, ivories and some valuable seals. In addition, the museum also expects 16 priceless Persian carpets, at present lying in the customs godowns, according to the museum authorities.

The objects handed over by the customs will enrich the Prince of Wales Museum, the museum authorities feel.

**13) COUPLE HELD FOR ANTIQUE THEFT**
**(The Times of India:** 12-1-1978)

A businessman was arrested here alongwith his wife in connection with the alleged theft of valuable antiques and Mughal paintings from a house in the Kamachha locality here in 1971.

The antique cell of the CBI claims to have recovered from the arrested couple 20 pieces believed to have been stolen in the sensational midnight theft seven years ago.

The couple owns a small factory and a curio shop in Vishwanath Gali in the city.

The theft case had been closed by the police after some days. However, a member of the aggrieved family succeeded in getting the case reopened. CBI took up the case last year and arrested a maidservant and a male servant of the household and on clues provided by them recovered some antiques from a curio shop in the Andesar locality some months ago. The curio dealer was also arrested at that time. CBI recently raided the house of the businessman and worked out the case following his wife's arrest.

The arrested couple was produced before a magistrate who, after refusing their bail applications, remanded them to police custody for a week.

CBI officials are looking for two sons of the businessman.

### 14) CBI SWOOPS ON RARITIES
**(Blitz: 26-5-1979)**

The recent recovery of rare paintings of the Moghul period, valued at anything between Rs. 5 lakhs and Rs. 10 lakhs, from a gang of antique dealers in Delhi and Varanasi, has added another feather to the cap of the Antiques Branch of the CBI, which has several noteworthy achievements to its credit during the short span of four years since its formation.

These peerless pieces of Indian art of high intrinsic value were stolen in 1971 from the Varanasi residence of the well-known antique collector, Dr. Dharam Pratap, former Dean of the Faculty of Law, BHU. The local police could not solve the mysterious theft and filed the case as closed.

The Antiques Branch of the CBI stepped in after a gap of five years, in 1977, and successfully established a conspiracy between the domestic servants of Dr. Dharam Pratap and some local criminals who specialised in this type of crime.

Sustained interrogation revealed that the latter had sold the paintings to dealers in Varanasi, Delhi and Calcutta. The efforts of these dealers over the years to smuggle the paintings out of the country had not borne fruit. Following raids conducted on the premises, the CBI recovered a number of paintings.

The latest success comes in the wake of several notable achievements like the recovery of the Ponaraja idol, a rare life-size bronze statue of 9th/10th century A.D., which compares favourably in workmanship with the famous Shivapuram Nataraja, sold in the US for a million dollars.

The CBI had also traced and brought back from London the famous Amin Pillars of the Sunga period (first and second century B.C.) which were being sold for 500,000 dollars. Two of the accused in the case were extradited after a year-long legal battle going upto the House of Lords.

The Antiques Branch of the CBI was also able to recover the 1,500 years old Buddha idol stolen from Haryana, and 14 miniature paintings from the Salarjung Museum.

### 15) GANG OF IDOL THIEVES BUSTED IN SIMLA
**(The Tribune: 8-4-1984)**

With the arrest of 12 persons and recovery of stolen idols worth Rs. 1.14 lakh, the police claim to have busted a gang of thieves which had been plundering ancient temples in Simla district.

Disclosing this to newsmen here today the Superintendent of Police, Mr. V.K. Malik, said that 14 temple thefts were reported from various parts of the district in 1983-84. Of these 10 cases had been solved.

Of the 12 arrested, four were Gurkha labourers forming a gang of five suspected to be involved in three cases of theft. The fifth member of the gang was absconding.

He said that all 12 persons arrested by the police were working as agents for antique dealers operating from the Jama Masjid and Sunder Nagar areas of Delhi. Most of the stolen idols were smuggled to foreign countries where these were sold at exorbitant prices.

Some of the temples in which thefts were committed were Gopeshwari temple in the Rohru area, Bhadrakali temple in the Markanda area and Thakur temple in the Kotkhai area. The stolen objects included idols made of gold, silver and ashtadhatu.

**16) ART THEFTS ON THE RISE WORLDWIDE**
**(The Times of India:** 8-3-1988)

In the 1964 film, "Topkapi", Peter Ustinov and Elina Mercouri played thieves who descended into a museum in Istanbul through a skylight to steal a jewel-encrusted dagger.

That plot was repeated with stunning accuracy last month when burglars broke into Manhattan's Colnaghi art gallery through a skylight, shinnied down a rope and plucked 27 old master paintings and drawings off the walls.

The stolen artwork was valued at $ 6 million, making it the biggest art heist in New York history. The most valuable pieces stolen were two panels by the 15th century Italian Renaissance master Fra Angelico, worth $ 4 million.

But unlike the cunning thieves in "Topkapi", those who broke into the Colnaghi gallery on Feb. 8 appear to have been unschooled burglars who had no clear idea of what they were stealing.

If so, their fate is ironic: their booty may be impossible to sell at anything resembling its face value.

Art theft, long romanticised as a genteel form of larceny, is on the rise worldwide. Some law enforcement officials and other experts believe it may rank second only to narcotics trafficking in value of ill-gotten gains.

"If you're talking about dollar value, it probably is", said one U.S. justice department official who specialises in crime statistics. The official, who declined to give his name, stressed that he was only speculating since art theft is not recognised as a separate category in federal statistics.

"It began to increase in the late '50s and the early '60s when the art market began to rise", said Milton Esterow, editor and publisher of *Arnews* magazine. More and more thieves began to wake up and say, "Hey, there's a lot of money here."

If there was a lot of money then, there's more now.

Masterworks often cost many times the value of the mansions where they are hung. Vincent van Gogh's painting, "Irises", set a record last November when it was sold for $ 53.9 million.

Art thieves usually fall into one of three categories, experts say.

One is the professional thief who is commissioned to steal specific works of art.

"Mr. Jones might have fallen in love with one of these paintings and he wants it so bad he can just taste it, so he goes out and hires someone to steal it", explained retired insurance claims investigator Jim Mellors, who specialises in fine art claims.

In these cases, Mellors and others said, the stolen item may wind up in a private collection for years—or even generations—and no money changes hands except the fee paid by the collector to the thief.

Less common is the collector who steals art himself, such as the Philadelphia doctor who was arrested in 1982 for "shoplifting" hundreds of thousands of dollars worth of art from New York galleries for his lavish personal collection.

And then, probably most common of all, is the professional thief who steals art and tries to fence it. Sometimes the thief is knowledgeable about art—often he is not, as appears to be the case in the Colnaghi break-in, law enforcement officials say.

"It's no secret that thieves who are knowledgeable about art don't steal well-known pieces", said Esterow, who is the author of the book, *The Art Stealers.*

Detective Thomas Moscardini, the New York police department's full-time art crimes investigator, agreed that the Colnaghi thieves may have blundered when they chose works by Fra Angelico, Jean Baptiste, Simeon Chardin and other old masters.

"I think it would be difficult to dispose of them because they were somewhat noted pieces", he said. "You're dealing with 15th-16th century works of art (and) that in itself would bring some attention."

According to the experts, smart thieves steal mid-range art, preferably works that are similar to others by the same artist. These works can be sold to unscrupulous or unwitting dealers who don't conduct thorough background checks. Sometimes they are used in place of currency in drug transactions.

**List of Stolen Items:** The International Foundation for Art Research maintains a list of art reported stolen. The list now contains 278,000 items and is regularly sent to law enforcement agencies, museums and galleries. Between 150 and 300 items are added every month.

In the case of a major theft, like that from the Colnaghi gallery, the Foundation puts out a worldwide alert, complete with photographs of the missing pieces. The glare of publicity makes it hard for a thief, particularly one without connections in the art world, to sell the stolen goods except at an extreme discount to a crooked dealer—or to an insurance company.

"What are you going to do with a Fra Angelico?" asked Esterow. "How are you going to get rid of it, except by making a deal with the insurance company?"

Esterow's remark brings up one of the touchiest subjects for those who deal with art theft.

Insurance adjusters routinely deny that they ever pay ransom to get back a work of art. "No, no, no, they don't pay ransom", said independent claims adjuster William Smith, who specialises in the fine arts. "They pay rewards, which are a different thing. They will pay to retrieve property under acceptable circumstances...if, for example, an innocent (party) comes forward and gives them information that leads to recovery."

But others say that policy is not strictly followed.

"In Europe, (artworks) have been held for ransom for the insurance company to pay", said Manhattan art dealer Arnold Herstand. "That's arranged frequently. It's even arranged in New York City. That's fairly common."

In the Colnaghi case, the gallery has announced that its insurance company was offering a reward—10 per cent of the value of the stolen pieces—for their return.

"Final determination of eligibility for payment of the reward will be made by the donor, not by the New York City police department or any other party", the announcement said.

A spokesman for the gallery, vice-president Alan Wintermute said he couldn't say if the thieves were among those eligible for the reward, which could amount to $ 600,000. It was up to the insurance company, he said.

The recovery rate for stolen art is probably no greater than 10 per cent, experts say. Enforcement is spotty. New York and Los Angeles each have one full-time police officer investigating art crimes—the FBI has one and the U.S. customs service has one. They represent the nation's war on art crime.

"It is a big business", said Charles Koezka, a retired U.S. customs agent who was that agency's specialist in fine art crimes. "It has a minimal risk of being caught or, if you are caught, of going to jail. And unfortunately, if you are a victim, you're very unlikely to recover your property."

**17) WHAT PRICE INDIAN ART?**
**(India Today:** 30-6-1983)

Auction houses in London and New York have recently come up with some answers to the oft-asked question—what is Indian art worth? Winter sales organised recently by the three big international art dealers, Sotheby's, Christie's and Phillips together realised about Rs. 2 crore and proved conclusively that interest in Indian art, at least in London and New York, is alive and well.

A Mathura Goddess, 10th-12th century, the most sensuous Indian sculpture at Sotheby's sold for Rs. 82,500. A 1570 Mughal miniature, an illustration for the Hamza Nama—belonging once to Akbar's own copy of Dastan-i-Amir Hamza—brought in Rs. 2.20 lakh. Phillips in its sale—held to a standing room only audience—realised Rs. 9 lakh. And at Christie's, a 15th century Nepalese gilt copper figure of Durga went for Rs. 7.15 lakh—that is, Rs. 4.6 lakh more than what Christie's had estimated the figure to be actually worth. Said Andrew Kahane, Christie's expert on Indian art: "The high prices achieved indicates that there is solid interest for important pieces of this area."

**Renewed Interest:** Various reasons have spurred interest in Indian, Himalayan and South-East Asian art—and for the feverish bidding it invites at auctions. One reason, of course, is that a lot of famous pieces have only been recently released on the commercial market. Descendants of British collectors have begun to sell at auctions. The affluent Iranians who left their country when the Shah fell have also turned to auction houses to liquidate some of their assets.

Further, awareness and acquisition of Indian art continues to grow in the US as Americans are exposed to new areas of Indian art. Gandhara sculpture, for instance, is always a sure sell, aided as it is by art shows, books and scholars who have focussed much attention on this school that synthesises the Greco-Roman and Mauryan-Gupta plastic traditions in sculpture. Similarly, the surge of interest in Tibetan and Nepalese art can be explained by three major exhibitions on Himalayan culture that were held in 1982-83.

Yet another reason offered for the heated bidding was Phillips's move into a new, untapped residential area, away from the fashionable art galleries of Madison Avenue. Said Cintra H. Huber, vice-president of Phillips in New York: "We have new clients from this district augmenting our established dealers-collectors clientele."

Yet there is a chemistry about how and why art objects and manuscripts are received at auctions. While an Indian Koran at Sotheby's in London fetched the highest price of Rs. 1.49 lakh—a two-volume Sultanate Koran dated 14th-15th century failed to sell, despite its rarity, in New York. Dealers attempt to explain this as a damaged Muslim image because of OPEC, the oil cartel, and Khomeini.

**Resilient Market:** On the other hand, ivory works, Gandhara sculpture, Oriental miniatures, Tibetan bronzes and Rajput and Islamic paintings continue to keep the cash register ringing. "For Pahari paintings there is a tremendous demand", said Michael Jones, Sotheby's expert on Indian miniatures, "but there are few works of high quality." A 1749 painting of a princess bathing, from Bikaner, sold for Rs. 31,900. A 12th century Chola bronze of Balakrishna fetched Rs. 3.08 lakh, while a head of Bodhisattva from 2nd century Gandhara went for Rs. 41,250. Buddhist art, especially the images of Buddha are very well received by Americans. And Indian miniature sales in America are, according to an enthusiastic British auctioneer, "simply...missionary work".

What, then, is Indian art worth? In its winter sale alone, Christie's of London realised Rs. 10.5 lakh selling 68 per cent of the lots displayed. Sotheby's of New York made over Rs. 1.02 crore over two specialised winter sales of Indian art. And Christie's of New York made Rs. 2.83 crore (Rs. 80 lakh being realised by the Pan Asian collection).

While the four very successful sales prove the resilience of the art market, awareness of Indian art in America has still a long way to go. Americans prefer simplicity. "The complex Indian iconography is a serious deterrent", lamented one well-known dealer while another felt sure that "Indian sculpture is bound to develop." Similarly, the market for Indian sculpture is highly specialised, and in America, a rather limited one. But when the art is superb, the market is bullish. Even during hard economic times as these, the best works of art continue to raise eyebrows—and hands—at auctions.

**18) MAJOR HAUL OF RARE ANTIQUES**
**(The Statesman: 13-4-1988)**

In a major haul of rare and priceless antiques, 52 pieces of archaeological importance have been seized by the Delhi police. Two persons have been arrested under the Antiques and Art Treasures Act, 1972.

Following a raid in a South Delhi colony on Tuesday the police caught Pritam Sharma red-handed while he was allegedly trying to dump some rare sculptures at a tented place being used as a godown by him. A resident of South Extension Part I, Pritam Sharma alongwith one of his associates had gone to East of Kailash with small antiques of terracotta and a big sculpture of a four-faced deity. Ashok Gupta of Aligarh was accompanying him with two sculptures in another bag. They were intercepted by the Lajpat Nagar police who were shadowing them on a tip-off. The keys of the place being used as a godown were allegedly found in the pocket of Pritam Sharma from where the police recovered 37 sculptures dating back to the prehistoric period.

The oldest of them was a 31-cm long harpoon of the Bronze Age. The police took the help of experts from the Archaeological Survey of India to identify the seized articles. The ASI has testified that they range right from the Bronze Age to the medieval period.

Some antique statues of the Buddha, Ganesha and Surya belong to the first century A.D. A Superintending Archaeologist (Antiquities) in the ASI, Mrs. Munira Khatun, said that the bronze harpoon could be as old as from 1500 B.C. She claimed that the seized icons belong to the Kushan, Maurya, Sunga and Gupta ages. They were of incredible importance and were priceless in the international market, she added.

The police claimed that Pritam Sharma had a chain of antique lifters spread all over the country. He started his career as an apprentice at an antique shop in Jor Bagh. The shop owner Bali Ram Sharma was himself charged with the pilferage of antiques several times. He took to the trade after giving up the job of a clerk in the ASI, said Mr. P.R.S. Brar, the Deputy Commissioner of Police (South).

Pritam Sharma developed his contacts while working in the shop. Soon he acquired a shop of his own in Lok Nayak Bhavan in Khan Market.

The police said that he had been using the shop as a cover for his clandestine deals with foreign tourists. The shop which dealt in artefacts had nothing objectionable in it. However, it was a meeting point for prospective customers. Mrs. Khatun said that the sculptures like those recovered were mostly exported as even the museums in India paid nothing compared to the prices they fetch in the West.

Interestingly the South Delhi police claimed that the atique haul which took place in East Delhi about a week ago had the same kingpin behind it. The East District police raided the place as a police team from the South had returned after locating the premises that housed antiques belonging to the gang. The DCP (South) said that his men were on a look out for Pritam Sharma and they did not disturb the place so as to avoid tipping off the culprits. But the East District police made no bones after getting an inkling about the antiques, said Mr. Brar.

Meanwhile, Pritam Sharma and Ashok Gupta were produced in the court of Metropolitan Magistrate, Ms. R. Kiran Nath, on Tuesday. Both were sent to police remand for 10 days.

### 19) ANTIQUES: AN ENDANGERED HERITAGE
**(The Times of India:** 20-2-1988)

Over three lakh antiques—exquisite sculptures, paintings and manuscripts—have been registered under the antiquities data bank of the Archaeological Survey of India (ASI) at Purana Kila. But as many if not more have not been registered. The fear that these priceless symbols of Indian art, culture and heritage are being smuggled out of the country despite the Antiquities Act being in force since April 1976, is genuine. Many of them lie unrecognised and uncatalogued in and near temples, excavation sites and in the homes of villagers who do not realise their value.

Others, recognised for their artistic and antique value, are secreted away in closets and godowns. They are all unregistered and waiting for a good customer—preferably a foreigner with his pockets jingling with dollars.

Within the country, too, hundreds of antiques are being bought and sold without registration and without the knowledge of the ASI.

But while the ASI has been trying frantically to catalogue and document every antique in the country in the hope that this would curtail smuggling and help scholars doing research on the pantheon of Indian gods, miniature paintings or temple art, the Central Advisory Board for Museums has passed a resolution against compulsory registration for State and Central Government museums in May last year.

The museums, and this includes the premier National Museum, are quitely buying registrable, unregistered antiques, some of which are even bought from antique dealers of doubtful integrity, and there is no guarantee that they are not stolen property.

The ASI is unhappy that its sister concern, sitting pretty just across its boundaries, should be purchasing unregistered antiques. If they must be bought, they should be registered right away. At one stage, the ASI even offered to send one of its officers to the meeting of the Art Purchase Committee so that at least at this stage the registration is done. Those coming for the meetings with priceless goodies would also be forced to register their wares irrespective of whether the Museum bought them or not.

The National Museum's argument, however, is that items that would have come to them for sale are no longer being offered because of the Antiquities Act. They argue that it is with considerable difficulty that the dealers have overcome their fears and are coming out with the antiques for sale. If the museums do not buy them, they fear they will be smuggled out and lost to the country forever.

A serious charge levelled against the National Museum is that just last December it bought unregistered antiques. While L.P. Sihare, the Museum's Director, refused to talk on the subject on the plea that he was a civil servant, there seems little doubt that the only ones who are really serious about the Act are the ASI.

The ASI wants to build up a national catalogue of antiquities so that at any given time information supported with photographs is available on India's heritage in sculptures, paintings and manuscripts. With this catalogue, the ASI could keep an eye on the important antiques in the country and if necessary, the documentation could prove invaluable for police sleuths tracking down stolen antiques. Transfer of antiquities is permitted but each transfer or sale is recorded with ASI.

The ASI's efforts notwithstanding, the Act has, for all practical purposes, already failed because the people who are supposed to be implementing it have been lax and public cooperation has been minimal. Now there is a move to waive it if not scrap it altogether. Several collectors, dealers and art lovers find the registration process cumbersome and time-consuming.

But surely the process itself could be simplified instead of waiving the Act. For reclaiming unregistered antiques once they are smuggled abroad is Herculean task. To establish legal claim it has to be testified that the object was registered or documented in an Indian collection. If this is not done, one can only claim that it is of Indian origin, not ownership.

Take the case of the Nataraja from Sivapuram in Thanjavur district of Tamil Nadu. It was found in 1951, disappeared from the country in 1956 and recovered and restored to India only last May.

The idol was discovered while a field was being dug up. Under the Indian Treasure Trove Act 1878, the Collector of the district handed it over to the temple authorities of Sivapuram in 1953. Being buried for a long period, it was in a bad state and in 1954 it was given for repair and restoration work to Ramaswamy Sthapati of Devei Silpasala.

The idol was with him for five years. During this period, five of the idols with him for restoration, including the Nataraja, were replaced by fake ones, and the originals changed hands.

They came into the possession of Lance Dane, an executive of an advertising firm. Dr. Douglas Barrett of the British Museum on a visit to India in 1964 saw the Nataraja with Dane. In his book *Early Chola Bronzes,* published at the end of his visit, he mentioned that the Nataraja of the Sivapuram temple was in a private collection in Bombay.

In 1967 the Tamil Nadu Government ordered an inquiry to find out if this was so. After the inquiry assisted by the crime branch of the CID, Madras, the Director, Madras Museum, declared that the existing idols of the Sivapuram temple were fake.

After changing several hands, the Nataraja reached New York via London in 1969. It was cleared at the British customs and subsequently sold to Norton Simon of the Norton Simon Foundation of Los Angeles for $ 100,000 in 1973.

After protracted litigation the matter was settled outside the court and an agreement signed that the bronze idol would remain with the Foundation for 10 years and then be returned to India.

Antiques have sometimes disappeared right from under the nose of the ASI. An exquisite terracotta Yakshi of the Sunga period discovered in Tamluk, West Bengal, in 1953-54, disappeared soon after it was brought to Delhi for the 1961 contenary exhibition of the ASI. It found its way to the British Museum in London. When it was offered for sale there, the British Museum referred it to India to determine its Indian origin. It was only then that its disappearance was noticed and thanks to the good offices of the British Museum it could be brought back to India in 1986. The tiny terracotta is now in the central antiquities collection of excavated objects at the Purana Kila.

But the Government has not yet been able to recover the standing Buddha of the Gupta period from the Metropolitan Museum of Art, New York. This piece of Indian artistic genius was picked from a housing site at Govind Nagar, Mathura, alongwith a number of antiquities in the mid-seventies. While some went to the Mathura Museum, the rest went to unknown destinations.

That antiques are disappearing from the country is a well-established fact. Yet the fact remains that it is easier to get back stolen property if it is registered, particularly if the countries involved are signatories to the UN convention on restitution of cultural properties.

At the antiquities data bank the largest number of registered antiquities are from UP, some 8,929 from Thanjavur alone—the series of thefts from temples in that district having brought home a realisation of the importance of registration. The three southern states of Andhra, Karnataka and Tamil Nadu are also doing excellent certification work. The registration certificates are forwarded to the data bank which in turn screens them for discrepancies and ensures that each antique registered is photographed. There is a move to publish a compendium of every 5,000 certificates so that the police as well as scholars know about the collections. On the basis of the compendium, the ASI can bring out a list of class A and class B antiques.

The resolution exempting State and Central Government museums from compulsory registration has dealt one blow to the efforts being made to prevent India's heritage from being smuggled, stolen or lost. Abolishing the Antiquities Act itself will allow the evil to flourish unchecked.

**20) ANTIQUES RECOVERED**
**(The Hindu:** June 26, 1990)

Priceless antiques smuggled out of the country and lying unclaimed in the Netherlands for the past several months have been recovered recently.

The centuries old artefacts—212 bronze statues, 66 paintings and over 500 wooden art pieces—were recovered by the Rotterdam Port Customs authorities earlier this year after the consignment remained unclaimed.

A case was registered by the Central Bureau of Investigation in this regard after the Indian Embassy in the Hague contacted it.

A first information report (FIR) was filed in the court of Delhi's Chief Metropolitan Magistrate, Mr. J.M. Malik, on June 22 regarding the theft of these antiques from different parts of India in the past two years.

A Delhi resident, Mrs. Malavika Gupta, 'and others' have been cited as accused in the case instituted under Section 120-b of the IPC (criminal conspiracy), read with Section 3 of the Antiquities and Art Treasures Act, 1972.

**21) CBI TO SECURE INDIAN ANTIQUES FROM DUTCH**
**(The Indian Express: July 2, 1990)**

A top official of the Central Bureau of Investigation (CBI) is in the Hague now holding talks with Dutch authorities for the transfer of priceless Indian antiques recently seized in Rotterdam.

CBI Joint Director, Mr. C.M. Sharma, arrived in Hague after attending an international police seminar in Lyons in France, CBI sources said here on Sunday.

The Rotterdam port customs authorities had earlier this year recovered the centuries old artefacts—212 bronze statues, 66 paintings and more than 500 wooden art pieces.

The 850 kg consignment sent by a New Delhi woman to a Netherlands address was shipped from the Madras port on August 10, 1988.

The sources said the Indian Government would have to satisfy the Netherlands Government that the stolen artefacts were its property. The artefacts would be released only after going through the legal process.

The Indian Government's request for the return of artefacts may have to go through a court of law.

Though the Dutch museum authorities have assessed the Indian antiques to be 200 to 300 years old; the sources said their age and value from the archaeological and legal points of view could be ascertained only after the same were handed over to India.

The antiques, stolen from different parts of the country, are however, believed to be worth several crores of rupees.

The CBI had registered a case in this regard after the Indian embassy in the Hague contacted it.

The CBI filed a First Information Report (FIR) in the court of Chief Metropolitan Magistrate on June 22 regarding the theft of these antiques.

The consignment, in two boxes, was described by the consigner as "used personal effects".

### 22) APPEAL IN NATARAJA CASE
**(The Hindustan Times:** July 5, 1990)

An appeal to stall the release of the Nataraja, stolen from a temple in Tamil Nadu in 1976, commenced here on Tuesday with the defendants seeking to produce new evidence to convince the court that the 12th century piece of art was not sacred to the Hindus.

The defendants Bumber Development Corporation made the submission that hundreds of such Natarajas were available in the world market and sought to produce a witness claiming having seen the same Nataraja in the London market in 1974—two years prior to the one now before the court was reportedly stolen from Tamil Nadu.

They have also sought to throw light on various aspects of Hinduism in their bid to demolish the Indian Government's case upheld in the Queen's Bench Division in February 1988.

The case is expected to continue till the second week of this month. The Nataraja will be presented before the court today.

A division bench in February 1988 upheld the Indian contention that the Nataraja was stolen from a temple in Tamil Nadu but before it could be released to the Indian Government, the defendants appealed against the judgement.

**23) THE 12TH CENTURY GARUDA STATUE IS BACK IN PURI**
**(India Today:** 30-11-1990)

The Bhubaneswar-bound flight from Delhi carried an unusual passenger. He had been given a warm send-off at the VIP lounge by high-ranking officials. Once on board, the cabin crew including the pilot came to pay obeisance with folded hands. At the other end, Bhubaneswar airport wore all the paraphernalia used to greet the high and mighty—a large posse of security guards and a noisy crowd of well-wishers.

None of the other passengers begrudged the VIP his special treatment. For he was more than a mere mortal. It was, in fact, a priceless 12th century granite statue of Garuda, the half-man half-bird vehicle used by Lord Vishnu. Known as the foremost disciple of Lord Jagannath, Garuda is believed to have whisked Lord Krishna to the hall in time to save Draupadi from the dishonour of being disrobed by the Kauravas.

Having been stolen by a gang of art thieves five years ago, the statue (weighing 40 kg and 15 inches high) was finally returning to its original home—the Sri Gundicha temple in Puri, Orissa. The home-coming had been long delayed. Although it was retrieved by the CBI three years ago, in a lightning strike just moments before the thieves put it on a flight out of India, the statue then fell into the much more tenacious clutches of the Indian legal system.

It was locked up inside a store-room while the CBI and the Orissa Government waged a protracted legal tussle over who its rightful owner was. The stakes were high. The one and a half feet high Garuda has been valued at Rs. 14 crore in the international antique market. And once back in its original pedestal it could continue to be a major temptation for art thieves. For the temple and the town do not exactly have the infrastructure to prevent yet another attempt at lifting the magnificent granite idol.

The Orissa Government eventually won the battle to regain possession of the prized 12th century relic after much difficulty. The battle is not yet over for it may be some months before the statue is restored to its pedestal at the Sri Gundicha temple from where the thieves chiselled it away. The case against the thieves is still pending in Delhi and since the idol itself is the main piece of evidence against them, it may have to be produced in court from time to time adding to the complications of the case.

But the temple authorities at Puri are determined not to let the statue suffer any further indignities, so they have filed a petition before the Supreme Court asking for the case to be transferred to Puri. Even if that happens, there are many legal hurdles left for the State Government to surmount.

Until the court announces its verdict, Garuda has been ordered to be kept within the precincts of the famous Jagannath temple, just three kilometres down the road from the Sri Gundicha temple. During the renowned annual rath festival at Jagannath, Garuda's absence had been badly felt, for his role in the ceremony is crucial. Once the three deities inside Jagannath have been carried to the Sri Gundicha temple, Garuda's role is to act as sentry during their one-week stay.

Although the statue is still waiting to be reinstalled to its rightful place, the people of Puri have heaved a collective sigh of relief that it's finally back. Their euphoria stems from a mixture of civic pride, religious devotion and self-interest. After its theft, a replica of Garuda was made, installed and worshipped every day. But there's been a nagging suspicion in the minds of the faithful that the replica has a somewhat malignant aspect. A spate of mishaps—the collapse of a couple of blocks from the top of the Jagannath temple and the embarrassing breakdown of the rath during this year's festival—have all been blamed on the replica.

But it won't just be a simple case of restoring the adored and much-missed original and discarding the suspect replica. Now that the legal niceties of ownership have been resolved, the statue has become the object of an equally unseemly theological wrangle.

In one camp are disciples who say that once a replica has been installed and worshipped, it cannot be discarded. In another are those who believe the original Garuda has been defiled as a result of its experiences in store-rooms and at the hands of the CBI. And in the middle are those who've never quite liked the look of the replica and want it removed before it does any more damage.

**24) INDIA WINS BATTLE FOR NATARAJA**
**(PTI:** 13-2-1991)

India today won the 15-year-old legal battle over a Nataraja statue and the precious 12th century antique piece would be handed over to India to be reinstated at Pathur temple in Tamil Nadu.

The court of appeal dismissed with costs the appeal by Bumber Development Corporation, a US firm, challenging the judgement of the high court of London in February 1988.

The high court had directed that the Nataraja be handed over to India.

Delivering this historic judgement in a crowded court room here today the judges said there was no ground on which we could differ from the judge in his assessment of the weight to be placed on the identification of the London Nataraja by Ramamoorthy.

On the contrary, a study of the transcripts certainly suggests that the judge might well have been justified in taking a view of his evidence that was less reserved.

The judges observed that we remain of the opinion that Mr. Justice Ian Kennedy came to the right conclusion on this part of the case, and we dismiss the appeal in relation to it.

"Whether the plaintiffs (India and others) have a title to the Nataraja", Mr. Justice Kennedy said, "I am satisfied that the pious intention of the 12th century notable who gave land and built the Vishwanathaswamy temple in Pathur, remains in being and is personified by the temple itself, a juristic entity which has a title to the Nataraja, superior to that of the defendent (Bumber Development Corporation)."

Court of Appeal verdict on this issue affirmed Mr. Justice Kennedy's judgement and dismissed the appeal by the Bumber Development.

Mr. Justice Kennedy in February 1988 upheld the contention of India that the Nataraja was stolen from the temple in Tamil Nadu and he concluded, "I am satisfied that the Nataraja has been proved to be that found and sold by Ramamoorthy in about September 1976 and so proved to a high degree of probability.

The issue ordered to be tried by the master was framed in the following question: Have any of the "claimants" established that they have a better title than Bumber to the Nataraja on the assumption that the London Nataraja was the same as the Pathur Nataraja?

Hereafter, we refer simply to "the Nataraja". For practical purposes the question must be considered in three separate stages. First, have any of the claimants a title recognised by the Courts of Tamil Nadu according to Hindu law as practised there? Secondly, assuming that one or more of the claimants would be acceptable in the courts of Tamil Nadu and would there have a good title to the Nataraja enforceable in those courts, then would that claimant be recognised as capable of suing and being sued in the English courts, and if so, would the claim be enforced by those courts? Lastly, if the answers to first and second are 'yes', would the claimant's title to the Nataraja be considered by the English courts to be superior to the possessory title claimed by Bumber?

**25) NATARAJA'S STATUE BEING SENT BACK**
**(ANI, London: 15-4-1991)**

After a prolonged 15-year legal battle over a Nataraja statue of the 12th century Chola age, which had been stolen from a temple in Pathur village in Tamil Nadu, India has finally won the case and the custody.

India's victory was upheld recently when a London High Court dismissed an appeal by a Canadian oil firm, challenging an earlier judgement of the High Court of London and the verdict ordered the reinstatement of the precious idol to the Pathur temple. The court of appeal upheld the earlier order of Justice Ian Kennedy of the London High Court that the idol was a 'stolen' property of India.

The Nataraja statue came into the custody of police in 1982. Although there is no indication as to who instructed the seizure, the statue was first purchased on June 10, 1977, in Britain from Julian Sherrier for $ 405,000 by the Oil Development Company for its chairman Robert Borden, a Canadian art collector. The statue went into the hands of Margaret Enderley, an expert conservator at the British Museum, under her private capacity, to enable the safe transportation of the statue to Canada.

The case came before the London High Court in 1984 before Justice Ian Kennedy. The central question of the case was whether the seized statue of Nataraja and the Pathur Nataraja were one and the same. Detailed examinations of its cultural identity and studies to determine its title were held.

# APPENDIX III

**UNITED NATIONS EDUCATIONAL, SCIENTIFIC AND CULTURAL ORGANIZATION**

**CONVENTION ON THE MEANS OF PROHIBITING AND PREVENTING THE ILLICIT IMPORT, EXPORT AND TRANSFER OF OWNERSHIP OF CULTURAL PROPERTY**

**(Paris, 14 November 1970)**

**List of the 65 States having deposited an instrument of ratification, acceptance or accession as at 15 June 1988**

| STATES | Date of deposit of ratification (R) acceptance (Ac) or accession (A) | Date of entry into force |
|---|---|---|
| 1 | 2 | 3 |
| ALGERIA | 24.6.1974 (R) | 24.9.1974 |
| ARGENTINA | 11.1.1973 (R) | 11.4.1973 |
| BANGLADESH | 9.12.1987 (R) | 9.3.1988 |
| BOLIVIA | 4.10.1976 (R) | 4.1.1977 |
| BRAZIL | 16.2.1973 (R) | 16.5.1973 |
| BULGARIA | 15.9.1971 (R) | 24.4.1972 |
| BURKINA FASO | 7.4.1987 (R) | 7.7.1987 |
| BYELORUSSIAN SSR | 28.4.1988 (R) | 28.7.1988 |
| CAMEROON | 24.5.1972 (R) | 24.8.1972 |
| CANADA | 28.3.1978 (Ac) | 28.6.1978 |
| CENTRAL AFRICAN REPUBLIC | 1.2.1972 (R) | 1.5.1972 |
| COLOMBIA | 24.5.1988 (Ac) | 24.8.1988 |
| CUBA | 30.1.1980 (R) | 30.4.1980 |
| CYPRUS | 19.10.1979 (R) | 19.1.1980 |
| CZECHOSLOVAKIA | 14.2.1977 (Ac) | 14.5.1977 |
| DEMOCRATIC KAMPUCHEA | 26.9.1972 (R) | 26.12.1972 |
| DEMOCRATIC PEOPLE'S REPUBLIC OF KOREA | 13.5.1983 (R) | 13.8.1983 |

| 1 | 2 | 3 |
|---|---|---|
| DOMINICAN REPUBLIC | 7.3.1973 (R) | 7.6.1973 |
| ECUADOR | 24.3.1971 (Ac) | 24.4.1972 |
| EGYPT | 5.4.1973 (Ac) | 5.7.1973 |
| EL SALVADOR | 20.2.1978 (R) | 20.5.1978 |
| GERMAN DEMOCRATIC REPUBLIC | 16.1.1974 (Ac) | 16.4.1974 |
| GREECE | 5.6.1981 (R) | 5.9.1981 |
| GUATEMALA | 14.1.1985 (R) | 14.4.1985 |
| GUINEA | 18.3.1979 (R) | 18.6.1979 |
| HONDURAS | 19.3.1979 (R) | 19.6.1979 |
| HUNGARY | 23.10.1978 (R) | 23.1.1979 |
| INDIA | 24.1.1977 (R) | 24.4.1977 |
| IRAN (Islamic Rep. of) | 27.1.1975 (Ac) | 27.4.1975 |
| IRAQ | 12.2.1973 (Ac) | 12.5.1973 |
| ITALY | 2.10.1978 (R) | 2.1.1979 |
| JORDAN | 15.3.1974 (R) | 15.6.1974 |
| KUWAIT | 22.6.1972 (Ac) | 22.9.1972 |
| LIBYAN ARAB JAMAHIRIYA | 9.1.1973 (R) | 9.4.1973 |
| MALI | 6.4.1987 (R) | 6.7.1987 |
| MAURITANIA | 27.4.1977 (R) | 27.7.1977 |
| MAURITIUS | 27.2.1978 (Ac) | 27.5.1978 |
| MEXICO | 4.10.1972 (Ac) | 4.1.1973 |
| NEPAL | 23.6.1976 (R) | 23.9.1976 |
| NICARAGUA | 19.4.1977 (R) | 19.7.1977 |
| NIGER | 16.10.1972 (R) | 16.1.1973 |
| NIGERIA | 24.1.1972 (R) | 24.4.1972 |
| OMAN | 2.6.1978 (Ac) | 2.9.1978 |
| PAKISTAN | 30.4.1981 (R) | 30.7.1981 |
| PANAMA | 13.8.1973 (Ac) | 13.11.1973 |
| PERU | 24.10.1979 (Ac) | 24.1.1980 |
| POLAND | 31.1.1974 (R) | 30.4.1974 |
| PORTUGAL | 9.12.1985 (R) | 9.3.1986 |
| QATAR | 20.4.1977 (Ac) | 20.7.1977 |
| REPUBLIC OF KOREA | 14.2.1983 (Ac) | 14.5.1983 |
| SAUDI ARABIA | 8.9.1976 (Ac) | 8.12.1976 |
| SENEGAL | 9.12.1984 (R) | 9.3.1985 |
| SPAIN | 10.1.1986 (R) | 10.4.1986 |
| SRI LANKA | 7.4.1981 (Ac) | 7.7.1981 |
| SYRIAN ARAB REPUBLIC | 21.2.1975 (Ac) | 21.5.1975 |
| TUNISIA | 10.3.1975 (R) | 10.6.1975 |
| TURKEY | 21.4.1981 (R) | 21.7.1981 |
| UKRAINIAN SSR | 28.4.1988 (R) | 28.7.1988 |

| 1 | 2 | 3 |
|---|---|---|
| UNITED REPUBLIC OF TANZANIA | 2.8.1977 (R) | 2.11.1977 |
| UNITED STATES OF AMERICA | 2.9.1983 (Ac) | 2.12.1983 |
| URUGUAY | 9.8.1977 (R) | 9.11.1977 |
| USSR | 28.4.1988 (R) | 28.7.1988 |
| YUGOSLAVIA | 3.10.1972 (R) | 3.1.1973 |
| ZAIRE | 23.9.1974 (R) | 23.12.1974 |
| ZAMBIA | 21.6.1985 (R) | 21.9.1985 |

# INDEX

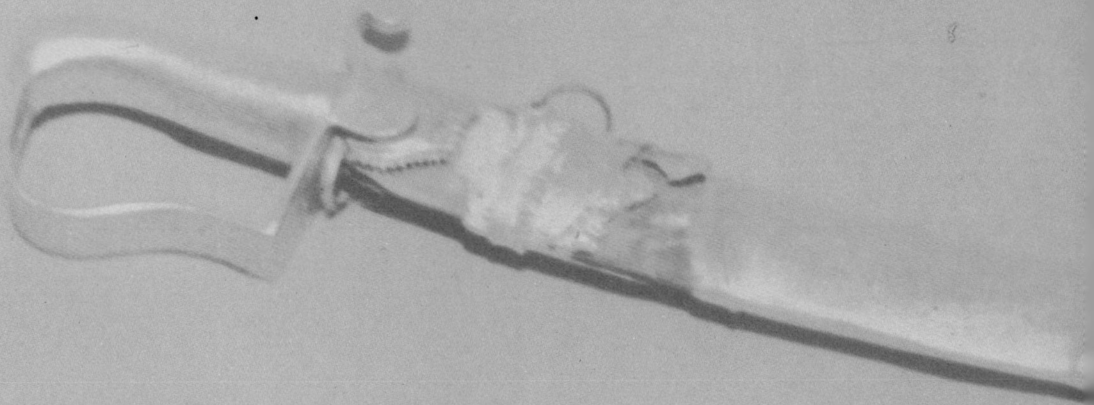